SEPTEN RIO
PARTE DI GRONLANDA
nord
OCEANVS SEPTENTRIONALIS

PICNEMAY REG TIERRA DE LABRADO

TIERRA DE BACCA LAOS

B.a de oros
Isola de Fuego
Buenauenturata de aues
Monte de trigo
Isola de freyluis
Isole de aues
B.a de S Ciru
Isola de bacallaos
B.a arcoryhcson
C. de Spera
Cabo Ralo

Onzemluirgines

Isola di Cruz

ISLAS DELOS AÇORES

Querno
Graciola
Tercera
Abreojo
Isola de flores
Faial
S. George
S. Miguel
Pico
S. Maria

Ilol de la bermud

Isola de brazil

Las maydas

Porto San

Isola de Madera

Saluator G

ISLAS DE CANARIA

Cana
Gomera
Palma
Ferro

La Catholica

TROPICVS CANCRI

OCEANVS

OCCIDENTALIS

Sombrelo
Anguilla
S. Martin
S.bo
Barnada
Antigua
Deleada
Marigalante

S. Vincente
S. Antonio
S. Nicolas
Isola de fal
S. Lucia
Bueuilla
ISLAS DE CAPO VERDE
S. Iacobo
Mayo

Incolę horum locorum mediter-
raneorum antropophagi sunt, nu-
di incedunt sagittandi arte peritiss.
natatores egregij; eoru diuitię sunt
variorum coloru auium plumę; solem
et lunā adorāt, domicilia ad instar
campanaru habent, frondib. contesta.

Abreojo
Isola fuerte
Isola de fuego

Baruodo
Gran
aa
Paria
Tabago
P.a la galea

Guadalupe
de aues
todosictos
Dominica
Matinino
S. Lucia
S. Vincete
Flaylos

Margarita

R.to duce

PARIA Viaparo

El grand rio de las amazones

NOVA ANDALVSIA

Penedro de S Pedro
LA FLOTA DE PORTVGAL
QVE VA PAR CALICVTE

Prouincia de
Comos Christi

Prouincia de los
Tiguadoz

3.10
3.20
33.o
34.o
35.o
La Trinidad

HIC SUNT DRACONES

THE **ATLAS** OF
LEGENDARY LANDS

THE ATLAS OF LEGENDARY LANDS

FABLED KINGDOMS, PHANTOM ISLANDS, LOST CONTINENTS AND OTHER MYTHICAL WORLDS

JUDYTH A. McLEOD

PIER 9

Contents

Frontispiece: 'Here be dragons' — The flat Earth, with toppling ships and lurking monsters.
Page 2: A galleon in a swarm of flying fish, by Theodore de Bry.
Pages 4–5: According to medieval travel records, the East was inhabited by dragons and other strange beasts.

Introduction

Beautiful man-hating Amazons flying astride griffins over the Island of California, the waters of eternal life, El Dorado, treasure islands and reefs of gold, the mysterious Mountains of the Moon, the Garden of Eden, Patagonian giants, sea-dwelling dragons, drowned lands, floating islands, the Great South Land counter-balance, a massive swirling oceanic black hole in the Arctic ... If this sounds like fantasy fed on a diet of hallucinogenics, it is just a tiny sample of the world portrayed by sober-sided, scientifically minded cartographers in our not so distant past. Gathered together in this book is the strange and fascinating history of the world as it never was, but as map makers once envisioned it. Unhampered by excessive facts, fired by fear of the unknown and inextricably tangled in the dogmas of the day, their often exquisitely drawn maps attempted to make sense of a world beyond the known.

We love to add a touch of mystery and a delectable shiver of fear to our lives. While our twenty-first century imaginations conjure up spine-chilling aliens, strange worlds beyond our solar system, monsters unleashed from the Id, parallel universes and interdimensional travel, our by no means remote ancestors were no different, creating in their maps and travel writings thrillingly fearsome monster-filled seas and lands beyond strangeness awaiting exploration.

From earliest recorded times to the beginning of the twentieth century, many maps and official histories of exploration have been filled with bizarre inaccuracies, glorious blunders and deliberate misdirections. Maps were created in early times as much on secondhand information—in effect on 'Chinese whispers'—as on sound knowledge gathered by expansionist empires, conquering armies and extraordinary early navigators and travellers. The intellectual Sargasso Sea in which Europe was trapped by religious dogma during the medieval period certainly added to the extraordinary cartographic errors of more than a millennium. A lack of technology including a reliable means of fixing geographical locations severely hampered navigators until after Columbus and led to many cartographic errors, not least a belief that the pesky barrier to the riches of the Orient posed by the inconvenient North American continent could be overcome in a couple of days march.

Information has always been the key to power, and many European countries in particular played arrogant political chess games across the new lands revealed by high risk taking explorers, aided by spy networks as ingenious and lethal as any Bond movie. International prestige, land acquisition and great wealth followed on the heels of magnificent navigational feats. But the political manoeuvring of international rivals also rewrote history to suit their own ends, diminishing or suppressing the extraordinary feats of many. Some of those historic canards are revealed here.

The world is anything but the stable place we believe it to be. Catastrophes happen from slow coastal subsidence to tsunamis, earthquakes and volcanic eruptions that both destroy and create whole lands, encounters with meteors, and massive climate changes that have both drowned and bared continents. Some of these events are within historic times, the memories of others have been passed down as oral histories distorted by time and retelling. These mythological lands, some now being discovered with the assistance of modern technology, are a fascinating addendum to this 'alternative geography' of our Earth.

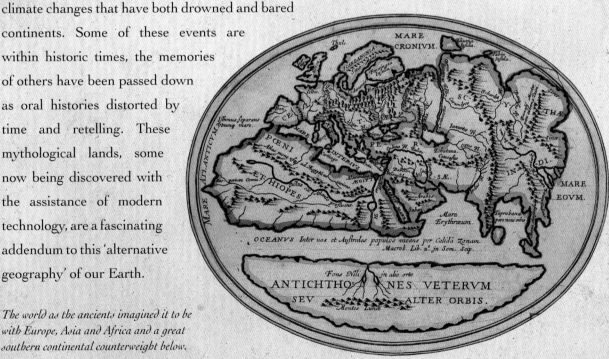

The world as the ancients imagined it to be with Europe, Asia and Africa and a great southern continental counterweight below.

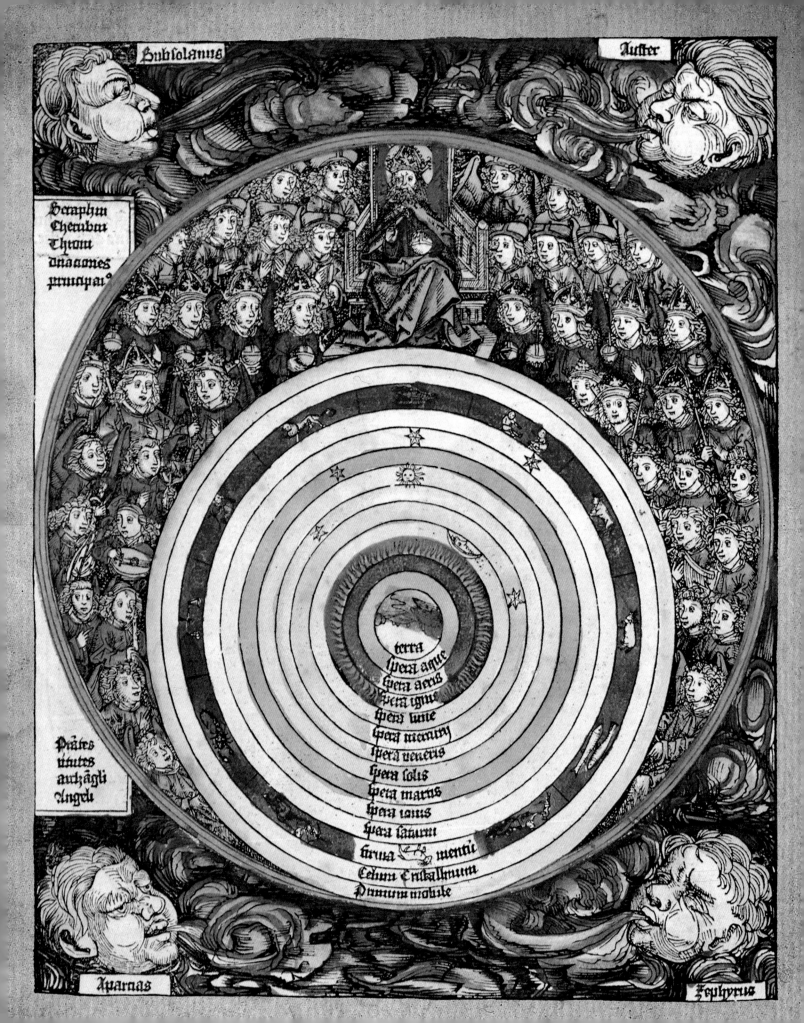

PART ONE

INVENTING THE EARTH

LEFT: The universe, according to Ptolemy, with the Earth at its centre. Reproduced in the Nuremberg Chronicle *by Hartmann Schedel, 1493.*

FOLLOWING PAGES: A mariner uses a navigating instrument to view stars to fix position, from a vellum manuscript of Jacques Devaulx, 1583.

Ensuict. L

Par le Midi du Solleil

Latitude Long. de lequin

stant en quelque terre estrange et nayant a

seroit soy se puist seruir du premyer bas

quil fera le solleil estant a son midy la

moyen · de · scauoir · treuuer

c le premyer baston treuué combien lon est de degrez de haulteur c
ial, et de longitude lomg de da ligne Diametralle · &c·c·cᴐ

una instrumentz propres pour treuuer la longittude z lattitude du lieu ou
treuué de quelque grandeur ou petillesse quil soit Et treuuer par lhon
gittude et lattitude du lieu ou loy est! Sont premyerement pou

A WORLD OF THE
IMAGINATION, MATHS
AND SCIENCE

What was our world like when its only boundaries lay in the human imagination? Beyond the known lands of the Mediterranean basin lay a world of infinite possibilities for the European explorer, filled with the strangest imaginable part-human beings like centaurs and moon-women, with unicorns and griffins, fire-breathing dragons and great sea monsters, fabulous treasure troves, disappearing islands, a long lost paradise, the fountain of youth ... everything the human heart longed for and everything it feared in its darkest nightmares might lie beyond that beckoning horizon. Or if theories of a flat Earth were correct, only a great thundering waterfall as the oceans of the world spilled over into the black abyss, taking with them every foolish sea creature and mariner who strayed too close.

When the world was still believed to be full of such wonders, Claudius Ptolemaeus built upon a centuries-long intellectual inheritance that used logic as a tool in understanding the universe.

Ptolemy, as he has become better known, has long been renowned as an astronomer, a brilliant mathematician whose work was fundamental to the development of trigonometry and one of the greatest geographers of all time.

Ptolemy was probably of Greek descent although even that is uncertain, born in Roman Egypt around 90 AD and dying in Alexandria around 160 AD. The only certain time fix we have on his life is the period between 127 and 148, when he worked in Alexandria, the ancient Egyptian centre of learning. He was a prolific author. Among his works were *Mathematical Syntaxis* (*Almagest*), a thirteen-volume text on mathematics and astronomy, his immensely influential *Geographia* (*Geography*), the *Tetrabiblos* (*Four Books*) on astrology (which was then a serious and important discipline), as well as books on music, optics, latitude and longitude and applied mathematics.

Ptolemy inherited the combined astronomical and astrological traditions of Sumeria, Babylon, Egypt, Ancient Greece, and later Hellenic Greece—knowledge that was assimilated through centuries of trade and conquest around the Mediterranean basin and the Middle East. Ptolemy codified the Greek view of astronomy, placing the Earth at the centre of the universe following the Aristotelian model, with the sun, the moon and the five planets known in his time (Mercury, Venus, Mars, Jupiter and Saturn) circling the Earth (see map, page 10). This became known as the Ptolemaic system and was overwhelmingly influential—and not a little appealing to both human ego and later medieval Christian beliefs. It was not until thirteen centuries after Ptolemy that Nicolaus Copernicus in 1543 stubbornly proposed the then heretical idea of a system of planetary movement in which the planets, including Earth, circled the sun.

If Ptolemy's system would eventually be proven wrong, he nevertheless used extensive mathematical logic to reach his conclusions, and his convoluted mathematics based on the work of his near contemporary Hipparchus actually did predict the position of the known planets with reasonable accuracy. The *Almagest* included a catalogue of 1022 fixed stars and forty-eight named constellations, and 'Handy Tables', which laid out methods for computing the positions of the sun, moon and planets as well as the timing of eclipses. The *Almagest* became the indispensable astronomical reference text in three languages—Greek, Arabic and Latin—and was in use at least to the end of the fifteenth century.

Ptolemy's interest in astronomy was more than cerebral. It was a great passion. He once wrote: 'I know that I am the creature of a day: but when I search out the massed wheeling circles of the stars, my feet no longer touch the Earth, but, side by side with Zeus himself, I take my fill of ambrosia, the food of the gods'.

If Ptolemy's writings on astronomy were immensely influential for almost a millennium and a half, then his *Geographia* was even more so. Had such terms been around then, he would have been a 'bestselling author' not only in his own era, but for at least fourteen centuries after his death. *Geographia* became the standard and virtually unchallenged textbook for centuries. Losing nothing of its following, *Geographia* was translated into Latin at the beginning of the fifteenth century and very wisely dedicated to successive influential

Ptolemy's work, written in the second century AD, would remain immensely influential for over 1000 years. This illuminated initial showing Ptolemy holding an armillary sphere is from the 1482 Ulm Edition of Geographia.

popes, Gregory XII and Alexander V. By the mid-sixteenth century the possession of beautiful manuscripts of *Geographia*, originating mainly from Florence, became a symbol of conspicuous wealth. The manuscripts were accompanied by exquisitely drawn maps of the inhabited world reconstructed from those drawn under Ptolemy's precise instructions (the originals were lost quite early). *Geographia* also included calculations of latitude (with measurements given relative to the equator) and, far more dubiously, in longitude, for approximately 8000 places in Europe, North Africa and Asia Minor.

Ptolemy's map was certainly not the first world map to be drawn. The oldest surviving map predates Ptolemy's by seven centuries. But like his

highly influential geocentric concept of the universe, Ptolemy's map (see pages 32–3) would become a benchmark for future cartographers. Many of his ideas about the world, although sometimes (and then inevitably very) wrong, were perpetuated for an exceptionally long time and had a remarkable influence on the exploration of the planet.

THE WORLD ACCORDING TO PLINY

If Ptolemy was the scientific face of the second century AD, Gaius Plinius Secundus, better known as Pliny the Elder, was the very human face of encyclopaedic scientific knowledge in the preceding century. Born in northern Italy during the reign of the emperor Tiberius, in a tumultuous period in history, Pliny was an accumulator of knowledge and fascinated by the odd and bizarre in nature. Nothing failed to interest him, from botany and zoology to astronomy, agriculture, geology, geography, history, metallurgy and magic. He was a voracious reader, famously saying that there had never been a book so bad that he could not gain something from it. He claimed to have quoted from 2000 works by one hundred carefully chosen writers in compiling his *Natural History*.

In reality, he considerably underestimated the breadth of his research efforts. In an era when books were still rarities and access to them a privilege, Pliny quoted 140 Roman writers and more than 330 others. His taste for exotica in the natural world was shared with those who had lived in the earlier Hellenistic period of expansion far beyond the eastern Mediterranean, which had opened up new lands and cultures filled with wonders real and imaginary.

Pliny's preoccupation with the natural world was not that of an emotionally detached scientist, but rather that of a philosopher trying to explain in rational terms the universe and the role of humanity within it. Living in an age when philosophy and science had not formally parted ways, nor had the arts and sciences, Pliny was the ultimate seeker of the answer to the great eternal 'Why?' He could not resist asides and essays on social issues. His work had much in common with that of the earliest narrative historian, Herodotus, who had preceded him by 500 years. Both men had an encyclopaedic approach, both were omnivorous gatherers and organisers of knowledge. Of the two, however, Herodotus based far more of his works on personal exploration and first-hand discussions—and he was also the more sceptical. It took much to convince Herodotus of a fact unless he could examine it at first hand or dissect it in detail to check its veracity. Pliny, living more within the world of books, and often dependent on second- and third-hand reportage, was more easily led astray. Pliny produced many more treatises than the *Natural History*, and on a very wide range of subjects, but this work is the only one to survive.

The world that Pliny depicted was necessarily a mixture of fact, misunderstanding and fantasy. The section on astronomy in the *Natural History* is a wonderful amalgam. Pliny concurred with the generally accepted Pythagorean theory that the Earth was spherical and divided into climatic zones. However, he deemed it 'madness, absolute madness' to want to know about worlds beyond our own, or to contemplate measuring the Earth. He regarded the sun as the soul or mind of the universe. In a reversion

to early Greek thinking, and basing his ideas on the four classical elements—earth, air, fire and water—he described the planets as being suspended by the element air, while Earth was balanced in space with the fourth element, water. Beyond the sun, he said, lay the fires of heaven, which were glimpsed as the 'great array of blazing stars'.

Pliny wrote of wonders, including a shrine to Venus in Cyprus, where no rain ever fell, and a similar shrine to Minerva in Asia Minor where not only did rain never fall, but sacrifices never decayed. He described a place where the earth healed all wounds. Other marvels he described are explicable to modern science, such as a balancing rock that can be moved with a touch of a finger, magnetic mountains and a stone that eats away bodies. Science would have more difficulty explaining the rock of Scylla in the Straits of Messina, however, where a six-headed monster lived in a cave, or the utopian land of Hyperborea, located at the 'hinges on which the world turns'.

Pliny dismissed (with that rather superior tone assumed by the modernist who belongs to the dominant empire of the day) as outrageous Greek nonsense a story told 'with great relish' by Cornelius Nepos, a Roman biographer from the first century BC, of snakes guarding the crossing to the Lixus River (now the Al-Araish River, in northern Morocco), which was said to wind around the legendary island where the garden of Hesperides and its trees of golden apples were located. But he did not reject stories that Mount Atlas in Africa rendered people speechless with mysterious apprehension, that it soared almost to the moon, that it flashed with fires and was inhabited by frolicking satyrs and goat-pans, or that the air at night was filled with the sounds of flutes, pipes, drums and cymbals.

Pliny stands on the cusp between the ancient world of myth and legend, and the modern world of fact. His writings were often accurate, but he was sometimes betrayed by his era and perhaps by a reluctance to forsake entirely a world so richly imagined. He made a substantial contribution to writings on zoology, quite a deal of it seeming to depend on careful first-hand observation, and to botany. He probably fared worst in the section on geography in the *Natural History*, although the section is a delightful literary exercise filled with colourful stories of people and places far away. Quite inexplicably he often followed the ideas of generations long before him, ignoring the new information resulting from the exploration and conquests of the Roman Empire.

Nevertheless, in some ways Pliny was a voice two millennia before his time. To him, the gods and nature were one. Although human impact upon the planet was very small compared to its impact in our times, he protested strongly at the destructiveness of humanity and the damage caused to nature as a result of demands for a more luxurious, consumer-oriented lifestyle. As a follower of the Stoic school of philosophy, he chose to live an essentially simple life, dedicated entirely to intellectual activity and public office.

Pliny was the complete workaholic from early in life, with fierce powers of concentration and sleeping very little. He lived by the creed 'To live is to be awake'; he was a member of an advisory council serving the emperor, practised as a lawyer, served in the military, and held a number of important public offices. According to his industrious nephew Pliny the Younger, certainly no slouch himself and a noted writer and bureaucrat, his uncle reproached him for walking when he might be carried to his destination in a sedan chair—walking was an unnecessary incursion on valuable research time. When travelling, Pliny the Elder kept a secretary constantly beside him to take notes.

Whether Pliny was heading for a health breakdown with this lifestyle we will never know, because his all-abiding curiosity killed him at the early age of fifty-five. In 79 AD Pliny was in an administrative position in command of the Roman fleet in the Bay of Naples. Fascinated with vulcanism, he insisted on observing Mount Vesuvius erupting at close quarters. Unfortunately, however, this was the eruption that destroyed Pompeii, Herculaneum, Stabiae and Oplontis. He was rowed in to Stabiae, and he died there like so many thousands, overcome by the deadly sulphurous fumes.

RIGHT: Frontispiece to Book I of a fifteenth century edition of Natural History *depicting Pliny the Elder doing astronomical calculations.*

CAII PLINII SECVNDI NATVRALIS HISTORIÆ
LIBER PRIMVS
CAIVS PLINIVS SECVNDVS NOVOCOMEN
SIS T. VESPASIANO SVO SALVTEM
PRAEFATIO

IBROS NATVRALIS HISTO
riæ nouitium camoenis quiritium tuoruz
opus natum apud me proxima foetura
licentiore epistola narrare constitui et
iucundissime imperator. Sit enim hæc
tui præfatio uerissima: dum maximo cose
nescit in patre. Nanq tu solebas putare ee
aliquid nofal nugas: ut obiicere mollia Ca
tullum conterraneum meum. Agnoscis
et hoc castrense uerbum. Ille enim ut scis:
permutatis prioribus syllabis durusculi
um se fecit: q uolebat existimari a uerna
culif tuis & famulis. Simul ut hac mea
petulantia fiat: quod proxime non fieri questus es in alia procaci epi
stola nostra: ut in quædam acta exeant. Scianq omnes: q ex æquo tecum
uiuat imperium. Triumphalis & censorius tu sextum q consul ac tri
buniciæ potestatis particeps. Et quod iis nobilius fecisti: duz illud
patri pariter & æquestri ordini prestas præfectus prætorii eius: omniaq
hæc rei pu. Et nobis quidem qualis in castrensi contubernio. Nec quicq
mutauit in te fortunæ amplitudo in iis: nisi ut prodesse tantunde pos
ses & uelles. Itaque cum cæteris in ueneratione tui pateant omnia illa
nobis ad colendum te familiarius audacia sola superest. Hanc igitur tibi
imputabis: & in nostra culpa tibi ignosces. Perfricui faciem: nec tamen
profeci. Quando alia uia occurris ingens. et longius etiam submoues
ingenii facibus. Fulgurat in nullo unq uerius dicta uis eloquentia. Ti
bi tribuniciæ potestatis facundia. Quanto tu ore patris laudes tonas.
Quanto fratris amas. Quantus in poetica es: o magna foecunditas aïmi
quenadmodum fratrem quoq imitareris excogitasti. Sed hæc quis posse
intrepidus æstimare: subiturus ingenii tui iudicium: presertim lacessitu
Neque enim similis est condicio publicantium: & nominatim e dicatium
Tum possem dicere: quid ista legis imperator. Humili uulgo scripta se
agricolarum: opificum turbæ: denique studioz ociosis. Quid te iudicez
facis: cum hanc operam condicerem: non eras in hoc albo. Maiorez te
sciebam: q ut descensurum hac putarem. Præterea est quædam publica
etiam eruditorz reiectio. Vtitur illa & M. Tullius extra omne inge
nii aleam positus. Et quod mirentur per aduocatam defenditur. Hæc
doctissimum omnium persius legere nolo. Lælium decimum uolo. Qd
si hoc Lucilius qui primus condidit stilnasum dicendum sibi putauit
Si cicero mutuandum: præsertim cum de re.pu. scriberet: quanto nos
causatius ad aliquem iudices difficilius. Sed hæc ego mihi nunc patroci
nia adero nuncupatione. Qd plurimum refert: fortiatur ne aliquis

EARLY VIEWS
OF THE WORLD

The Ancient Greeks envisioned the Earth as being encircled by a great river of fresh water known as Okeanus (also later known as Oceanus), the source of all underground water, springs and rivers. The River Styx, the River Eridanos of the utopian land of Hyperborea and the Nile of Ethiopia were all said to arise directly from Okeanus. It formed the boundary of the Earth, a nine-fold stream beyond which lay only impenetrable mist and darkness, where the rim of the great bowl of the sky settled upon the Earth. Some believed that Hades lay within the outer darkness, while others thought it lay within the subterranean places of the Earth. Each night the moon and stars would emerge from Okeanus, while the sun god travelled in a golden chariot from the west to the east of the mighty river, to rise again in the morning in the eastern sky.

The Earth itself was a flat disc on which humanity dwelled. Above was a hemispherical dome of light—the realm of the gods. Below the disc, below

Hades, was a twin inverted hemisphere of darkness called Tartarus.

The Greek historian Herodotus, writing in the fifth century BC, would have none of the prevailing cosmology, stating in Book II of his *Histories* that 'the opinion about Okeanus is grounded in obscurity and needs no disproof; for I know of no Okeanus river; and I suppose that Homer or some older poet invented this name and brought it into his poetry'. And to leave his readers in no doubt, in Book IV of the *Histories*, sounding much like a professor irritated by an obdurately dim student, Herodotus added, 'As for Okeanus, the Greeks say that it flows around the whole world from which the sun rises, but they cannot prove that this is so'.

Herodotus was correct in thinking that Okeanus was but a suspiciously useful literary device. Homer placed all manner of marvellous places within the streams of Okeanus in his seventh century BC *Odyssey*, including the Elysian Fields where the weather was always pleasant and the cooling breezes were borne from Okeanus, the Land of Dreams and the Gates of the Sun. In the same period the poet Hesiod placed the Islands of the Blessed within Okeanus — a place where heroes lived untouched by sorrow. He also described gorgons living on a rocky island called Sarpedon (Isle of the Sword), and Hesperia, the Evening Isle at the very edge of the world where the Hesperides guarded golden-fruited apple trees. The dramatist Aeschylus creatively supplied the writhing snake-haired gorgons with near neighbours, the three Phorcides maidens and also added Erytheia, the Red Isle, to the lands that lay beyond the Pillars of Hercules where Heracles completed the tenth of his great labours, overcoming the three-bodied monster Geryon and stealing his crimson-coloured cattle. One can quite see why Herodotus might despair of Greek notions of geography, no matter how inspiringly described.

FLAT OR ROUND?

One of the great schisms in early philosophical thinking was caused by the debate between the flat-Earthers and spherical-Earthers. Philosophy and aesthetics may seem to be somewhat unusual bedfellows, but many early scientific debates tended to involve the sense of order, balance and symmetry that it was thought should epitomise the creations, if not the behaviour, of the gods.

Pythagoras of Samos, a Greek mathematician of the sixth century BC, was as much a mystic as a philosopher, although today he seems to be remembered largely, and dryly, for his theorem. For him, the purity of numbers and the patterns to be found in numbers were the very basis of a universe ultimately based on logic and perfection. He was certainly an early advocate of the idea of a spherical Earth and is said to have developed his concept from the belief that the Earth and the planets would be based on the most perfect and most balanced geometric form, the sphere. The Pythagorean cosmology also included spherical planets and planetary axes. Pythagoras originally supported the concept of a geocentric system, in which the planets and stars circled the Earth, but later advocated a system in which the planets revolved around a central fire. His writings have been lost and his achievements are known largely by repute, but it would seem reasonable that the fire he referred to was the sun. It was certainly a remarkable insight, when the prevailing notions of earlier centuries had not progressed beyond the idea of a flat, circular Earth floating on a vast sea. Very early Greek maps, such as those of Anaximander in the sixth century BC certainly reflected that idea.

The dominant belief among intellectuals in Greece from the fifth century BC onward was that the Earth was spherical. Plato, who together with his teacher Socrates and pupil Aristotle founded philosophy in the Western world, studied in the Pythagorean school, and both he and Aristotle taught their followers that the Earth was spherical.

Aristotle added real substance to the argument with his practical observations. He noticed that the Earth cast a rounded shadow against the moon during a lunar eclipse, which suggested that the Earth was a sphere. Aristotle also made logical deductions regarding the relative positions of particular constellations observed in different parts of the world and correctly concluded that such observations could only be made if the Earth's surface was curved. He also divided this spherical world into climatic zones, recognising an equatorial torrid zone, frigid zones at the polar extremities, and two temperate regions lying between. By the third century BC, the Greek scholar and geographer Eratosthenes, in a bravura display of trigonometry and logic, had calculated with remarkable precision the circumference of the Earth, coming within 5 to 10 per cent of the correct figure.

RIGHT: According to Cosmas Indicopleustes and some of his early Christian contemporaries, the Earth was not only flat but enclosed in a box with a curved lid—modelled on the Tabernacle in the Bible (c. 540 AD).

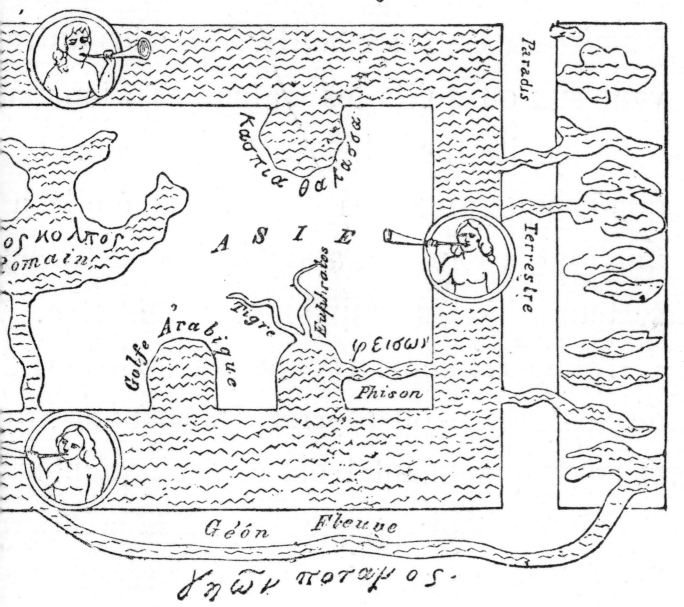

In the first century AD, Pliny the Elder wrote forcefully that 'the shape of the Earth is the first fact about which there is general agreement. At any rate we call the Earth a sphere and admit that it is included within poles'. He did, however, differentiate between the knowledge of scholars and that of the general public, adding that 'scholars assert that men are spread out all around the Earth and stand with their feet pointing towards each other … An ordinary person, however, inquires why men on the opposite side do not fall off—as if there is not an equally good reason for them wondering why *we* do not fall off'.

But later, the Christian Church was not entirely in accord with the opinions of Pliny's scholars. The highly intellectually influential St Augustine of Hippo, who spanned the fourth and fifth centuries AD, would have found himself in some more than robust debate with both Pliny and Ptolemy. He made it very clear in Book XVI of his theological opus *De Civitate Dei* (*The City of God*), that the idea of human beings living in the, as he called them, 'fabled Antipodes' was absurd. He based his argument on the belief that Adam fathered the human race in the northern hemisphere. It was therefore inconceivable that humanity might have subsequently populated the southern hemisphere, for 'it is too absurd to say, that some men might have taken ship and traversed the whole wide ocean and crossed from this side of the world to the other'. Other theologians of the time declared no descendants of Adam could have crossed the equatorial zones as they were too hot for a ship to survive.

Other Christian intellectuals more or less contemporary with St Augustine made it very clear that, in their opinion, the Greek scholars were entirely mistaken to believe in a spherical Earth. Many churchmen seemed to form their opinion as a result of bias against pagan science. After he became a convert to Christianity in the early fourth century AD the 'Christian Apologist' sometimes called the 'Christian Cicero', Lactantius, became a leading voice and author of scathing ridicule within the church against the theory of a spherical Earth. In his book *The Divine Institutions* he derided the idea that there might be inhabitants of the Antipodes 'whose footsteps are higher than their heads'. His voice was all the more effective for his having been the head of rhetoric at Nicomedia under the Emperor Diocletian. Other critics within the Church went even further, supporting the much earlier pagan belief in a flat disc-like Earth floating on the sea. Among these were the very influential Severian, the Bishop of Gabala, St Athanasius and St John Chrysostom.

The strangest concept of all, based on some wonderfully convoluted arguments, came from the sixth century Greek merchant turned Nestorian monk, Cosmas Indicopleustes, who reasoned that the Earth was not only flat but was enclosed in a box with a curved lid (see map, pages 22–3). Indicopleustes had made a number of long and genuine journeys as a trader, which he recorded in his richly illustrated book *Topographia* (printed in English under the title *Christian Topography*).

Despite the odd ideas he generated on the form of the Earth, Indicopleustes remains valuable to historians for his record of travels to the Malabar Coast of India and observations on the Syrian Christians who had settled there, as well as journeys to Taprobane (modern-day Sri Lanka, which was quite well known to the West from the time of Alexander the Great), Ethiopia and Eritrea. His writings provide a unique perspective on an eventful era.

Early medieval opinion among theologians about the form of the Earth appears to have been quite divided. The contraction of the Roman Empire and the loss of access to texts from the classical world led many to support the more ancient flat-disc model. Others, however, who perhaps had greater access to texts from the classical period, appear to have fully supported the spherical Earth concept. Some who supported the theory of a spherical Earth, including Bishop Vergilius of Salzberg in the eighth century AD, were reputedly threatened with persecution by the pope of the day, Pope Zachary, who described the theory of a spherical Earth peopled in both hemispheres as a 'perverse and sinful doctrine' and adhered to the belief that even if humans did exist in the Antipodes they could not be descendants of Adam and were therefore not entitled to redemption.

It is often claimed that few scholars in the medieval period denied that the Earth was spherical. As far as it goes, that is probably a fair statement. It is also fair to say that intellectuals may well have exaggerated their influence on the thinking of the masses, or for that matter of the Church. As Pliny lamented in the first century, the knowledge of learned men is not necessarily shared by people on the street. Even today, belief in a flat Earth has never quite disappeared. There is a Flat Earth Society that still perpetuates the concept. The original society declined in the 1990s, but a new Flat Earth Society was founded in 2004, despite decades of observations from space by satellites of a spherical Earth spinning on its axis.

Taprobane, the spice island

It might seem strange that the island of Sri Lanka was known to the ancient world, but it appeared on very early Greek maps, including those of Eratosthenes and Strabo, under the name Taprobane. The island was an important producer of spices and a trading centre for cinnamon, cloves, pepper, ginger and cardamom. It was represented as much larger than it actually is in relation to India, perhaps in response to its significance to trade at the time, and it was located at the tip of the Indian subcontinent rather than to the south-east.

Early information seems to have come from stories told by Indian merchants who traded regularly with Taprobane as well as with Europe. The exploits of Alexander the Great proved it was an island. An admiral in Alexander's navy called Onesicritus wrote in the later part of the fourth century BC about his time there and described elephants that were larger and 'more warlike in spirit' than those he had seen in India. Megasthenes described Taprobane as divided by a river and tantalisingly added that more gold and giant pearls were to be found there than in India.

The elder Pliny, in his *Natural History*, said that Taprobane had long been considered another world,

RIGHT: Map of the world according to the third century BC Greek geographer Eratosthenes, showing a disproportionately large Taprobane (modern-day Sri Lanka).

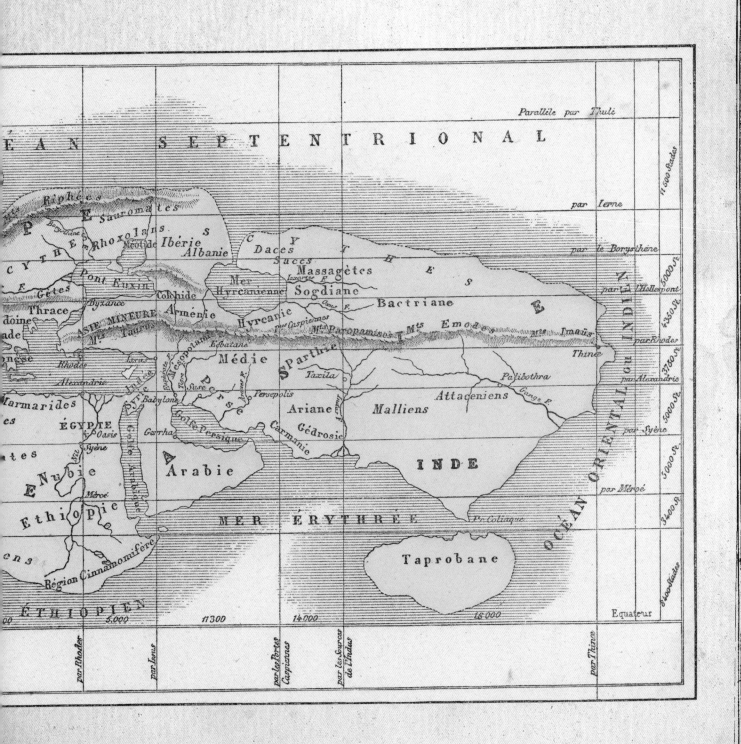

the Land of Antichthones—the place where everything is upside down. At least two journeys to Taprobane were recorded by the Romans: one by Annius Plocamus in the first century AD, and another by Sopatros in the fifth century. The sixth century Greek writer and traveller Cosmas Indicopleustes also gave first-hand accounts of Taprobane and described it as a significant stop on various trading routes: 'The island being as it is, in a position, is much frequented by ships from all parts of India and from Persia and Ethiopia and it likewise sends out many of its own and those from remote countries like China and other trading places'.

The geography of Taprobane was quite vague. The Romans believed it was located in the eastern ocean, its long axis aligned east–west and at right angles to the Indian subcontinent. The sea between Taprobane and India was thought to be very shallow in most places, no more than around five metres (sixteen feet), but with deep channels that ships' anchors could not reach. Accordingly ships with a prow at each end, were used so that they did not need to turn around in the narrow channels, and these ships were steered not by the stars, but by releasing birds, which guided the sailors to land. It was also reported that they did not put to sea for one hundred days from mid-summer onward—which would have coincided with the monsoon season and typhoons. The capacity of the ships was measured by the number of amphorae, or pottery storage jars, they could hold. The ships of Taprobane were rated at 3000 amphorae, a considerable cargo.

Pliny told the story of Annius Plocamus, who was contracted by the treasury of the Emperor Claudius to collect taxes from the Red Sea. (There was no escaping the taxman, no matter where you went, even in that era.) One of his men, while sailing around Arabia, was blown off course by northerly winds, and fourteen days later he made landfall in Taprobane, in the harbour of Hippuri. He received a generous welcome, and within six months had mastered the local language. Annius Plocamus's stories of Rome and its emperor intrigued the king of Taprobane, who eventually sent four envoys from his court. When they reached Rome, they in turn told wonderful stories about Taprobane. They described the 500 towns on the island and a royal city built on a south-facing harbour that had a population of 200,000 and a palace. India was four days sail from the island via the Island of the Sun, which was submerged beneath waters of deepest emerald. Trees grew there in clumps so that their tops were grazed by the rudders of passing ships. Was this a reference to the giant brown seaweed *Sargassum* that grows in great beds around western Sri Lanka? The envoys located Taprobane south-east of India and estimated the length of the western side of their island to be 2000 kilometres (1250 miles). They also gave valuable geographical clues about China, a place they traded with regularly, which lay beyond the Himalayas. But they described the Chinese as being of above-average height, and having golden hair and blue eyes.

Pliny disapproved of any unnecessary plunder of the Earth and of frivolous, ostentatious living, and he expressed his disappointment that Taprobane was not entirely free of the vices of the West, as gold and silver were highly valued there, together with precious stones, pearls and marble. Nonetheless, it would seem that Taprobane came close to modern ideas of a democratic Utopia. There were no slaves; no one slept in or took a siesta, as the privileged of Rome did, the people were instead diligent farmers. Their buildings were modest; prices were never subject to inflation; and Taprobane had neither lawsuits nor law courts. The king was chosen by the people from among the elders, for his forbearance and preferably childless state to prevent successional arguments. If a king had a son, the son was forced to sign away all hereditary rights. The king was supported by thirty wise counsellors, and if he betrayed his people he was condemned to social death—the equivalent of being sent to Coventry. Holidays were spent hunting for tigers and elephants, or fishing for turtles. The average life span on Taprobane was one hundred years. Even if only some of the stories Pliny reported were correct, ancient Sri Lanka came as close to the perfect kingdom as this Earth is likely to see.

In fact, Taprobane was seen as a de facto paradise, a storybook kingdom, and a place of the miraculous, said to have been visited by Gautama Buddha, the god Vishnu, Sinbad the Sailor, Alexander the Great, the Chinese pilgrim Fa Hien in the early fifth century, and Marco Polo in the thirteenth century. It was also a place where Noah's Ark was said to have come to rest after the great flood, and where Adam ended his days. The island has been known under many names, including Serendib, and its propensity for being a place of fortuitous, happy discoveries led to the word *serendipitous*.

THE FIRST MAPS

If the prevailing world view would eventually support the spherical Earth theory, exactly what was on the surface of that sphere would prove to be even more contentious. Time travelling through the great maps of the Western world, whether they are based on scholarly precision or are delightfully intricate works of art and imagination, provides a powerful insight into the evolution of the West's increasing wealth and influence. While the maps chart the progress of explorers and traders, incorporating expanding geographical understanding, they also demonstrate that knowledge can truly equate to power.

The oldest surviving attempt to create a map of the known world, the *Imago Mundi*, is a sixth century BC map that placed Babylon on the Euphrates (in modern Iraq) at the centre of the world, surrounded by a circular land mass. Both Armenia and Assyria are featured, together with a number of cities.

The renowned Greek philosopher and teacher of Pythagorus, Anaximander, created a map of the world at some time in the first half of the sixth century BC which was also circular but centred on the Aegean Sea. The land mass was divided into three portions, the largest being Europa, and the others Asia and Libya (as Africa was then known). The three lands were surrounded by a circular ocean.

Not long after, in the fifth century BC, Hecataeus of Miletus wrote a two-volume work entitled *Ges Periodos* (*Travels Around the Earth*) in which he described the world as it was known to the West at the time, and refined and added detail to Anaximander's map. The first volume was based on the Mediterranean world as far north as the fearful land of Scythia, the second was devoted to Asia. The earliest remaining copy, existing in fragments, dates to the first century AD.

By the early third century BC, the world as Eratosthenes knew it was already more complex than the one represented by Anaximander. The *mappa mundi* of Eratosthenes (see pages 26–7) is certainly more recognisable to us today, though still distorted. It had benefited from the knowledge gained through the campaigns of Alexander the Great, and from the many explorers and traders who were pushing back the boundaries of the known world. His map became a benchmark for cartography, depicting the entire world then known to Westerners. If the proportions are not correct, the Mediterranean is nevertheless represented largely accurately and includes the Iberian Peninsula and the Pillars of Hercules (Gibraltar). The northern shores of Africa are shown, along with the important islands of Crete, Sicily, Sardinia and Corsica, and great cities, including Athens, Byzantium,

Alexandria, Carthage and Cyrene. Rivers, such as the Danube, Nile, Tigris and Euphrates, are somewhat less accurately drawn.

Africa was terminated not far south of the Arabian Gulf, and at its southernmost extension lies Cinnamon Land, a reflection of the spice trade that was already well established. Traders landed their precious cargo on the eastern shores of Africa, where the spices were offloaded and shipped north for sale. For centuries many thought that Africa itself was the source of the spices that traders brought from India and the East Indies.

On Eratosthenes' map the northern portion of Africa is labelled Libya, and the south is labelled Ethiopia. To the north-west, off the European coast, lies Britain, although it is shown lying parallel to the mainland, and somewhat enlarged. Beyond Britain lies the mysterious land of Thule. To the east of the Mediterranean countries lies the vast Persian Empire, which at its peak was the largest in the classical world, encompassing all of modern-day Pakistan and Afghanistan, Asia Minor, Central Asia (including ancient Tajikistan, Uzbekistan with its famed cities of Samarkand, Tashkent, Bukhara, Khiva and Kokand on the ancient Silk Road, Kazakhstan, Kyrgyzstan and Turkmenistan), the Black Sea region, Saudi Arabia, Lebanon, Israel, Jordan, Syria and northern Egypt. Ancient Greece itself was fortunate not to be added to this vast empire, turning the Persians back in the fifth century BC. Still further east, at the limit of Eratosthenes' map, lay India.

North of the Mediterranean countries on this map lie the expansive lands of the fierce and feared tattooed Scythians, a group of nomadic tribes owing their allegiance to a single ruler and renowned for

PREVIOUS PAGES: Ptolemy's remarkable world map — this version is from Gerard Mercator's 1578 edition of Geographia —*shows the extent of the ancients' knowledge of the globe and applies an understanding of latitude and longitude that would not be surpassed until the seventeenth century.*

their great victories in war. They belonged largely to areas now occupied by Ukraine, southern Russia and Central Asia. One of the first groups of Scythians to move south were the Cimmerians, who gave their name to Crimea. In the seventh century BC they invaded and devastated Urartu (modern Armenia) and Phrygia (in modern Turkey). According to Herodotus, the Scythians also reached Palestine and ruled Medea for a number of years. Diodorus recorded that the women were covered in tattoos, just like the men, and fought just as bravely. Their use of hemp, which was recorded by Herodotus and confirmed by twentieth century archaeology, was both ceremonial (smoked particularly during burial ceremonies) and practical, as they wore clothing woven from hemp fibres.

The very pro-Roman Greek geographer Strabo is mainly remembered today for his seventeen-volume *Geographia* (*Geography*). Like Herodotus before him, whom he seems to have had little time for, Strabo was a born traveller (with the wealth to indulge that passion) as well as a geographer, making his works extremely valuable to modern historians. His books are full of fascinating insights, if rather drily written. For instance, he provided a remarkable account of the Nile River, travelling as Herodotus had done to the island of Elephantine in the Nile, opposite Aswan, as the official geographer for a Roman exploratory expedition. He also travelled through the region of the Tigris and Euphrates rivers, recording the levelled

remains of the biblical city of Nineveh in Assyria (but with no specific directions so that it remained lost for a further 1900 years), and the Hanging Garden of Babylon, which was then flourishing, built on a ziggurat, planted with trees and watered from the Euphrates by 'engines'. He described the equivalent of a four-lane highway around the top of Babylon's city walls.

Strabo's world map (c. 18 AD), which was probably produced in Alexandria, provides a link between Eratosthenes' map and that in Ptolemy's *Geographia*, a century and a half later.

The map is remarkable for the extent of its geographical knowledge. The proportions of land masses and their orientation are often incorrect, and eastern Asia largely indicated as the mysterious land of the Hyperboreans, a place akin to an earthly paradise where the sun shone all day and, according to the Greek Pindar 'neither disease nor bitter old age is mixed in their sacred blood', but the African continent and the Indian subcontinent are recognisable, together with Sri Lanka (Taprobane). Arabia and the Persian Gulf, the Mediterranean basin, and the area around the Caspian Sea all seem to be well known.

The world map created by Ptolemy has been long lost but a number of maps were reconstructed from the early medieval period onwards, using his book *Geographia* (c.150 AD) together with the extensive catalogue of latitude and longitude calculations that he made. Like Strabo's map, that of Ptolemy is clearly based on the earlier work of Eratosthenes, although Africa has been slightly increased in size and Europe has been extended northward. Ptolemy's map shows a greater knowledge of the eastern world than Strabo and includes China (Sinai), the China Sea (Magnus Sinus) and the Indian Ocean (Indicum Pelagus). The northern coastline of Asia is not depicted. The Crimean Peninsula is shown as Aurea Chersonesus. Ptolemy's knowledge of the western fringes of the known world was also more detailed than that of Strabo. Britain (Albion) is shown off the west coast of Europe together with Ireland (Hibernia) displaced to the north, and what was probably Scandinavia shown as two islands named respectively Thule and Scandia. With a demonstration of mathematical genius, Ptolemy had also produced a treatise, the *Analemma*, which dealt with the concept of orthographic projection—the mathematical projection of a sphere upon a flat surface, a problem with which cartographers would

struggle for many centuries—and his mapping skills incorporated that knowledge. Although the calculation of longitude would not be fully solved for many centuries, Ptolemy incorporated latitude and longitude in his maps long before the seventeenth century mathematician René Descartes (remembered by many for his quotable 'I am thinking therefore I exist'), who is usually given credit for the use of mapping coordinates.

Ptolemy rejected speculation and dogma, together with most travellers' yarns unless they were well corroborated. His concerns were purely scientific and impersonal, and it would be centuries before sieving truth from unsupported beliefs would again become the norm. The distortions in Ptolemy's maps arise largely from the lack of reliable data available to him.

MAPS OF THE
MIDDLE AGES

Unlike the maps of the Roman period, those of the Middle Ages were often more symbolic than practical, and they were much influenced by religious belief. Jerusalem was often depicted at the centre of the world, just as sacred Delphi had been in some ancient Greek maps. The Garden of Eden was generally thought to be located in Asia and was therefore placed at the uppermost limit of many maps, with Europe and Asia below. The tripartite map created in the early seventh century by a leading European scholar St Isidore of Seville in his *Etymologiae*, or *Origines* (*Encyclopaedia*, or *Origins*) was the first to be printed in Europe and it differed disturbingly little from Anaximander's map of more than a millennium before. Isidore's map clearly reveals the desire and struggle to reconcile deeply held religious beliefs with scientific observation in the medieval period. His map depicts a circular world surrounded by ocean, the Mare Oceanus. The land mass was divided into three portions – Asia occupies the upper half, with Paradise located at

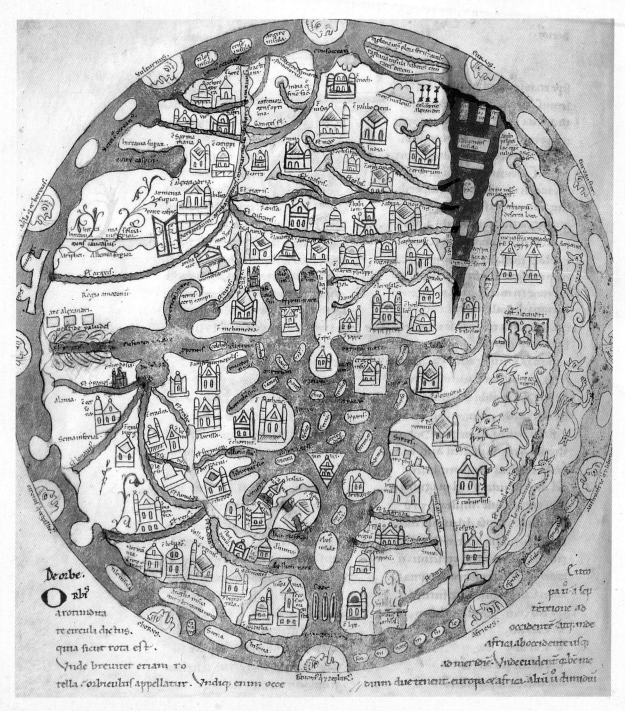

This eleventh century version of St Isidore's tripartite map reveals the struggle to reconcile Christian teachings and scientific understanding during the Middle Ages. Jerusalem is at the centre of a circular world with Paradise at the top of the map beyond Asia, and Europe and Africa separated in the lower half by the Mediterranean Sea. The red wedge shape is the Red Sea.

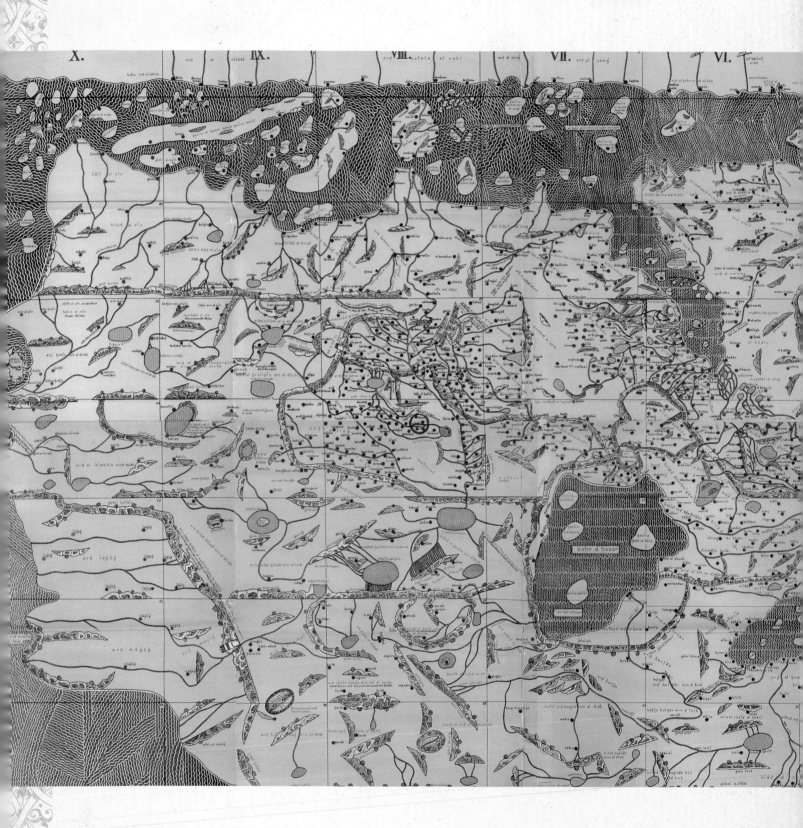

the extreme top of the map, and Europe and Africa shown equal in size in the lower sector. The three lands are divided from each other by a very stylised Mediterranean Sea, Red Sea and River Tanais (the Don). At the centre stands Jerusalem. Below it St Isidore seems to have leaned heavily on early classical writers, and also on the Church's teachings in his work. The feared Scythians of the ancient world and the Goths are presented, together with biblical Magog. The River Ganges is identified along with the River Phison, shown flowing from Paradise. Winged griffins, wonderful leaves from which fleeces are cut and clothes fashioned (perhaps a distorted reference to cotton plants), and other wonders described by the ancient writers all received mention in Isidore's *Etymologiae*.

An elaborate eleventh century version of Isidore's map reveals a further decline in knowledge compared with Ptolemy's time. Or perhaps it is fairer to say that what was known in practical terms could not be expressed in publications for fear of charges of heresy.

In the fifteenth century a highly stylised map again derived from that in the *Etymologiae* was published in Augsberg, depicting sixth century beliefs with the world peopled by the descendants of Adam through the sons of Noah—Europe by Japheth's descendents, Africa by Ham's, and Asia by Shem's. Isidore's work was so pervasive and so long-lived that the original classical references

LEFT: Detail from the Tabula Rogeriana, *drawn by the Arab geographer al-Idrisi for Roger II of Sicily in 1154, showing Europe (at the bottom) and Africa (at the top). Islamic maps during the Middle Ages reveal an understanding of the world far in advance of the West, which was stifled by Christian dogma.*

from which he borrowed heavily, and sometimes most ineptly, were no longer copied and were lost for all time.

The *mappa mundi* (world map) of the Beatus of Liébana codex (see pages 70–1), created by the Spanish monk, geographer and theologian Saint Beatus, was drawn in the eighth century, and is another example of a map so stylised that it is barely recognisable as planet Earth. The theological dictatorship that ruled European thought in the Middle Ages clearly had its effect in stifling genuine scientific scholarship. As a result, the centre of the progressive intellectual world inevitably moved eastward once more.

The *mappa mundi* created by the famous Arab cartographer and geographer Abu Abd Allah Muhammad al-Idrisi in the mid-twelfth century court of King Roger II of Sicily, depicted the real world far more accurately than any maps produced at the time in Western Europe (see previous pages). While scientific research was virtually comatose in Western Europe, intellectuals in the Arab world rediscovered and studied the great works of the past, building on them to create a golden age of science and research, supported by knowledge gained from within the cultures of their vastly expanding empire.

For some time Arab culture dominated the Mediterranean, and if any good was to come from the endless Crusades it would lie in the access that Western Europe finally gained to the great stores of knowledge locked up in lands such as Syria and Egypt. It is a too often repeated tragedy that the acquisition and retention of real knowledge of the world has been suppressed by narrowly confined outlooks of many religious persuasions.

The beautiful Hereford *Mappa Mundi* (see page 54), created around 1300, is the largest and greatest illustrated medieval map in existence. It is held in Hereford Cathedral, and is attributed to Richard of Haldingham and Lafford, also known as Richard de Bello, who was at the time of its creation a canon in Lincoln Cathedral. Like other medieval Christian-based maps, it was at least as much a spiritual interpretation of the world as a geographical one. Jerusalem lies at the centre of this tripartite world, with the Garden of Eden placed, as usual, at the top. The map is very richly illustrated with around 500 images including fifteen biblical events, approximately 420 medieval towns and cities, and many plants, animals, and birds. The map of Beatus of Liébana, the Psalter map (probably from London or Westminster c. 1265) and the very richly detailed tripartite Ebstorf map (see page 64) created by Gervase of Tilbury (c. 1234) bear a close resemblance to the Hereford *Mappa Mundi*. They are immensely important examples of medieval European Christian cartographic tradition.

MAPS DURING THE AGE OF EXPLORATION

The fifteenth century, which marked the Age of Exploration, produced some of the most important maps of the world. The Kangnido world map, produced in 1402 and painted on silk, was perhaps the perfect beginning for such an age. It emerged from Korea and represents a fusion of the geographical knowledge of two great cultures—that of the Arab world, brought to the East by Arab scholars living in the Mongol Empire, and that of the Far East, centred on China. The map depicted China, Japan, Korea, South Asia, Africa, the Middle East and Europe, and is considered as fine as any produced up to that time in Western Europe. Only two copies of the Kangnido world map are known to exist and both are preserved in Japan.

A circular *mappa mundi* was produced in Venice between 1411 and 1415 by the Venetian Albertinus de Virga. The map is particularly ornamental and beautifully coloured, incorporating a calendar and two tables, but it is the content that is remarkable. Africa is recognisable before the Portuguese were

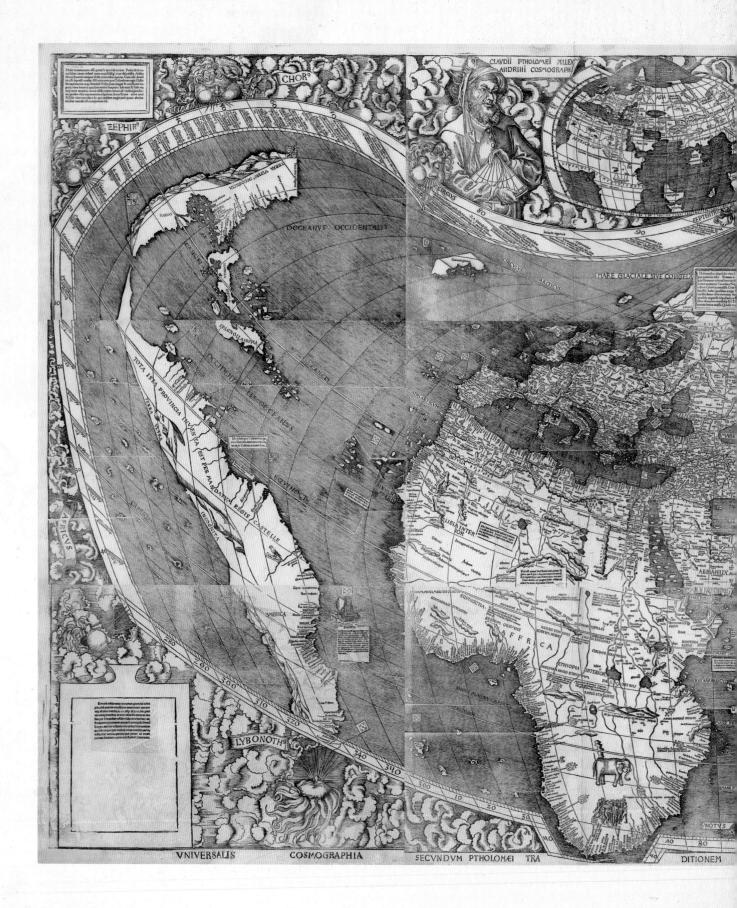

UNIVERSALIS COSMOGRAPHIA SECVNDVM PTHOLOMÆI TRA DITIONEM

AMERICI VESPVCII

AQVILO

CECIAS

SVBSOLANVS

GLACIALE

CIRCVLVS ARCTICVS

TAGVI PROVIN CIAMAGNA

CHATAY

SERICA REGIO

SCITHIA EXTRA IMAV

ASIA

INDIA MERIDIONALIS

CVAM PROVINCIA MAGNA

OCCEANVS ORIENTALIS INDICVS

REGNVM AIRVM

WITVRI EVRVS

SINVS GANGETICVS

INDIA

EQVINOCTIALIS

OCCEANVS INDICVS MERIDIONALIS

CAPRICORNIVS

JAVA MINOR

EVRONOTVS

TROPICO CAPRICORNI

MADAGASCAR

AVSTER

110   120   130   140   150   160   170   180   190   200   210   220   230   240   250   260   270

ET   AMERICI   VESPVCII   ALIORV QVE   LVSTRATIONES

PREVIOUS PAGES: Arguably the most famous map of all time, Martin Waldseemüller's 1507 Universalis Cosmographia *was the first map to include the name 'America' on the lands reached by Christopher Columbus in 1492. It is housed in the US Library of Congress.*

to explore its coasts (however, ancient Phoenician records of travel along African shores still existed). The Azores appear, although officially and dubiously they would not be discovered until 1427. As well, the Canary Islands, which were almost certainly the Fortunate Isles known to the world of antiquity—but 'discovered' in the fourteenth century, according to Las Casas, by a French (or possibly English) vessel blown off course by contrary winds. Greenland also appears to be indicated on Virga's map, together with Norway (Norveka). The mythical Kingdom of Prester John is placed in Ethiopia and Jerusalem is marked, but it is no longer at the centre of the map. The Garden of Eden is relocated at the southernmost part of Africa (which would have been roundly denied by St Augustine). The feared lands of Gog and Magog are located in Northern Europe. Locations within Asia are consistent with the knowledge of the Mongols. Even more remarkably, the northern shoreline of Australia appears to be located, and depicted from northern Western Australia to the Gulf of Carpentaria.

Virga's map was followed by a significant atlas on ten sheets of vellum produced in 1436 by Andrea Bianco (see page 88), the commander of a Venetian galley and a cartographer. The atlas includes eight sheets of navigation charts and is believed by many to contain the first correct representation of Florida as a large peninsula which is shown projecting from the legendary island of 'Antillea'—fifty-six years

before Columbus' voyage. Bianco also assisted in the production of the *mappa mundi* which was commissioned by King Afonso (also Alfonso) V of Portugal and made between 1457 and 1459 by the Venetian monk Fra Mauro (see pages 118–19). The original was lost, but a copy that Fra Mauro was working on before his death in 1460 was completed by Andrea Bianco, and remains.

In 1492, the year Christopher Columbus sailed to the Americas, Martin Behaim, a German navigator who later worked as a geographer for the court of King John II of Portugal, produced a globe overlaid with a world map in which there is an all but virtually empty ocean between Europe and Asia (which was excessively enlarged on the globe). But there is an oddity worth noting on the map. Antillia was placed on this map too, together with a notation by Behaim that it was also called Seven Cities, perpetuating the myth of the island and further influencing explorers of the day, including Columbus. Clearly Behaim had faith in its existence. He added that 'in 1414 a ship from Spain got near it without being endangered'.

Early maps that incorporated knowledge gained from the journey of Columbus to the Americas included the 1500 *mappa mundi* of the Spanish cartographer Juan de la Cosa (see pages 72–3). It is the earliest known surviving European map to have depicted the Americas, although other maps had almost certainly been made as a result of Viking explorations, and possibly other early European landfalls on Newfoundland and Canada.

Two years later, an important benchmark map was named after Alberto Cantino, an agent of the Duke of Ferrara. Industrial espionage is not a modern phenomenon and spies abounded in the world of exploration. Knowledge of new geographic finds became the foundation of many great fortunes made in trade, and kings and queens, let alone dukes, were not above retaining the odd spy in foreign courts to gather information on new discoveries. Cantino smuggled the map that bears his name out of Portugal and into Italy. It depicts the world known to the Portuguese, and most significantly part of the coast of Brazil, which Portuguese explorer Pedro Alvares Cabral accidentally discovered in 1500.

The Brazilian coast would be further mapped by the Italian cartographer and explorer Amerigo Vespucci during two important expeditions in 1499 and 1502, and by the Italian cartographer and the Portuguese explorer Goncalo Coelho, also in 1502. With the information gained, together with various land explorations by the Portuguese, Lopo Homen produced a manuscript map of Brazil in c. 1519 (followed by a *mappa mundi* in 1554 which incorporated new knowledge from Portuguese explorations), while Diogo Ribeiro produced a manuscript map of Ferdinand Magellan's celebrated circumnavigation of the globe in 1527.

No discussion of the exploration of America and cartography is complete without mention of the world map produced by the sixteenth century German scholar, humanist and cartographer Martin Waldseemüller in 1507, because it provided the accidental reason for naming America. The map (see previous pages) is often referred to as America's birth certificate. Waldseemüller was a great admirer of Amerigo Vespucci, whose Latinised name was Americus Vesputius, and for quite inexplicable reasons Waldseemüller credited him with discovering the New World and proposed the name 'America' for this new land. Gerard Mercator used the name on his world map of 1538, and the rest is history.

Waldseemüller, seems to have undergone a sea change in his admiration of Vespucci in later years, however, as a result of a published letter by Vespucci that generously acknowledged Columbus's achievements. In the 1513 edition of Ptolemy's *Geographia* and the 1516 *Carta Marina* Waldseemüller removed the name 'America' and replaced it with 'Terra Incognita' and 'Terra Nova' respectively. Waldseemüller's 1507 world map, of which 1000 copies were printed, and his *Carta Marina* are today among the world's most valuable maps. Just one copy exists of each.

The oddest and most controversial of the maps created by the old cartographers is the Piri Reis map (see page 215), made in 1513 by the Ottoman Turkish admiral and cartographer of that name. Only about one-third of the original map has survived, but what remains depicts the Atlantic shorelines of Europe and North Africa, an accurate depiction of the coast of Brazil, the island groups of the Azores and Canaries, and the mysterious large island of Antillia. What is quite extraordinary is the depiction south of Cape Horn at the tip of South America (known to have been explored by Portuguese navigators before 1507) of what many take to be the first record of Antarctica.

MAPPING THE ANTIPODES

If the African and South American continents had yielded many of their coastline secrets to explorers and cartographers by the sixteenth century, the remaining Antipodean lands remained conjecture, an unsolved jigsaw formed from the scraps of vaguely charted coastline. Medieval dogma-based theories opposing the very existence of the Antipodes had given way to a forceful if simplistic argument that a Great South Land must exist in the south to act as a counterweight to the land masses of the northern hemisphere. The continent of Australia was an idea long before it was a reality for the Europeans.

The Dutch *Itinerario* map of the world showing the two hemispheres, created by Jan Huyghen van Linschoten in 1596, depicted the Great South Land as a massive single continent more than counterbalancing the land mass of the northern hemisphere. It dipped below South America and Africa but rose to include much of the southwest Pacific Ocean, engulfing the yet to be mapped Australia, New Zealand and Antarctica.

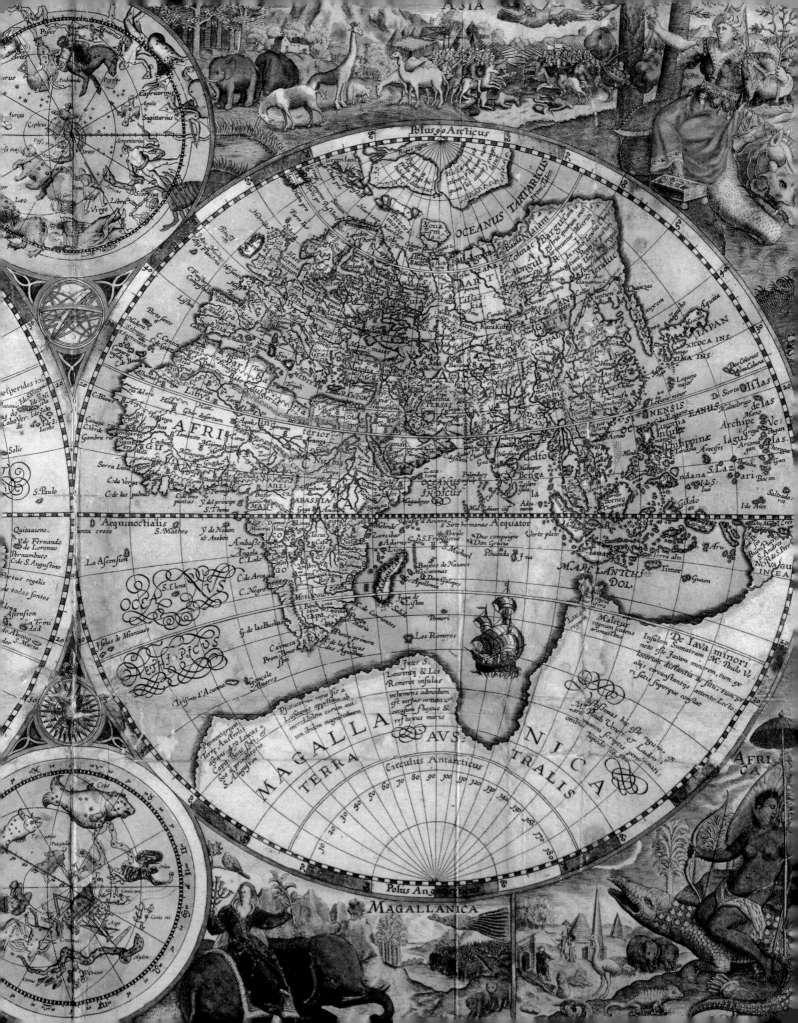

PREVIOUS PAGE: In 1598, Jan Huyghen van Linschoten's Itinerario *was published in English. The map detailed Portuguese knowledge of the East Indies and represented Australia as part of a huge southern continent.*

In 1627 a 'New Map of East India' appeared in English cartographer John Speed's last edition of *Prospect of the Most Famous Parts of the World*. If India is somewhat robbed of stature and the arrangement too compressed, the map is entirely recognisable to modern eyes, remarkably accurate and detailed, and included western New Guinea.

In 1636 a map produced by William Blaeu called *India quae orientalis dicitur et Insulae Adiacentes* revealed that an intimate knowledge of South-East Asia had emerged. It was evidence of the intense interest the Dutch now had in trading with the region. The individually mapped peninsulas, land masses and islands are distorted in terms of relative size, but coastlines are mapped with considerable accuracy. It is the first map to unambiguously depict a part of the Australian coastline.

Frederick de Wit's 1680 map of the known Pacific Ocean, *Mare del Zur cum Insula California*, published in Amsterdam, provided more pieces of the Australian (Hollandia Nova) jigsaw puzzle, including as it did virtually the entire coastline of the Northern Territory, the western coast of Cape York in Queensland (named 'Carpentaria' on the map), together with western New Guinea to the north and the southern two-thirds of Tasmania, which had been charted by Abel Tasman and named by the Dutch 'Anthoni van Diemen's Landt'. Vincenzo Coronelli's 1696 map of the Pacific repeated much the same features of Australia and New Zealand

but was notable as one of the maps which depicted California as an impressively large island lying to the west of virtually the entire coast of the modern United States.

By c. 1689, the Johannes van Keulen chart of the East Indies revealed a remarkably detailed and accurate knowledge of the Australian coastline, from the approximate region of York Peninsula in South Australia clockwise around the Western Australian and Northern Territory coastline to western Cape York and New Guinea (incorrectly attached to Australia), together with the lower two-thirds of Tasmania, including Schouten Island off Swansea on the east coast. Thanks to Dutch exploration, the great southern counterweight was all but resolved by the continental masses of Australia and Antarctica together with Tasmania and New Zealand.

HERE BE DRAGONS

A famous map notation that has descended to us from the great cartographers is 'Here Be Dragons'. Ancient maps were full of beautifully drawn serpents and fearful monsters that lurked in waters where no sensible man would dare take his boat. But only once does this warning actually appear on a surviving map, on the 13 centimetre (6 inch) diameter Lenox Globe, c. 1503–07, made from copper.

Almost as famous is the notation Terra Incognita, 'Parts Unknown'. It was a useful and much used phrase to describe regions of the world unknown to the West. Australia was once placed on maps in that vaguest of all regions, becoming Australia Incognita in an 1803 chart of the Indian Ocean issued in London by the publisher William Faden, fifteen years after settlement in Sydney. So incognita was Australia to

England that a parcel of extra names were added to the Faden map, such as 'New Holland' and 'Maletur', to ensure that the continent would be recognised. It was not until Matthew Flinders circumnavigated Australia and printed charts labelled 'Terra Australis' or 'Australia' that the Great South Land was finally awarded a proper name.

As for the term Terra Incognita, it finally became redundant as the last major explorations of the nineteenth century filled in the gaps on the world map.

Terra Incognita disappeared from maps at the end of the nineteenth century, and with it went the last vestiges of the impossible but thrilling wonders conjured by medieval minds. But it would survive elsewhere, in our modern dreams of travel among the stars, with all the attractions of the unknown for the imaginative and adventurous.

Detail from the Carta Marina *by Olaus Magnus, 1572, showing strange monsters and sea creatures in the waters west of Scandinavia.*

By sun and by stars

While a natural desire to fill the unknown with fictions both probable and improbable led to the creation of many mythical places in early maps, the mathematical concepts and technology necessary to the cartographer were painfully slow to evolve and aid exploration. This was at least in part responsible for the records of those mysterious places that never existed, or were distorted or displaced, and continued to appear on even relatively modern maps.

The Babylonians, Syrians, Egyptians and Greeks had all studied the movement of celestial bodies and had learned to chart a position and navigate by the sun and stars. The earliest and most primitive instrument to measure geographical position was a vertical shaft known as a *gnomon*, one form of which was invented by the Babylonians. Anaximander is credited with introducing it to the Greeks in the sixth century BC, when he was said to have placed one on a sundial. The gnomon was independently invented in China, perhaps even earlier than in the West, being mentioned in a second century BC Chinese text entitled *Nine Chapters on the Mathematical Art,* which stated that it had been in use since the eleventh century BC.

Early gnomons were vertical and their shadows could be used to determine the exact moment of noon, and the altitude of the sun, particularly the meridian (line of longitude). Later, gnomons on sundials were inclined to the horizontal at an angle equal to the latitude of the sundial's location. The gnomon cast a shadow across a surface marked with time intervals so that the sundial became a timepiece. Not until the eighteenth century would the ship's chronometer make accurate time measurement possible on sea voyages.

By the second century BC geographers had established the convention of describing a location by latitude and longitude according to rectangular coordinates. Credit for the notion of latitude and longitude is generally attributed to the Greek geographer Dicaearchus of Messina, who was born in the mid-fourth century BC. Ptolemy used rectangular coordinates to plot the position of places, and the latitudes he determined were serviceable, if not perfectly accurate, for shorter journeys.

Longitude, however was another story. Until accurate time measurement became possible, the precise measurement of longitude for long-distance travel remained an unsolvable problem. And an accurate method for measuring time would not be invented until the eighteenth century. For all their shortcomings in a world that was inconveniently spheroid rather than flat as once envisioned, Ptolemy's maps were destined to be the benchmark for geographers for more than a millennium.

It has been remarked that Columbus set out to discover the East Indies and pepper, and instead found the West Indies and chilli peppers, which might seem to indicate a certain inaccuracy in his navigational skills. But given the instrumentation of the day, his use of Ptolemy's maps, which indicated a much larger Asia than actually existed, and lack of an accurate timekeeper, Columbus must be applauded not only for his discoveries but also for surviving the voyage.

Columbus possessed a compass, which had been invented in Europe at the end of the twelfth century, and a sextant. The compass assisted sailors to determine their position by using a freely moving magnetised pointer that swung to align itself with the Earth's magnetic field. The pointer was suspended on a pivot or floated in a liquid. The face of the compass was marked with the cardinal points and intervals marking angles from zero at magnetic north to 360 (back to zero) degrees of the circle.

The sextant in Columbus's time was a large clumsy instrument that required the user to sight directly into the sun. It was not improved until c. 1600 by John Davis, whose Davis quadrant mercifully allowed the sighter to stand with his back to the sun. Not until later in the seventeenth century were refined calibrations made possible, with the use of a screw-based vernier scale invented by Pierre Vernier. Its ease of use and accuracy had been widely adopted by the first quarter of the eighteenth century.

But still the mariner's technology betrayed Venier. The octant, as the quadrant had become, was so large it was constructed of wood, which warped on long sea journeys, giving rise to sizable inaccuracies. Not until Jesse Ramsden invented the

By sun and by stars

dividing engine in the eighteenth century could smaller instruments with more accurate scales be developed, and made from much more serviceable brass.

Once a ship's navigator was equipped with a marine chronometer and a compass after the mid-eighteenth century, longitude could be calculated. A sextant provided the latitude. At last, those who ventured to sea could know with a high degree of accuracy where they were—unless they ran into a magnetic anomaly. That problem would not be overcome until the twentieth century, when compasses that operated independently of the Earth's magnetic field would be available—known as gyrocompasses on board ships, and astrocompasses on planes. Global positioning satellites now provide instant information on the position of anything, and anybody, on the planet, something beyond the wildest imaginings of those early sailors hugging the shoreline and placing their faith, and lives, in their knowledge of the sun and stars.

RIGHT: Navigators using an astrolabe in the Indian Ocean, *by the manuscript illuminator Boucicaut Master.*

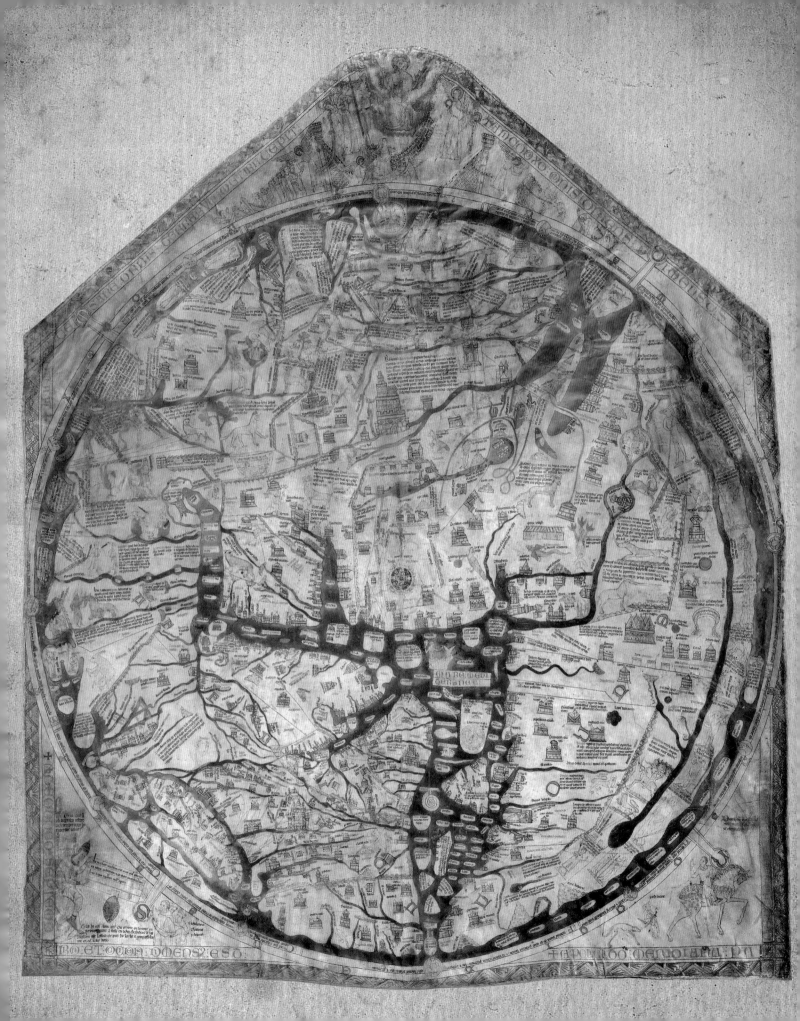

PART TWO

PARADISE ON EARTH

∾ ❦ ∾

THE UNIVERSAL DREAM OF PARADISE

THE CHRISTIAN WORLD OF THE MIDDLE AGES

FINDING THE GARDEN OF EDEN

THE QUEST FOR THE FOUNTAIN OF YOUTH

HELL ON EARTH

LEFT: The c. 1300 Hereford Mappa Mundi *placed Jerusalem in the centre of the known medieval Christian world. East is at the top of the map with the Garden of Eden in a circle at the edge.*

FOLLOWING PAGES: A sixteenth century painting of Paradise by Lucas Cranach the Elder showing God with Adam and Eve in the Garden of Eden.

THE UNIVERSAL
DREAM
OF PARADISE

Paradise is perhaps the most ancient of all human archetypes. It is universal to all places, all peoples and all times, and it is consistent as a cultural concept. Its geography and era may change, but its qualities never. Here there is eternal youth; nature provides everything any human sanely desires; there is no sadness and no sickness. It may be no place for moulding character but it is a reward and a refuge from the eternal strife of the real world. The waters are fresh and sweet, luscious fruits abound on every tree, the sun shines warmly and gentle breezes cool the skin. The ground is soft with lush grasses and spangled with flowers, the animals gentle and fearless—true companions of those who occupy such a blessed world. Here there is love and bliss and innocence and security, and rest in a place hidden from the remainder of the world.

St Basilius of Caesarea, also known as Basil the Great, was a fourth century theologian, recognised as a saint in both the Eastern Orthodox and Roman Catholic churches, and immensely influential not only through his work as a theologian but also through his political adroitness, steering a well-chosen course through the turmoils engendered after the first conference of the Christian Church, the Council of Nicea. His life was focused on the care of the needy and the poor. The dream of Paradise as described by St Basilius is based on the experiences of a man almost too familiar with the sufferings of the world and the stress of high office:

There the earth is always green, the flowers are ever blooming, the waters limpid and delicate; not rushing in rude and turbid torrents, but welling up in crystal fountains and winding in peaceful and silver streams. There no harsh and boisterous winds are permitted to shake and disturb the air and ravage the beauty of the groves; there prevails no melancholy nor darksome weather, no drowning rain nor pelting hail, no forked lightning nor rending and resounding thunder; no wintry pinching cold nor withering and panting summer heat, nor anything else that can give pain or sorrow or annoyance; but all is bland and gentle and serene; a perpetual youth and joy reigns throughout all nature and nothing decays or dies.

THE GARDEN OF EDEN

The story of Adam and Eve was only one of many creation stories found in ancient cultures. The ancient Persian creation myth was based on seven creations, rather than the seven days of the biblical Genesis, seven being one of the ancient sacred numbers. The sky was the first part of the cosmos to be created and was made of rock crystal and shaped like a sphere. Then water was created, followed by a perfectly flat Earth. The sun was placed directly above the Earth, fixed in the noon position. Plants and animals were then created, followed by humanity and fire. When all was in place the great cycle of day and night began.

The Prometheus story first appeared in c. 700 BC in Hesiod's epic narrative poem *Theogony*—a Greek creation story which encompassed the emergence of the gods and the cosmos. Hesiod's narrative began with the emergence of Chaos (air) and Tartarus (the underworld), which both sprang spontaneously into existence. Chaos gave birth to Eros (the life bringer), Gaia (earth), Erebos (darkness) and Nyx (night). The Titans, a group of minor gods of which Prometheus was a member, arose from particularly fertile matings between Gaia and Ouranos (the sky).

The Greeks held that in the Golden Age man was immortal and lived a happy life. The entire world was their paradise. But when Prometheus sought to challenge the great Zeus and stole from him the secret of fire, giving it to man, Zeus created a terrible and typically devious divine punishment. Hesiod described how Zeus ordered Hephaestus to create a woman, Pandora, so beautiful she would prove irresistible to all men. The gods Aphrodite, Hermes, Horae and Charites endowed her with gifts that added to her already ample attractions. She was walking temptation.

Prometheus was very aware of the desire for revenge harboured by Zeus and warned his brother Epimethius to have nothing to do with Pandora. His advice of course fell on deaf ears, and Epimethius married her. Zeus had given Pandora a sealed pithos (a storage jar, not a box as is often related) and armed her with the fatal gift of excessive curiosity. Inevitably Pandora opened the pithos and released

The tree of life and the tree of knowledge

Two trees were associated with the Garden of Eden in the book of Genesis in the Old Testament. One was the Tree of Knowledge of Good and Evil. In the Christian and Jewish traditions the second tree, the Tree of Life, was said to grow in the heart of both the heavenly and earthly Edens, a link between the two. It was the ultimate source of the four great rivers that watered Eden. An inverted Tree of Life was another powerful symbol, representing the upward path of spiritual growth.

Trees dwell simultaneously in three worlds, the subterranean, the Earth and the heavens. Together with their frequent great longevity, these attributes have given rise to a belief in their sacred nature common to many religions and cultures. In the ancient Norse cosmos, the sacred ash tree, Ygdrassil, Tree of the World, had its roots in the underworld while its branches supported the kingdom of the gods. The first man, named Ask, was said to have been carved from a log of ash (*Fraxinus excelsior*). The Mayas shared that cosmology, portraying the Tree of Life, Yaxche, with its branches lifted to support the heavens. The Holy Sycamore of Egypt connected the worlds of the living and the dead.

The Tree of Life was the source of great spiritual and earthly gifts. The Toomba Tree of the Qur'an is the source of flowing honey, milk and wine. The Tree of Life, bearer of fruits, was also a symbol of fertility and immortality in many places. In ancient Persia, the peach bestowed immortality. The Norse gods ate of the apples of immortality, which were guarded by Idunna. Sacred trees also conferred gifts. Buddha received enlightenment beneath the branches of the Bodhi tree, while the Norse god Odin received the gift of language. Gods even became trees or were personified as trees, like the Hindu Brahman and the Sumerian Dammuzi.

Finding the Tree of Life, and passing by its guardians was virtually impossible. Ancient images from China depicted a dragon at the base and the phoenix, symbol of resurrection, at the top. Other trees were guarded by griffins, angels or creatures of nightmares. Mortal man was unlikely to gain access.

The Tree of Life, from a thirteenth century Hebrew Bible and prayer book.

its contents, the instruments of death and sorrow. An infinitely vulnerable world was suddenly rendered mortal.

The Garden of Eden of the Abrahamic religions became synonymous with a place of innocence, the promised land of the after-life, the reward of those who lived valiant and blameless lives. The word Paradise itself comes from *pairidaeza* in the ancient Persian language, referring to a walled pleasure garden filled with beautiful fruitful trees, fragrant plants like lilies and roses, and cooled with streams and fountains.

The Garden of Eden is portrayed in the first book of the Old Testament of the Bible. After Adam was created from dust and Eve was created from Adam's side (or rib in the King James translation), the couple were placed in a garden eastward of Eden and instructed to become its stewards. Adam was given the strictest warning not to eat of the Tree of the Knowledge of Good and Evil, not even to touch it. A snake sinuously writhing in the forbidden tree, and usually understood to be the Devil in disguise, tempted Eve to taste the luscious fruit hanging from the boughs. Though Eve argued against picking one of the fruits, eventually her resistance was overcome and she picked a single perfect fruit, taking it to share with Adam. He too put up token resistance before sampling it. From that moment both became aware and lost their innocence. Adam and Eve were cast from the Garden of Eden so that they might not partake of the Tree of Life, and the entrance to the garden was closed to them forever, guarded by the cherubim and a flaming sword.

In the New World, one creation story, found in the Mayan epic *Popol Vuh* is perhaps the most touching of all and demonstrates the universality of human morality. The four creator gods in the heavens agreed to make 'man'. They each chose different materials. The first three chose clay, wood, and gold with which to fashion him. The clay and wood men were too easily destroyed. The gold man was very handsome, but cold. On the fourth attempt, one god fashioned man from his own flesh. The man of flesh brought great joy to the gods but the man of gold remained cold and unresponsive. The man of flesh showed kindness to the man of gold, warming his heart and bringing him to life.

From that time the gods ruled that no man of gold, a rich man, could enter heaven unless accompanied by a man of flesh, a poor man. The parallels with teachings in the Old World are obvious, but were ignored by the West in its crazed rush for gold and other forms of wealth when it reached the New World.

THE CHRISTIAN WORLD OF THE MIDDLE AGES

The Christian Church's all-pervasive dominance in Europe during the Middle Ages shaped almost all critical thought, and in turn map making. Orthodoxy rather than science and logic created a world view that became increasingly difficult and complex to defend as the facts were made to fit beliefs. Excommunication was a very grave and real threat and few were inclined to speak against accepted beliefs. One intellectual sticking point resulted from the story of Noah, descendant of Adam, and after the flood considered to be the father of the human race through his three sons. All had escaped death together with their wives by being safely gathered aboard the Ark during the biblical flood. After the flood their descendants populated the world—the biblical lands of Europe, Asia and Africa.

The very idea of a southern hemisphere, let alone one that was peopled, was anathema to many theologians based on this information, and also in conflict with the known world of the ancients. Christians knew that Noah and his family belonged

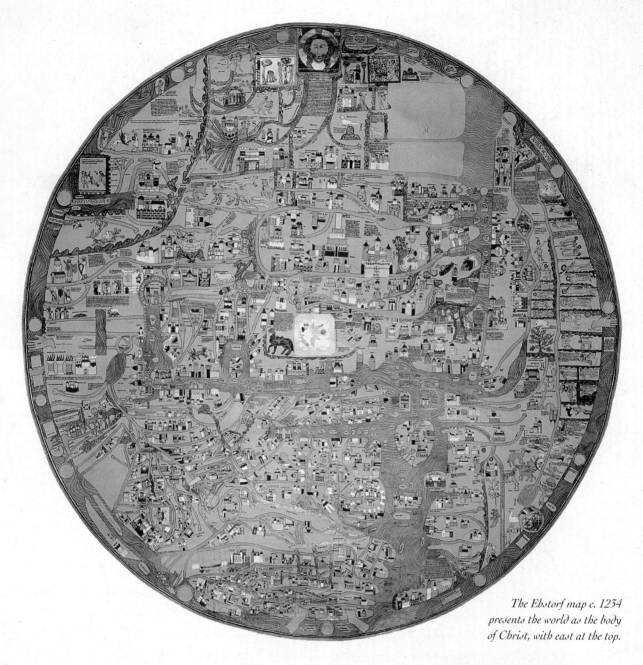

*The Ebstorf map c. 1234
presents the world as the body
of Christ, with east at the top.*

to the northern hemisphere. If any descendants had attempted to travel to the southern hemisphere the torrid equatorial zone would have shrivelled them to death while their boats burst into flames. And it was in any case inconceivable that men could sail so far from the shore to reach lands below the Earth where they would certainly fall off. And if for some inexplicable and astonishing reason there were people on the 'bottom' of the world, they clearly could not be descended from Adam through Noah, so were not entitled to redemption. (This attitude persisted for some time, with the support of various medieval popes, and goes some way to explaining the totally unchristian behaviour and prejudices of many in the sixteenth century and later against the inhabitants of the Antipodes.)

A strictly literal interpretation of Genesis, the first book of the Bible, provided a narrative to explain the origins of the peoples who inhabited the ancient world and reflected common linguistic inheritances. Seventy countries were recognised in Genesis. Noah and his wife Emzara (grand-daughter of Methuselah) had three sons, Shem, Ham and Japheth. After the flood, Noah was said to have assigned the world in three parts to his sons. Their three wives became known as the mothers of the human race. Shem was assigned western Asia and together with his wife Sedaqetelebab, through their sons, gave rise to twenty-six Semitic nations. Ham was apportioned Africa and together with his wife Na'eltana'uk became the progenitor of thirty Hamitic nations through their descendants. The youngest son, Japheth, was awarded lands largely associated with modern Europe, and he and his wife Adataneses would through their descendants found fourteen nations.

The total of seventy nations (allowing for natural intermingling) became another sticking point for those seeking to reconcile discoveries of lands beyond the ancient world with strict biblical interpretation. As the centuries rolled by it became undeniable that more countries existed but equally the problem arose as to how their existence could be interpreted through theologically determined geography.

Medieval *mappae mundi* were for centuries inferior to those of the Arabic world as they sought to interpret geography through the prism of religious orthodoxy. A brave attempt was made to create a geographical fit for the literal words found in the book of Ezekiel in the Old Testament: 'This city of Jerusalem I have set in the midst of nations, with other countries around her'. Such theological interpretations of real-world geography resulted in maps in which Jerusalem was placed precisely in the centre of the world leading to awkward distortions and maps that were as much fantasy as reality (and of very little practical value to travellers to the Holy Land).

One of the earliest Christian world maps to depict Jerusalem at the omphalos (navel, centre) of the world was included in a late eighth century manuscript titled *Commentary on the Apocalypse*, a somewhat turgid document written by Saint Beatus of Liébana, the Spanish theologian and geographer (see pages 70–1). It appeared to be inspired by the existence of Islam in Spain which was widely and wildly interpreted at the time as the Antichrist.

Jerusalem-centred maps did not come into great favour, however, until the thirteenth century when the Crusades had made Jerusalem such a prominent focus of Christian attention. The famous c. 1234 world map created at Ebstorf Benedictine abbey, possibly by Gervase of Tilbury (opposite page), demonstrated the dominance of Jerusalem-centric maps in that century. Careful examination shows the world depicted as the body of Christ with the head next to Paradise. The c. 1300 Hereford *Mappa Mundi* (see page 54) continued to place Jerusalem at the centre, and as late as 1581, Heinrich Bunting's *mappa mundi, Die gantze Welt in ein Kleberblat*, persisted in following medieval tradition with Jerusalem at the epicentre.

FINDING
THE GARDEN
OF EDEN

The medieval world tied itself in theological knots in an attempt to find an earthly location for Eden that would fit with the description provided in the Bible. It was often placed vaguely in the east, and sometimes on a very high peak so that it would have survived the biblical flood. The illustrations in the Hereford *Mappa Mundi* provide a location for various places within the Bible—a common attempt of cartographers of the time to simultaneously depict the world of the Bible and the geographical world—with Jerusalem at its centre (see page 54). The illustration of Adam and Eve covering their newly discovered 'interesting bits' while Eve introduces two inquisitive young animals to each other is naïvely drawn but engaging. Also included are the rivers Phison, Gihon, Tigris and Euphrates, all arising from a common source, together with the gates of the Garden of Eden, located at the top of the map.

The four rivers were generally interpreted in the medieval period to be the Ganges, the Nile (Gihon was one of the names for the Nile), the Tigris and the Euphrates. No wonder theologians were faced with a geographically insoluble puzzle in finding a common origin for these four great rivers that lie so far apart. But they certainly made every effort with some inventive explanations.

Sir John Mandeville (see page 106), an intrepid medieval explorer and teller of fine tales, was ever ready with explanations. According to him, some of these rivers travelled long distances underground from Paradise before surfacing far away from their origins. As for Paradise itself, it could not be located for all manner of reasons, which varied from the strength of the currents in the great rivers to fierce wild animals and, if all else failed, a high strong wall which excluded all who would search for the longed-for land. Mandeville told how:

Many great lords have tried at different times to travel by those rivers to Paradise, but they could not prosper their journeys; some of them died through exhaustion from rowing and excessive labour, some went blind and deaf through the noise of the waters, and some were drowned with the violence of the waves. And so no man, as I have said, can get there except through the special grace of God.

As exploration of Asia continued and Africa became less mysterious, like the Kingdom of Prester John (see page 101) the earthly Paradise moved from place to place, always on the edge of the known world. *Mappae mundi* regularly placed it where ready disproof was impossible, often at the North Pole (as with the Hereford *Mappa Mundi*).

Others located the Garden of Eden in the far-flung regions of the East, or near Jerusalem.

Some located Paradise on a mountain on the equinoctial line.

Many believed that Jerusalem, as the centre of Christianity, must have been near to the earthly Paradise, and there were some amazing explanations of the way in which the River Jordan travelled under the Earth, then split off first as the Nile which emerged to the south, then as the Tigris and the Euphrates, which eventually rose out of the Earth in the north, and as the Ganges in the east. The ancient prophet Ezekiel described a holy river flowing beneath Mt Moriah where the Temple Mount is built in Jerusalem. It was said that it would bring life back to the Dead Sea. A spring in Jerusalem is named Gihon, and is said to be connected to an underground river. It has been linked to both Ezekiel's vision and the Gihon River of Eden, but there is no convincing evidence for the river's existence.

Quite a few thought that the Garden of Eden was situated on various remote islands such as Taprobane (Sri Lanka) (see page 26). They were undeterred by the geographical difficulties of transporting the waters of the four great rives said to emerge from the Tree of Life over a vast distance to the East. Where there was imagination in the medieval period, there was a way. Almost without pause, two solutions were offered. Either the rivers would immediately plunge underground following a course of thousands of kilometres to reappear again, or rivers of fresh water, being lighter than sea water, could travel across the ocean to their biblically appointed places. St Brendan was said to have found his blessed land, his Eden, on an island after wandering across the Atlantic Ocean for seven years (see page 129).

Some would argue that the Garden of Eden was never an actual place but an archetypal memory of fruitfulness and plenty deeply embedded within the human memory. Others would claim that the story of the Garden of Eden was intended to be purely symbolic. Early neo-Platonist philosophers like the Philo of Alexandria and Origen interpreted the story with high intellectualism, as representative of man cultivating his soul and resisting all sensuous pleasures and temptations. This certainly eliminated many very knotty questions, not only theological but also geographical, in a single stroke. But most would have nothing of such explanations. If Adam and Eve were flesh and blood, then the Garden of Eden had been a real place on a solid earth, not an abstract theological concept. Here the blessed saints would live for a thousand years before the final judgement. Here mortal time began and mortal time would end.

SOME MODERN DETECTIVE WORK

Archaeology has substantiated the existence of many places described in the ancient world of the Bible. For instance, Jericho and its famous defensive walls that came (partly) tumbling down, as described in the Old Testament, has been excavated on the West Bank and dated to 8300 BC. Accordingly, any serious search for the Garden of Eden must begin with the geographical clues provided in Genesis 2:10–14:

And a river went out of Eden to water the garden; and from thence it was parted, and became into four heads: The name of the first is Pishon: that is it which compasseth the whole land of Havilah, where there is gold; And the gold of that land is good: there is bdellium and the onyx stone. And the name of the second river is Gihon; the same is it that compasseth the whole land of Ethiopia. And the name of the third river is Hiddekel [which was the Hebrew name for the Tigris]: *that is it which goeth toward the east of Assyria. And the fourth river is the Euphrates.*

This has left us with a geographical conundrum of the first order. The Tigris and the Euphrates are well known, and run through the modern country of Iraq. However, they arise separately, not from a Tree of Knowledge nor from a single spring. As the Tigris arises in the Taurus Mountains of eastern Turkey it has been suggested that the Garden of Eden may have been located there.

But what then were the mysterious rivers known as the Pishon and the Gihon? Some have argued that the four great rivers flowing through Iraq were the Tigris, its two major tributaries the Diyala and Zab rivers, and the Euphrates. Satellite imagery would certainly allow for that interpretation. Other biblical interpreters have nominated the Tigris, the Murat, and the Euphrates and its northern tributary. The region certainly bristles with ancient biblical names such as Nineveh and Babylon, and is the site of the first known great civilisations in the Old World. The Euphrates is particularly included in a number of biblical references.

Neither of the two suggested modern-day interpretations of the four great rivers of Genesis fits well with the biblical description, but the text in Genesis provides other clues. If we could locate 'Havilah', then perhaps we could discover where the Pishon flowed.

Havilah has traditionally been located by scholars in the north-west of Yemen. However, strong arguments have recently been advanced advocating a location in the Hejaz Mountains about 640 kilometres (400 miles) north of Yemen. Initial clues obtained from examination of alluvial deposits coupled with satellite imagery of the Arabian Peninsula provided strong evidence that a major ancient river rising in the Hejaz Mountains once channelled water through what is now desert and dunes to the Persian Gulf near the estuary of the Tigris–Euphrates. The river dried as a result of climate change somewhere between 3500 and 2000 BC. This river, which certainly existed within historical times, may well have been the Pishon, described in Genesis as encompassing 'the whole land of Havilah where there is gold; and the gold of that land is good'. It has now been named the Kuwait River.

Gold was first mined in the area approximately 5000 years ago and there is strong speculation that this was the true location of King Solomon's Mines. An enormous mined site of great antiquity has been discovered, with thousands of abandoned stone hammers, vast quantities of piled-up spent soil and rock still with traces of gold. The bdellium referred to in Genesis is also to be found in quantity in this area—it is an aromatic gum associated with myrrh and exuded from the tree *Commiphora wightii*.

But what of the fourth river in the Garden of Eden, the Gihon? The translators of the King James version of the Bible located the Gihon in 'Ethiopia'. The source of the Blue Nile lies in Ethiopia, but it is obviously too far south in northern Africa to be relevant. This conundrum might bring us to the end of any logical pursuit of the Garden of Eden, but Ethiopia is a result of a translator's misunderstanding. The word actually used was 'Cush' or 'Kashshu'. Certainly the Hebrews used the name Cush for Ethiopia (then a much larger area than it is today), but Cush also relates to the tribe of Cush, and the Bible contains references to the Cushites (Kashites) in Asia. In modern times people are associated with the place they live, but in this ancient period lands were named for the people who occupied them, not the other way around.

Genesis is notorious for its genealogy and endless 'begettings', but it contains fascinating clues to ancient history and places. Wherever the people of Cush dwelt, that became the land of Cush. The three sons of Noah, survivors of the biblical flood, were Shem, Ham and Japheth. In turn, the sons of Ham were Cush, together with Canaan, Put and Mizraim. The tribe founded by Cush were known as the Cushites in the Bible, and wherever they dwelt became the land of Cush. The Bible mentions both a Cush in Africa and a Cush in Asia, possibly inferring that the tribe at some stage had divided, with part emigrating northward to Asia. The empire of Kush lay to the south of Egypt and was first mentioned around 1970 BC, although it may have been much older in origin. The Asian Cushites are associated with the Kassites who inhabited Mesopotamia and the ancient Sumerian city of Kish, which would in turn locate the River Gihon somewhere in the vicinity of the Euphrates, not in Ethiopia at all.

As further confirmation that we now have the right general location for the fourth river of Genesis, the Bible records that Cush's sons included Nimrod, who was said to have founded Babel, Sumer, Akkad and possibly Asshur (the biblical account is open to dual interpretations with regard to Asshur). Havilah, another son of Cush and a tribal leader, gave his name to the area Havilah (which as previously mentioned is now thought to be around the Hejaz Mountains north of Yemen). Sabta, a third son, has been connected to the area of eastern Yemen. A fourth son, Raamah, is associated with the south-western area of the Arabian Peninsula. There is ample reason, given the location of many of Cush's sons, to believe that the land of Cush referred to in Genesis was not Ethiopia but the lands of the Kassites in Mesopotamia, an area occupied by modern Iraq. Thus, the Gihon could be the modern Karun River, which runs through neighbouring Iran.

The Mesopotamian Plain has a tangled history of 30,000 years of human occupation. Over that time a slow revolution took place from an ancient nomadic hunter–gatherer existence to a settled agrarian lifestyle and paved the way for the rise of urbanised peoples. These originators of our modern world were not the brilliant ancient Sumerians, but a pre-Sumerian culture, perhaps the Ubaidians whose culture goes back to 6000 BC. If these interpretations of the biblical clues to the location of Eden are correct, then this once lush, beautiful and fertile region is synonymous with the place where human civilisation truly began.

Our detective work cannot move past this point. We are probably as close as we will ever be to locating the Garden of Eden, at least until future archaeologists offer us more clues. But if the location of the Garden of Eden cannot yet be precisely fixed, other places suggested in the past can definitely be eliminated. It is

RIGHT: The mappa mundi *of the Beatus of Liébana codex. At the top of the map is the Garden of Eden, with Adam and Eve and the Tree of Life, and the four rivers of Paradise — the Tigris, Euphrates, Pishon and Gihon.*

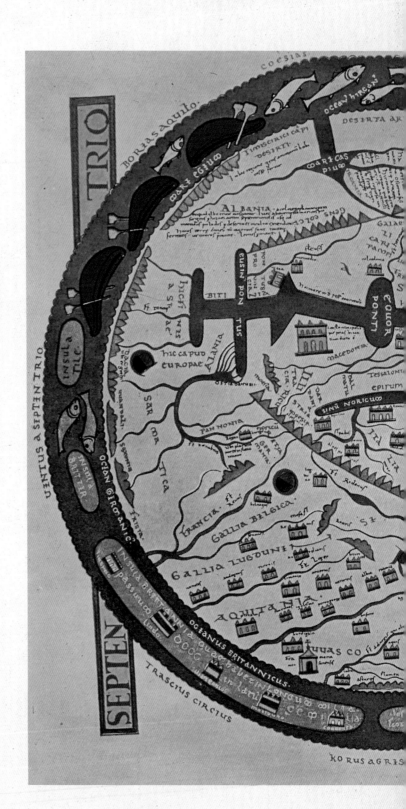

Columbus's search for Paradise

Even at the end of the fifteenth century, all kinds of beliefs continued to circulate about the location of the Garden of Eden. Christopher Columbus was a man with a quite strong mystical streak, not uncommon in his day. In his era, the Garden of Eden was quite regularly placed at the top of many *mappae mundi*, and like many others Columbus shared the belief that Paradise was located in some very high place. But Columbus went much further and developed a theory that the Earth was not so much round as pear shaped, and that Paradise lay at the very top of the pear. His writings towards the end of his career were that of a widely read and widely travelled man of his time, one with a philosophical bent and the deep religious belief that governed the lives of almost all Western Europeans in the fifteenth century. He read the various debates on Paradise among the most influential writers such as Strabo, St Isidore of Seville, the Venerable Bede, Scotus and St Ambrosius. He rejected 'heathen' locations such as the Fortunate Isles (Canary Islands), but could find no earthly location for Paradise among writings in either Greek or Latin. He became convinced that by sailing south of the equator he would encounter Paradise. He neither expected to be able to sail to the summit of this paradise nor to be admitted there other than by God's will, but he made it quite clear that he believed that Paradise lay to the south of his initial discoveries in the New World.

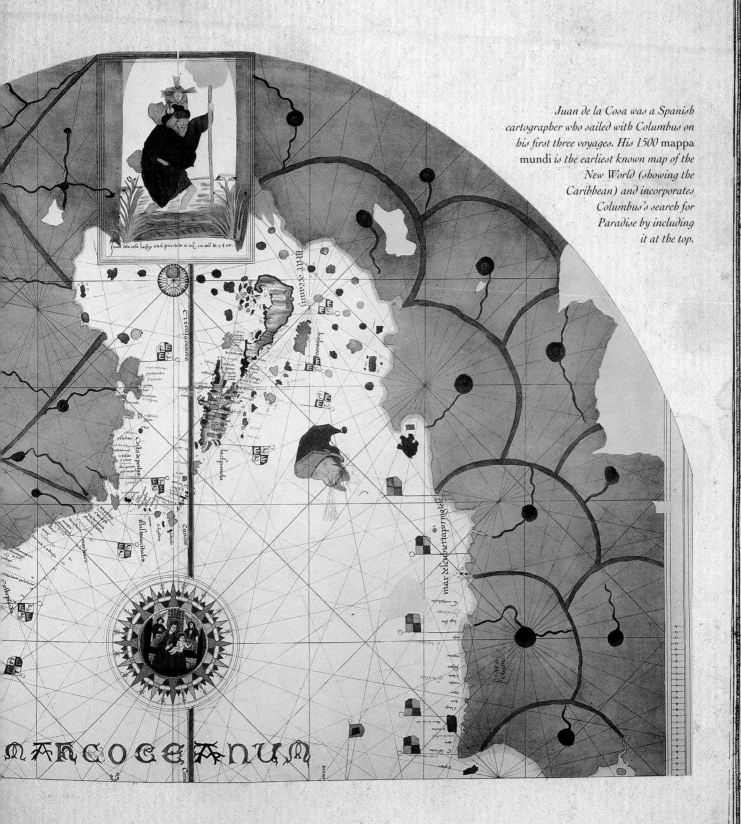

Juan de la Cosa was a Spanish cartographer who sailed with Columbus on his first three voyages. His 1500 mappa mundi *is the earliest known map of the New World (showing the Caribbean) and incorporates Columbus's search for Paradise by including it at the top.*

MARCOCEANVM

In 1498, after Columbus's third journey to the New World, he was imprisoned in Hispaniola and returned home in chains to Cadiz—his crime and that of his two brothers, in particular Bartolome, was a common one in the New World. They had failed to please other Spaniards with their efficiency in mining for gold while governing the fledgling colony.

Columbus was left to languish in prison from where he wrote many missives to Ferdinand and Isabella, king and queen of Spain. In a long letter, he described how during his approach to Paria in Trinidad the Pole Star's rotation had given the impression to him that the ship was climbing. He spoke of how mild the climate was, and of the enormous outflow of fresh water far out to sea in the Gulf of Paria. Putting the evidence together he drew the conclusion that they had been on the very outer edges of the earthly Paradise and the great output of fresh water could only have come from the rivers of Paradise. (The Gulf of Paria lies between Trinidad and the coast of Venezuela and receives the output of several arms of the huge Orinoco River delta.) Columbus was wise enough to add in his missive that he was sure he was therefore also very close to finding the great treasure in gold that their majesties had commanded him to find. The mention of Paradise no doubt struck a suitably religious note in a court where the Inquisition was active, but it cannot be doubted that their majesties were better persuaded by the word 'gold'. Nevertheless, Columbus was allowed to languish for some further time. He was finally released from gaol and received at court in late December of the year 1500, and in 1502 their majesties finally graciously acquiesced to Columbus engaging in what would be his fourth and last expedition to the New World.

He made a record-breaking time across the Atlantic, and carried out a quite remarkable exploration of the Caribbean and the Panamanian area. Far from finding his earthly Paradise, however, Columbus's last voyage was rewarded with nothing of great value. He died in 1506, having spent his last few years battling pain but in relative financial comfort in Seville. Isabella had died but Ferdinand continued to be petitioned by the explorer who felt he had been badly treated and poorly rewarded for his extraordinary exploits and great loyalty to his sovereigns.

not in the New World, and particularly not at the top of a pear-shaped planet as Columbus believed (see page 72). It is not in Egypt or Ethiopia or Israel, or for that matter at the North Pole, in sunken Atlantis, at the top of Mount Atlas, on Mount Ararat where Noah's Ark was said to come to rest as the waters of the Great Flood abated, or within the Fortunate Isles. Its location has certainly been narrowed to the northern end of the Persian Gulf in the area of present-day Iraq which has now ironically been turned into hell on Earth, or the region of the Taurus Mountains, source of the Tigris, in eastern Turkey, and close to the Iraqi border.

COULD A BIBLICAL FLOOD HAVE DESTROYED THE GARDEN OF EDEN?

The biblical flood described in Genesis was used by many Church figures, including Martin Luther, to remove any knotty problems associated with finding the physical location of the Garden of Eden. However, if there was indeed an event that shook the world, perhaps several thousand years ago, it must have left some traces behind, both physical and recorded.

There are two major contenders for the biblical flood. The first was a phenomenon which certainly happened across the entire world—the Flandrian Transgression. During the last glacial period global sea levels were more than 110 metres (360 feet) below their current level. The sea retreated and the Persian Gulf was almost dry. Over several thousand years as the ice sheets of the last great ice age melted, sea levels rose once more. The Gulf filled to its present level about 4000 BC. It is quite possible that the original Garden of Eden is now lost in the waters of the Gulf. The problem with equating the Flandrian Transgression with the biblical flood is that it took place over thousands of years and was not associated with endless flood rain.

Substantial fragments of the oldest surviving stories in the world, the rich poetic narrative of the ancient *Epic of Gilgamesh*, still exist. With an origin possibly as far back as 3000 BC in Sumeria, the saga probably had a much longer oral tradition. Among the stories it tells is one about a great flooding rain which lasted for seven days and nights before light returned to the Earth. The gods had decided to destroy the Earth and humankind but Utnapishtim, the hero of the story, was forewarned and filled his boat with all kinds of creatures living in the world, and gold and silver.

Eventually his boat settled on the very tip of Mount Nimush. Utnapishtim sent out three birds one by one. When the third bird failed to return he knew it had found land. It was safe to release all the living creatures back onto the Earth. The gods were angry that they had been tricked and that humans had survived but were finally inclined to show mercy. They granted Utnapishtim and his wife immortality on the understandable proviso that they settled far away at the head of the rivers. This is clearly a very old version of the biblical flood story. (The Sumerians also had a parallel and earlier story to that of Moses in the bullrushes.)

What could possibly have caused such an apocalyptic event within historical times? And could it have significantly changed the geography around the Middle East? Recent scientific studies have revealed a catastrophic encounter between Earth and a huge meteorite 4800 years ago, and proposed that this could be the historic event recorded in the Bible and the *Epic of Gilgamesh*.

The oldest meteorite crater known on Earth dates back to 3.5 billion years ago. The upper levels of the oceans would have boiled to steam, leaving only deep-water anaerobic bacteria to survive, and mega-tsunamis on an unimaginably mountainous scale would have repeatedly swished backwards and forwards across the land masses of Earth, like water slopping out of huge buckets.

The asteroid responsible for that event was estimated to have been between 19 kilometres and 48 kilometres (12 miles and 30 miles) wide, about twice the size of the asteroid which caused the extinction of the dinosaurs. The latter roared through our skies around sixty-five million years ago, slammed into the ground in the Yucatan of Mexico at Chiczulub, pulverising both itself and an equal volume of rock, impacting with around one-tenth the energy of the earlier impact event. Even so, what is known as the K-T event which ended the Cretaceous age and began the Tertiary period was on an unimaginable scale. The Earth was plunged into the equivalent of 'nuclear winter' by particulate smoke and dust, and none of the mega-fauna with their need for vast quantities of food survived.

It was once conventional wisdom that only huge asteroids or comet chunks such as those monsters could survive entry through our atmosphere. Smaller rocks would simply burn up. But in 2005 a crater 29 kilometres (18 miles) wide, was discovered 3800 metres (12,500 feet) below the surface in the Indian Ocean. Subsequently named the Burckle Crater, it is located approximately 1600 kilometres (1000 miles) south-east of Madagascar. This event, thought to have occurred nearly 5000 years ago, may not have been on the scale of that which ended the Cretaceous period but it was sufficiently large to have wiped out a quarter of the world's population, as it would have impacted on the densely populated coastal regions of Asia and Africa. The resulting tsunamis which smashed into the coasts of the Pan-Indian region were in the order of at least 180 metres (600 feet) high.

Legends of the great flood which was recorded in Genesis and the *Epic of Gilgamesh* are very widespread, and not limited to the Middle East. They are consistent in describing enormous gale-force winds which swept around the world, and a period of total darkness. Half the myths describe endless torrential rain, a third describe huge tsunamis. All report events which were consistent with a massive asteroid impact into oceanic waters. Enough of the myths include solid traceable events to provide a possible fix — 10 May 2807 BC — and a logical cause for the flood.

THE QUEST FOR
THE FOUNTAIN
OF YOUTH

Paradise and the Fountain of Youth have long been coupled together. The extraordinary twelfth century and later story circulated around Europe about the mythical Kingdom of Prester John (see page 101) is a clear example of such a linkage. Prester John was supposedly a Christian priest-king of unimaginable wealth and power with a vast kingdom placed very vaguely in the East, and in later centuries in Ethiopia. The story was based in part on a letter said to be written by Prester John and addressed to a number of heads of state, in which Prester John claimed that his land was filled with milk and honey, that it literally lay in close proximity to the biblical Garden of Eden, and that among its many extraordinary wonders was the Fountain of Youth, which lay at the foot of Mount Olympus (towards the north of Greece). He claimed that if the waters were sipped three times, a man's body would be returned to that of a thirty-year-old and remain that way forever.

Stories about the Fountain of Youth or at least of waters of immortality have inspired seekers of eternal life for millennia. The third century AD *Alexander Romance* which was rather vaguely based on the heroic deeds of Alexander the Great was particularly popular in the medieval period and firmly implanted the idea of such miraculous waters in the minds of those in the Western world.

In the *Alexander Romance* Alexander and his servant Andreas undertook a quest for the Water of Life, travelling across Russia and through the Land of Darkness, a mythical place shrouded in eternal night and thought to be the Forest of Abkhazia or Hanyson in Georgia. The Land of Darkness was a fearful place where none would dare to venture, but according to the highly inventive medieval bestseller *The Travels of Sir John Mandeville* (see page 106), voices could be heard within the darkness of this kingdom. They belonged to the descendants of the Persian Emperor Saures and his men, who were trapped there forever. Saures had been persecuting Christians in Abkhazia 'to destroy them and to compel them to make sacrifice to his idols, and rode with great host, in all that ever he might, for to confound Christian men'. The Christians attempted to flee into Greece but on the plain of Megon 'anon this cursed emperor met with them with his host for to have slain them and hewn them to pieces'.

The Christians' prayers for deliverance were answered. 'And anon a great thick cloud came and covered the emperor and all his host. And so they endure in that manner that they may go out on no

LEFT: The Fountain of Eternal Youth, from the De Sphaera d'Est *codex, c. 1470.*

side; and so shall they evermore abide in darkness 'til the day of doom, by the miracle of God.' Alexander was unable to negotiate the impenetrable darkness within this terrible land, but his servant succeeded, drank of the wonderful waters, and became immortal.

The quest to find the Fountain of Youth was strongly pursued until the end of the Age of Exploration, with occasional tales of its supposed location being mentioned ever since. For some Christians, water drunk from the Holy Grail, if it were ever to be found, would confer immortality. It was a clear concatenation of eternal life as promised by the faith and immortality on Earth. The search for the Holy Grail became both sacred and very much of this world as the centuries rolled on.

THE NEW WORLD FOUNTAIN OF YOUTH

The story of the Fountain of Youth in the New World appears to have been based on stories told at the time of Columbus and the Spanish conquistador Juan Ponce de León, contemporaries and explorers of the New World. An Arawak chief was said to have heard of miraculous restorative waters in Florida and travelled there with some companions from Cuba. They never returned and it was assumed that they had discovered their wondrous land and not wished to come back.

Variously described as a fountain or spring or river, it was located in Bimini, which was not, it seems a geographical fixture, being in Florida at times and the Bahamas at others. A number of islanders on various occasions attempted to locate these desirable restorative waters. The story is said to have reached Ponce de León when he was Governor of Puerto

Rico. As was the way of the times, the temptation to restore masculine vigour was conveniently coupled to tales of a land where gold ingots lay on the ground for the taking. For Ponce de León there would also have been the temptation of taking slaves. It is notable, though, that Ponce de León began his journey in the Bahamas before sailing north and encountering what he thought to be another island, the peninsula of Florida, landing north of St Augustine.

The Italian historian and geographer Peter Martyr reported the story to Pope Leo X in 1513: 'Among the islands of the north side of Hispaniola [now divided into the countries of Haiti and the Dominican Republic], there is about 325 leagues distant, as they say who have searched the same, in which is a continual spring of running water, of such marvellous virtue that the water thereof being drunk, perhaps with some diet, maketh old men young again'. It is noteworthy that Martyr slipped in a sensible proviso regarding the possible helpful effect of diet. Even in an age of considerable belief in the miraculous he was clearly not necessarily accepting the story, although he reported that many in upper society did.

Oddly, on his last and fateful visit to Florida Ponce de León landed near the site of present-day Port Charlotte. Nearby lies the township of Warm Mineral Springs, whose springs have been in use for millennia.

There is an unusual twist to the story of the New World Fountain of Youth. The islands of Bimini lie within the Bahamas, the two largest known as North and South Bimini. In the time of Ponce de León, the Fountain of Youth was originally rumoured to lie within the shallow pools of South Bimini, and a small pool marked with a plaque lies just off the road to the airport—though there is no reason to believe that its waters are in any way magical.

However, on North Bimini an unusual find was made in the twentieth century in the mangrove swampland—a pool fed by a series of underground channels with cool, mineralised waters rich in sulphur and lithium, a pool which those who have bathed in it claim has curative and regenerative properties. No elderly men have been known to instantly perform energetic aerobic exercises or cast themselves enthusiastically and purposefully in the direction of young women as the legend promised, but it certainly is not without effect. The pool is known to the local inhabitants as the Healing Hole and the island has become a site for New Age Earth-healing rituals.

HELL ON EARTH

If an earthly Paradise could exist, humanity has managed to create a number of versions of the opposite. It has to be wondered why as a species we produce such imagery. Was it originally a form of social engineering? Was it some perverse gene that sought the dark night of the soul? Was it a comforting thought of ultimate revenge on those who made the lives of their fellow humans a misery? Some religions have created a perpetual hell, others a more temporary place of correction. For others it is a grey 'non-life' akin to zombiism. Hell is usually visualised as being underground. The Hades of the ancient Greeks was the realm of the god Hades together with all its mineral wealth. In mythology Hades was the son of Cronus and Rhea, but in time he developed a slightly less uncompromising aspect in the form of the god Pluto. His companion in this dark and gloomy place is the three-headed dog Cerberus.

An account said to be spuriously attributed to Josephus, *Discourse to the Greeks concerning Hades*, and possibly adapted from the writings of Saint

Hippolytus of Rome (a self-proclaimed pope who was much preoccupied with discovering the identity of the Antichrist, who ironically was named the first antipope), described Hades as a place of darkness where souls were given temporary punishments by angels appointed as their guardians. In part of Hades was a lake of unquenchable fire reserved for the last judgement. He described the eternal horrors of the Christian Hades in terms which would have shaken a congregation to its very boots. He was one of the original preachers of fire and brimstone and provided a model for the Christian concept of hell for centuries to come.

Not all early Christian writers were so filled with fearful promises for the ungodly, but the upper layers of hell appear to have been generally populated with those whose lives offered them no chance of a Christian conversion. All who preceded Christ were allocated to a kind of netherworld. Children who died unbaptised were destined to a part of hell, according to Augustine of Hippo, where they would be less tormented than those who died unbaptised as adults. The hell of the Christian world was a remarkably structured place with various levels and various hideous fates. The Church became the ultimate power in Europe as the Christian religion spread. Sadly, it was not so much by saintly example and loving pastoralism that the Church would persuade its flock to a virtuous and holy life but by the fear of being outcast from the Church and its promise of salvation to the terrible torments of an horrendous and everlasting hell.

LEFT: Aeneas and the Sibyl in the Underworld, *1598, by Jan Brueghel the Elder.*

Religions that believed in the concept of reincarnation saw the period after death as a review of a life, a time when the soul is rewarded or punished for its actions. In the 'Myth of Er', which appears at the end of *The Republic*, Plato expresses neither the ancient Greek idea of Hades nor the world of eternal torment that Josephus described. Instead he portrays an intermission between lives, a time to correct immorality, arguing that the soul cannot die from a defect—rather the defect will die as a result of self-improvement. He did, however, believe firmly that lives morally led would be rewarded while those that had been immoral would be punished.

THE ENTRANCE TO THE UNDERWORLD

Humanity, of course, can create hell on Earth with wars and oppression and what is only too accurately described as man's inhumanity to man in places like Darfur, but there was another hell that was visualised in the real world—the world of vulcanism. Volcanoes were often viewed as an entrance to the underworld.

The Phlegraean Fields, or Campi Flegrei as they are now known, are the remnants of a giant caldera about 13 kilometres (8 miles) wide, largely submerged beneath the sea to the west of Naples in the region of Campania. The volcano which created the caldera has had two massive eruptions, one approximately 40,000 years ago, the second 12,000 years ago. Within the caldera lie the ancient town of Pozzuoli and the Solfatara Crater, said to be the home of the Roman god of fire, Vulcan. Despite the obvious dangers and continuous thermal activity in the area, the Greeks and later the Romans built magnificent summer villas there enticed by the beauty of the sea and the thermal baths, which had a healing reputation. Naples sits on a similar potential powder keg, just as Pompeii and Herculaneum did in the first century when Vesuvius erupted with such devastating consequences. Then, as now, the beauty is so devastating, the soils so fertile, that it is seen as well worth the risk to live with the potential danger.

The area around Solfatara became part of a Greek colony in the eighth century BC. Under their occupation Cumae, on the edge of the Phlegraean Fields and approachable by boat, became a thriving city. As Greek occupation continued down the coast other cities were founded, including Naples. The region finally came under Roman rule in 421 BC.

The huge caldera contains a number of crater lakes, including the shallow Lago d'Averno which was associated with the entrance to Hades. Averno is Greek for 'birdless' and the lake had a reputation for emitting gases so toxic that no bird could fly over it and survive. The entrance to Hades, the Antrum of Initiation, lay on the shores of the lake together with the cave of the famed Sybil of Cumae who acted as the prophetess of the god Apollo.

Those who know Virgil's *Aeneid* will recall the meeting between the Sibyl and Aeneas and her prophecy of the coming glory of Rome. Virgil described the strange Avernus cave, the entrance to the underworld. Here the Sibyl guided those into the underworld who wished to visit the dead. It was described as a huge, deeply recessed cave with sharp stones and pebbles underfoot surrounded by a dark wood and the equally dark waters of a lake. Virgil described disorienting twists in the path and the need to make various offerings to the gods.

Strabo also wrote about the Sybil of Cumae and described the physical geography of the area in his epic *Geographia*. He confirmed the existence of an Oracle of the Dead who dwelt there, and commented that Odysseus had visited the site. He described a spring of drinkable water on the shore but said that visitors avoided drinking from it as it was thought to come from the River Styx, the river crossed by the dead on entering the underworld. He also described how only those who had made the appropriate sacrifices to the gods were admitted to the Sibyl. Priests had apparently leased the site. The Cimmerians, who had lived in the area before the Euboean Greeks arrived, lived a fearful mole-like existence underground, earning their income as guides and miners, supplemented by a pension paid by the king in payment for carrying out their duties. They were never admitted into the sunlight and could only emerge at night.

(Although Pliny the Elder was in charge of the nearby naval station at Naples, he sadly had no particular comment to make about the Sibyl of Cumae, his only mention of Cumae being admiration for its pottery.) With time the story of the famous Sibyl would become the stuff of legend along with the entrance to the Greek Hades.

CUMAE

A visit in the modern world to the site at Cumae begins with less romance and drama than in the times of the Sibyl, via a ticket office. Until 1932 nothing seemed to remain of Virgil's famous tunnel of a thousand mouths, called the Antrum of the Sibyl. In one of those modern ironies the ancient entrance to the Antrum was discovered behind the oven of a pizza maker.

Virgil had not suffered from an overactive imagination, he had described the site perfectly. There are actually several side tunnels and the Sibyl made her prophecies in the final chamber. It must have been a nerve-wracking experience to witness her. Virgil described one encounter: 'The sibyl sang her fearful riddling prophecies, her voice booming in the cave as she wrapped the truth in darkness, while Apollo shook the reins upon her and dug the spurs into her flanks'.

While the Antrum of the Sibyl was discovered in the 1930s it was not until the 1960s that the Antrum of Initiation was located. The tunnel excavated into volcanic rock was known to archaeologists at Baia (the ancient Roman resort of Baiae) but had remained unexplored as poisonous fumes emanated from it. The tunnel is associated with an extensive complex of temples. Entering the tunnel revealed passageways, chambers, a pivoted door designed to shut off various pathways, two springs and a stream—almost certainly designed to represent the River Styx—which had flooded some tunnels. Here laid out was a representation of the passage of the dead, and the voyage through the underworld.

Lands of heroes

In legend, a very special place was reserved for the most valiant of warriors, a Utopia that eased their bodies and minds, and rewarded them with perfect pleasure. Many cultures seem to have devised their own version of a Utopian world for heroes, perhaps unconsciously rewarding them for deeds that have saved a country or a community, or encouraging further valiant sacrifices from the living.

In Norse legend, Valhalla was more of a stopover than an everlasting place of rest—a place to recover the spirits and heal wounds before re-entering future battlefields. Valhalla literally meant the Hall of the Slain and referred to the god Odin's hall. The most glorious warriors slain on the fields of battle were carried away by the Valkyries, fierce corpse goddesses in the guise of carrion-eating ravens, and welcomed to Valhalla by Bragi, the god of poetry. Beyond the sacred gate and holy doors stretched the great hall, said to contain 540 doors, each wide enough to accommodate 800 warriors marching abreast. They wait in the hall for the day when they will fight the final great battle of Ragnarok between the gods and giants, which will take place on the fields of Asgard. All who die in battle will be restored to life and returned to Valhalla to feast on the boar Saehrimnir and drink deeply of potent brew. To some of us, more timid mortals, the ancient Valhalla sounds more like a recipe for hell than a Utopia for the brave. There was an ancient Norse *hel*, but unlike later concepts of a place of divine retribution it was simply a place beneath the underworld.

The Elysian Fields of Greek legend also accommodated great warriors, but there was room too for the virtuous. The Elysian Fields were said to lie on the very western edge of Okeanus, the great river that encircled the world. Mortals were transported there to share immortality and everlasting bliss with the gods. Hesiod called these fields the Isles of the Blessed. Virgil's *Aeneid* created a particularly pleasant version of the Elysian Fields which he referred to as Elysium, where Aeneas, one of the 'wanderers', encountered his father Anchises. Despite the resistance of early Christian writers to borrowing from pagan writing and ideas, Elysium became synonymous with the idea of Paradise.

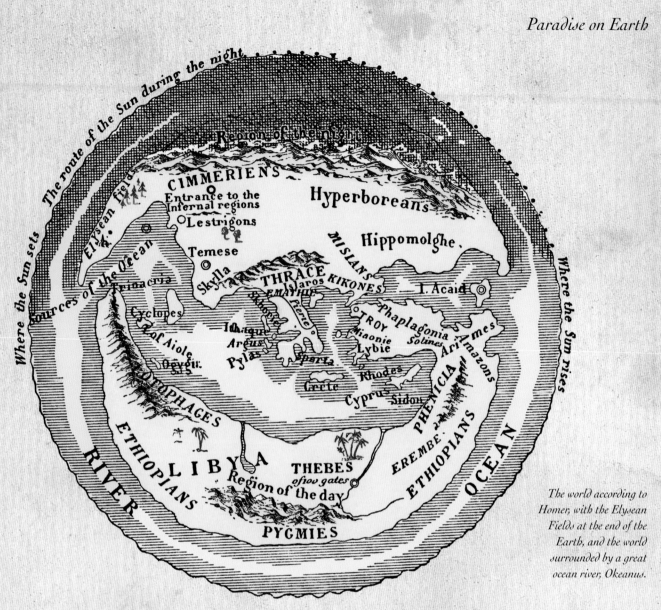

The route of the Sun during the night

Region of the night

CIMMERIENS

Entrance to the Infernal regions

Hyperboreans

Elysean field

Where the Sun sets

Lestrigons

Temese

MISLANS

Hippomolghe

Skylla

Sources of the Ocean

Triuacria

THRACE

Jaros

KIKONES

I. Acaïa

Where the Sun rises

Cyclopes

EMATHIE

Phaplagonia

Solines

Pierie

TROY

Miaonie

Ithaque

Argeus

Pylas

Sparta

Lybie

Ames

Amazons

Aries

I. of Aiole

Oeyou

Crete

Rhodes

Cyprus

Sidon

PHENICIA

LOTOPHAGES

EREMBE

ERATHIOPANS

ETHIOPIANS

LIBYA

THEBES

of 100 gates

Region of the day

ETHIOPIANS

OCEAN

RIVER

PYGMIES

The world according to Homer, with the Elysean Fields at the end of the Earth, and the world surrounded by a great ocean river, Okeanus.

The Irish realm of glory was known as Mag Mell, the Plain of Joy. It was a delightful Paradise, located rather vaguely, either west of Ireland or beneath the sea. In Mag Mell immortality was something to look forward to, a place where its inhabitants were blessed with eternal youth, beauty and strength, a place of pleasurable pursuits and music, abundant delicious food and drink, and where happiness was everlasting. This world was supposedly ruled by Manannan mac Lir. Mag Mell survived the changeover from the Celtic religion to Christianity, becoming an earthly Paradise—perhaps the one described to St Brendan by a visiting monk at Clonfert Monastery.

PART THREE

FABLED LANDS AND KINGDOMS

CAMELOT AND THE ISLE OF AVALON

THE LOST LAND OF LYONNESSE

THE KINGDOM OF PRESTER JOHN

BEYOND THE WALLS OF GOG AND MAGOG

LEFT: Andrea Bianco's world-map of 1436 presents a circular world surrounded by the Ocean Sea. Paradise is shown at the top, and on a peninsula to the left are the tribes of Gog and Magog, held in check by Alexander the Great.

FOLLOWING PAGES: Marvels of Canaan, seen on the journey undertaken by Marco Polo to China, from c. 1400 manuscript Li Livres du Graunt Caam (Travels of Marco Polo), with miniature by the artist Johannes and his school.

CAMELOT AND THE ISLE OF AVALON

The mists of time eddy around history, myth and truth so that sometimes there is no knowing where one ends and the other begins. No story, with the possible exception of Atlantis, is more powerful than that of King Arthur and his knights of the round table, his great love for the beautiful Guinevere, and his lost kingdom of Camelot.

Legend places the birth of Arthur, the son of Uther Pendragon, King of the Britons, in Cornwall. Arthur became king at quite an early age and was crowned either at Caerleon or Winchester. That in brief is the most common account of his beginnings and it is likely that it goes back to the sixth century. But there are many far more elaborate versions, and for that matter far more interesting ones. Some stories say that he was born at Tintagel, on Cornwall's west coast, where today there stands the extensive and dramatic ruins of a thirteenth century castle that has partly crumbled into the sea. The castle was built over the site of a Roman settlement which was established for the active tin trade operating out of Cornwall.

After the Romans departed Britain, it was said to have become the site of a castle built as the summer residence for the Cornish kings of Dumnonia and it is just feasible that it might then have become the home of Arthur as legend claims.

At the bottom of the cliffs is a large cave that has become known as Merlin's Cave. In one version of the legend, the baby Arthur was washed up by the waves at the feet of Merlin as he stood at the entrance. Arthur's conception was less than regular, said to have resulted from a union between Uther Pendragon and Igerna, the wife of the Duke of Cornwall. To preserve the proprieties, Merlin was said to have magically disguised the errant Uther Pendragon to look like the duke, so that, at least technically, Arthur's mother could not be held to blame. Arthur was reputed to have grown into an immensely strong, tall man, and the magical sword he carried into battle, Excalibur or Caliburn, was equally huge and heavy. Some legends say it was given to him by the Lady of the Lake, others that, while still a stripling, he had pulled it easily from a rock in which it was embedded, although great warriors in the full flower of manhood had failed. Arthur was a great warrior, successfully leading many battles against the invading Saxons, and some of his great prowess on the battlefield was attributed to the magical Excalibur. He owed his wisdom and knowledge of esoteric matters, however, to the patient, and sometimes not so patient teaching, of the greatest wizard of all time, Merlin.

Arthur married the young, blonde and beautiful Guinevere, daughter of King Leodegrance of Cameliard. According to some versions of the Arthurian tale, the original round table, which

Merlin had originally created for Uther Pendragon, was a wedding gift from Leodegrance. It became the symbol of the utopian world of Camelot where a king sat not at the top of a table but as an equal with his most trusted knights, and all aspired to live honourably, with humility, and to care for the weakest members of society.

There is a also strong tradition in the Arthurian legend of a chalice with legendary powers that was originally associated with the Great Goddess of the Celts. In its various incarnations the chalice was a symbol of plenty, of everlasting youth on the earthly plane and of spiritual perfection. With time it became associated with the Holy Grail from which Christ drank at the Last Supper. The Grail was said to be too pure for a wicked world to contemplate and that only those of the purest heart, such as Sir Lancelot, one of the Knights of the Round Table, might be permitted to see it.

Arthur's eventual betrayal and death, and the end of a golden age, came at the hands of powerful magic and of family. Arthur received a prophecy that a child born on May Day would destroy him. Mordred, the son of Arthur's half-sister, the powerful enchantress Morgause, was born on magical May Day with a heart apparently already filled with hatred and deceit. Morgause was married to King Lot of Orkney, although some versions of the legend hint at an incestuous relationship with Arthur. Other versions of the story claim that Mordred was crazed with lust for Guinevere and thus hated the ageing Arthur. Whatever the reason for his burning hatred, enchantment, genes or jealousy, Mordred was a thoroughly unengaging character, destined to cause chaos.

Arthur met his death as predicted at the hands of Mordred, at the Battle of Camlann. In some versions of the story Arthur is said to have killed Mordred in the battle, but himself received a mortal wound. In others, Mordred survives to continue his evil ways.

The most common version is that the fast fading Arthur returned Excalibur to the Lady of the Lake before his knights carried him to the Isle of Avalon (Glastonbury) where he was buried in the great medieval abbey in c. 642, said to be the holiest place in all England.

The knight Sir Bedivere returns Excalibur to the Lady of the Lake at the command of King Arthur, from Le Roman de Merlin, Lancelot du Lac, *c. 1300–13.*

WAS THERE A REAL CAMELOT?

The strongest evidence for the existence of a real Camelot is found around Glastonbury in Somerset, in the form of various local names, a very strong oral tradition, and the reputed discovery of the remains of the king and his consort at Glastonbury Abbey, although a remarkable number of places in Britain understandably lay claim to Arthur, including Winchester. Much of Glastonbury Abbey Church and the adjacent church of St Mary's were destroyed by fire in 1184 on St Urban's Day. In the course of excavations to reconstruct the abbey a grave was found that was said to contain the remains of both Arthur and Guinevere, exactly where an ancient Welsh ballad declared the king's remains lay or, according to Gerald of Wales reported, a soothsayer had prophesised to the then ruler of England, King Henry II.

At a depth of just over two metres (7 feet) a huge slab of stone was found and beneath it a lead cross inscribed: 'Hic jacet inclytus Rex Arturius in Insula Avalonia' (Here lies King Arthur in the Isle of Avalon). A further 2.7 metres (9 feet) below, a hollow contained the body of a very tall man, the skull bearing evidence of wounds that had healed and one massive unhealed wound which had caused the man's death. Nearby were the remains of a woman with braided golden hair that crumbled to dust when touched. Her name was carved, and spelled 'Guinevere'.

That at least was how the Abbot and his monks described their find. The bones were lifted from the grave and reburied in the now-destroyed mausoleum. The spot is still marked in the grass in front of the site of the high altar. The cross was not reburied. It was drawn c. 1607 by William Camden and appeared in his book *Brittannia*. Its existence was recorded up to the eighteenth century in Wells Cathedral, but it has since disappeared.

The strongest claim for the site of Camelot itself is the Iron Age South Cadbury Castle, which lies only a short distance from Glastonbury on a defensive hillside location. It was certainly never a grand castle, but rather a fort, as would be expected of a local king in that period. There is strong evidence of its use as an encampment.

As for the Battle of Camlann, again there are many suggestions but the River Camm in Somerset seems a likely location. And as for Arthur's knights who survived the terrible battle, the favoured version is that they lived on after Arthur's death, setting up an encampment on Glastonbury Tor around the site of the ancient and holy Chalice Well. The spring that feeds the well was mentioned in both the thirteenth century *High History of the Holy Grail* and Sir Thomas Malory's fifteenth century *Le Morte d'Arthur*. It is said that Arthur did not die, but will sleep eternally in a cave until England's darkest hour when he will once again come to his country's aid.

The legend of King Arthur permeates the very fabric of England. His name is perpetuated at endless sites as far north as Scotland. Perhaps there was a Camelot, a dream that almost came true where noble deeds were done and a good and courageous king ruled with justice and promoted equality. Perhaps there was a company of warriors with knightly virtues, and a round table, and a beautiful woman called Guinevere. If there wasn't there should have been. It is the closest we came to Utopia, and like all Utopias it was betrayed by human frailties, lust and hatred.

THE LOST LAND
OF LYONNESSE

So many stories of lost lands are based on real happenings that have been romanticised or distorted by time. If climate change continues, many more lost lands will enter into future mythology, just as they have in the past.

The fabulous and fertile lost land of Lyonnesse, lying beyond present-day Lands End in Cornwall, was certainly romanticised by its associations with the lost world of Atlantis, Arthurian legend, and the story of Tristan and Iseult. Lyonnesse was said to have been ruled by Tristan's father, who passed on the crown to his son.

It was inhabited by a people called the Silures, who had a reputation for being exceedingly industrious and very religious. Legend reports with unusual precision that there were 140 churches within the land and several towns. The City of Lions, the reputedly large capital city, was said to be built around a hill that sank to become the treacherous Seven Stone Reef of modern times, known to the Cornish people as Lethowsow.

Belief in its existence is still firm in England and is supported by a strong oral tradition. All the legends appear to indicate a dramatic and unexpected event that led to Lyonnesse's sudden and violent demise. Fortuitously for Tristan at least, he was away visiting his uncle King Mark of Cornwall, where he remained safe when the land of Lyonnesse slipped below the sea.

IS LYONNESSE SIMPLY A LEGEND?

The story of Lyonnesse is still told of an ancestor of the originally Cornish Trevelyan family, who was said to have escaped the sinking of Lyonnesse by outriding a terrible wall of water that flooded the land behind him, reaching safe ground at a cave in Perranuthnoe on the Cornish south coast. Trevelyan was the only survivor of the final terrible event; though he had already organised the evacuation of his family and livestock.

A small oratory known as Chapel Idne once stood in Senan Cove in Cornwall, said to have been built by a Lord Goonhilly in order to give thanks for his deliverance from the destruction of Lyonnesse, where he had owned lands. Again, though a tiny piece of evidence, it seems to refer to a real catastrophe.

There was certainly a widely known tradition dating to the thirteenth century of a catastrophic event which submerged coastal lands and forests, and a fifteenth century account of the travels of the Earl of Worcester made detailed references to the sinking of land from St Michael's Mount to the Isles of Scilly, 45 kilometres (30 miles) south-west of Land's End.

There is no doubt that sunken land exists beyond Land's End. The seas are often tumultuous in the area, where the waters of the Bristol Channel, the English Channel and the Irish Sea meet, and storm winds often further increase their ferocity. But when the waters are particularly calm, many have claimed to have seen the remains of a sunken forest on the sea floor of Mounts Bay in West Cornwall. An old Cornish saying was: 'Six miles south of St Michael's Mount waves, from Clement's Isle to Cudden Rock, a wood'. Fishermen have reported seeing the tops of houses, domes and spires beneath the water near Longships Lighthouse, and have brought up domestic artefacts in their nets. Persistent stories dating from at least the sixteenth century claim that the church bell can still be heard tolling under the water on stormy nights.

Gaius Julius Solinus, the Roman author of a geographical compendium of the third century AD, recorded the existence of a handsome island off the Cornish coast separated from the mainland by nothing more than a dangerously turbulent narrow strait. It is certainly not there today. In 1769 the Reverend Dr William Borlase pointed out that the Cornish name for St Michael's Mount, *Careg cowse in clowse*, was translated as 'the hoary rock within a wood', but the lofty island with its one time monastery now stands 800 metres (half a mile) into the sea at high tide, due to land subsidence. In the sands between St Michael's Mount and Penzance, Borlase had observed the remains of the trunks of large trees, still in their original position, exposed by storm tides.

THE ISLES OF SCILLY AND LYONNESSE

Evidence of sunken land around the Isles of Scilly is thought to be the last surviving remnants of the land of Lyonnesse. The islands have been occupied since Neolithic times and there are more than 500 archaeological sites just above the high-water mark. Investigation of sites that are now normally under water are possible only when tides are extremely low, and many field walls, hut circles, graves and other sites are exposed. At extreme low tides the islands of Tresco, Bryher and Samson are still united, so that it is possible to walk on dry land from one to another. A fall of around 10 metres (33 feet) in water level would join most of the fifty or so islands, with the exception of Agnes and Annet islands. In the time of the Roman emperor Maximus in the fourth century AD, the Isles of Scilly were still described as a single island, called the *Sylina Insula* or *Siluram Insulam*, and Roman maps show them as a single land mass.

The islands are just visible from the coast at Land's End. It is possible that there was a land bridge between the two which was lost after the last Ice Age melt-off around eleven millennia ago and that ancient memories have been passed on about the inundation of the coastline. The process was relatively rapid in the first few millennia after the end of the Ice Age, and would have been traumatic as familiar shorelines were inundated and villages swallowed, particularly during storm surges which would have driven the sea ever further inland. However, at least one if not more additional catastrophic events seem to have been involved in many land-loss events, and it is just such an event that surrounds the legend of Lyonnesse.

Just when such a dramatic incident might have occurred is difficult to identify from the literature of the past. The *Saxon Chronicle* recorded a remarkably high tide in November of 1099, when the sea was said to have overflowed the shore, destroying many towns and drowning many people and innumerable oxen and sheep. This is a classic description of the effects of either a tsunami or a massive storm surge along a coastline. Could the story of Lyonnesse relate to that extraordinary tide of 1099?

The sixth century has also been nominated as a time when major land loss occurred. It is recorded that the waters of Crow Valley in the Isles of Scilly became navigable only from Tudor times. Local earthquake activity could have caused one or more periods of rapid subsidence.

Similar stories to that of Lyonnesse occur in Celtic Brittany, which lies across the English Channel from Cornwall. Breton legends indicate a final inundation of Lyonnesse in the sixth century AD, when the land of Caer Ys was also drowned. The Bretons have a parallel story to that of the Trevelyan family, telling of a King Gradlon who escaped on horseback by outriding the flooding waters rushing behind him, although Gradlon's daughter, who accompanied him, was drowned.

Caer Ys was said to be the most wonderful city in the world. It was built on a site that had gradually been submerged below sea level and was protected by dykes and sluice gates. King Gradlon owned the only keys to the dyke. The Devil persuaded Dahut, his daughter, to steal the keys and give them to him, whereupon he unlocked the dyke and flooded the great city. Everyone perished with the exception of Gradlon. With typical medieval relish, it was said that all the souls of the dead children of Caer

RIGHT: Tristan and Iseult setting sail, folio 234 of Béroul's Le Roman de Tristan, c. 1150.

Ys were swallowed up by the ocean as a divine punishment. Gradlon survived to found the city of Quimper near the coast in Brittany having been converted to Christianity; a statue of him riding on horseback and forever looking back to his long-lost city surmounts the Saint Corentin Cathedral to this day in Quimper.

The Breton story shares the detail that the bells of Caer Ys can still be heard ringing out a warning of coming storms. As with the Cornish story there appears to have been a gradual long-term inundation of the coast. It seems to be a sign followed by sudden catastrophe.

Brittany and Cornwall have much in common, including medieval religious affiliations with shared saints and their Celtic heritage. But long before the Celts arrived, there is a very strong Neolithic link. Brittany is an extraordinarily rich site of megalithic avenues of menhirs marching down to the sea around the town of Carnac, dolmens and other massive structures, which are matched on the other side of the English Channel in Cornwall. Long before the Celts, and British and Roman occupation, Cornwall and Brittany appear to have shared a common heritage and tradition indicating that at least a partial land bridge may once have existed.

THE KINGDOM OF
PRESTER JOHN

The mysterious kingdom of Prester John is difficult to disentangle from its medieval trappings, and begins with a secondhand account provided in a document of 1145, the *Chronicles* of Otto, Bishop of Freising in Bavaria. While at the papal court at Viterbo in 1144, Otto fell into discussion with Hugo, the Syrian Bishop of Jabala. Hugo had been sent as an emissary to Pope Eugene II by the Christian prince Raymond of Antioch, after the bloodbath that accompanied the fall of the First Crusader state, Edessa in Turkey, in 1144. Hugo's mission was to persuade the Pope to call for a second crusade among the countries of Western Europe and bring relief to Jerusalem.

Hugo described a powerful Christian king of incalculable wealth and influence who had visited not many years before. Otto's *Chronicle* named this priest-king as Prester (Presbyter) John, a Nestorian Christian who lived in the Far East, somewhere beyond Persia and Armenia. Prester John claimed that he had led battles against the Samiards, brother

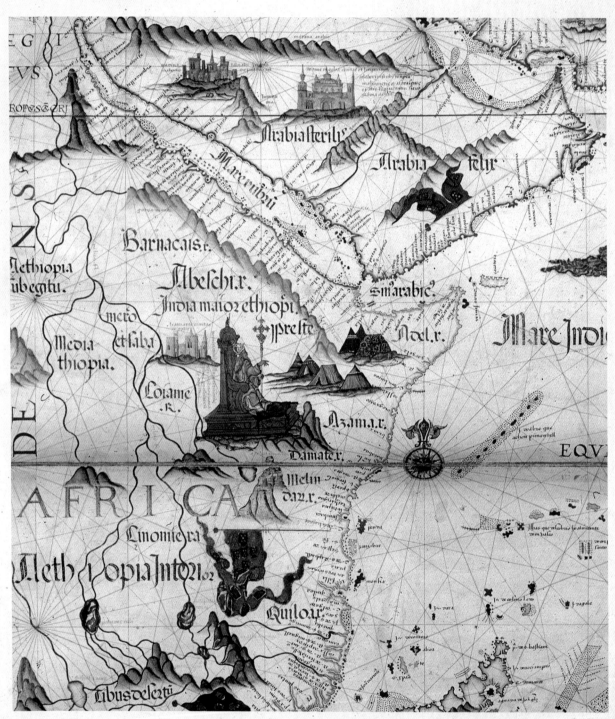

Detail from a portolan (navigation) chart of the Indian Ocean by Diego Homen, c. 1558, showing Prester John on his throne in Northern Africa.

kings of the Medes and Persians. Despite the eventual reinforcement of his enemies by armies of Assyrians, Medes and Persians, Prester John had finally emerged triumphant after three terrible days, during which he had also attacked the capital of their kingdom, 'Ecbatanus' (Ecbatana, once the capital of Media, is now the city of Hamadan in modern Iran). Prester John had then marshalled his forces to march onward to Jerusalem, but the Tigris River proved to be impassable and the depleted army had finally returned home.

Somewhat fired up after presenting this stirring account, the Syrian bishop then claimed that John was a descendant of the Magi, and his excursion to Jerusalem had been fuelled by his wish to emulate his forefathers, who long ago had come to worship Christ in the manger. Hugo also added, perhaps to reinforce the immense wealth of Prester John, that he used no sceptre except one contrived from pure emerald, and that he governed the same lands as had the original Magi.

It is possible that a widely circulated rumour about a visit to Pope Callistus II by Patriarch John of India in 1122 may have formed the germ of the bishop's anecdote. When that rumour was put together with the well-known historical spread of the Nestorian Christian Church into India and beyond, and stories which had been widely circulated since the third century about Thomas the Apostle's travels and proselytising in the Indian subcontinent, the entire story appeared to be at least possibly true. The great battle described so vaingloriously by Prester John did take place in 1141 AD, although not with Prester John at the head of the victorious army.

The Khitai tribe had ruled over northern China, Manchuria and Mongolia in the tenth century, establishing the Liao Dynasty or Khitan Empire in 905. When their dynasty was weakened and overcome by the Jin Dynasty, part of the imperial Khitan family escaped westward, establishing a new Turko–Mongol empire called Karakhitan in central Asia. The kingdom's expansionist activities finally led it into a clash with the Seljuk Turks of Persia. A battle took place near Samarkand in 1141 in which the Sultan of Sanjar, the Seljuk ruler of Persia, was completely defeated. The warrior who led the mighty army against him was Yeh-lu Ta-shih, not Prester John. The empire of Karakhitan itself was completely destroyed in 1218.

THE LANDS OF THE MAGI

This was the first and least corrupted version of what was already a cobbled-together story, placing Prester John's kingdom in the realm of the Magi of the Bible. But the account of the Magi, found in the Gospel of Matthew, is very vague regarding the origin of these wise men, describing them only as coming from the East and returning there. Matthew is not even specific about the number of Magi, only that they brought with them three gifts: frankincense, gold and myrrh.

The term *Magi*, however, is helpful. It was specifically used to refer to the priests of the ancient religion of Zoroastrianism who were learned in mathematics, astronomy and the then important science of astrology. The Magi were led to the birthplace of Christ by a star, which fits with their advanced knowledge of astronomy and astrology. If they were indeed Zoroastrian priests, they are most likely to have come from Persia, or Babylon (in present-day Iraq), which was the centre of astrological knowledge at the time.

The names Gaspar, Melchior and Balthazar were accepted as those of the Magi by the Christian church in the West, based on a sixth century manuscript found in Alexandria, and had become well entrenched by the eighth century. The Alexandrian manuscript places the home of the Magi in Syria.

In the thirteenth century, Marco Polo claimed that he was shown the tombs of the Three Magi in three 'very large and beautiful monuments, side by side' in the small Persian city of Saveh (called Saba by Marco Polo, who also said it was the city from which the Magi set out to follow the star). Saveh is about 100 kilometres (60 miles) south of modern-day Tehran. In another story, St Helena found the bones of the Three Magi when she was on pilgrimage to Palestine and the Holy Land; they were eventually interred in the Shrine of the Three Kings in Cologne.

Zoroastrianism is a monotheistic religion and philosophy more than 3000 years old, and the first world religion. It was spread by the Persian teacher and prophet Zoroaster, also known as Zarathustra. It taught that there was one god, a personal god, Ahura Mazda the Wise Lord, representing the power of good in the universe. The teachings of Zoroaster—of the struggle between good and evil in this world, and the way in which humanity should live by good thoughts, good words and good deeds, by being generous, honest, modest in one's desires, kind and law abiding—would also be the essential moral messages of later major religions. Zoroastrianism

was the religion of the Medes and Persians and it spread to both the East and West.

So even with the clue embedded in the word *magi*, a very wide area is indicated in which the Kingdom of Prester John might have been located. At the centre of Zoroastrianism was the ancient kingdom of Persia. Sometimes called Greater Iran, this once included Armenia, Azerbaijan (which the oldest texts describe as the birthplace of both Zoroaster and Zoroastrianism), much of Georgia, Bahrain, western Afghanistan, most of Iraq, including Iraqi Kurdistan, and beyond. Much of this territory was lost from Persia due to the wars with the Ottoman Empire in the sixteenth and seventeenth centuries, the southern advance of Imperial Russia in the nineteenth century, and the activities of the British. Tajikistan and Uzbekistan also have an ancient Zoroastrian past. The oldest centres of Zoroastrianism included Baktria in northern Afghanistan, where Zoroaster was said to have spent his last days, Sogdiana and Margiana (the site of ancient and highly advanced Margush in Turkmenistan, which is thought to be one of the five oldest centres from which civilisation emerged).

A MOVABLE KINGDOM

But where was Prester John's Kingdom within this broad area? The chronicler of the *Annals of Admont's Monastery*, written in 1181, placed the kingdom in Armenia. While this land had been part of the ancient kingdom of Persia and within those territories associated with the Magi of the Bible, it was not so remote or unknown to the peoples of Eastern Europe, criss-crossed by trading routes as it was, for a kingdom of Prester John to have remained undiscovered.

Could Prester John then have come from beyond Persia and Armenia? After the fall of the Sassanid Empire in 651, a mass migration of Zoroastrians led some of them into western India, largely around Mumbai (Bombay), where they are known as the Parsees. A story concocted in the later medieval period might well have placed the home of the Three Magi, and therefore also of Prester John, in western India where the Zoroastrians had settled. But as they did not migrate to the Indian subcontinent until the seventh century, and as Prester John's country supposedly lay within that of the New Testament's Three Magi, it could not have been located in India.

Prester John's story entered the world of truly fantastical medieval mythology with a letter known as the *Epistola*, supposedly written by Prester John eighteen years after Otto's *Chronicle* and sent in 1163 to Manuel I Comnenus, the Byzantine Emperor of the time, as well as to the ageing Frederick I Barbarossa, and various other European princes. Copies began to circulate mysteriously in Europe around 1165, many of them enhanced to create an even wilder story than the original.

In this letter, claiming humility as the reason for accepting the lowly name and rank of Prester (as nice a form of inverted snobbery as one is likely to find), Prester John nevertheless ensured his importance would not be overlooked by referring to himself in such terms as 'the Lord of Lords', 'our Magnificence', 'our Supreme Eminency' and 'our Exaltedness', and in case the message had not quite registered with the reader, as surpassing 'all under heaven in virtue, in riches, and in power'. He claimed that his domain stretched from Babylon to the three Indies and beyond India, suspiciously taking in most of the lands famously conquered by Alexander the Great. Seventy-two kings supposedly owed him their complete allegiance. His entire missive is the most wonderful and colourful concoction of recognisable medieval myths and beliefs. It might well be considered the quintessential medieval document of unfettered imagination.

In describing the many strange wonders to be found in his kingdom, he begins with an interesting and vaguely possible list of animals, including elephants, dromedaries, camels, red and white tigers, crocodiles, lions, hyenas and wild horses, but enters dangerous territory by adding centaurs, griffins, satyrs and the phoenix. He repeats medieval myths by describing salamanders that live in fire and spin cocoons of silken thread from which the ladies of his palace create clothes that can only be washed in flames. Fish in his wonderful kingdom supply him with a purple dye made from their blood, perhaps a reference to the murex sea snail. (There were two species of *Murex* involved in ancient dyes. The spiny murex was the source of the colour Tyrian purple, so long traded by the Phoenicians.)

His subjects appear to be equally diverse, ranging from the ten lost tribes of Israel, Brahmans and Amazons to incredible giants, pygmies, Cyclopes, horned men and those with eyes both in front of and in the back of their heads. They also included cannibal tribes, such as Gog and Magog, which he claimed came from the region beyond Alexander's Gate, and had proved useful in removing the untidy bodily remains of enemy armies he had conquered. These same tribes, he said, would be released upon the world when it ended at the coming of the Antichrist.

Sir John Mandeville

The medieval author Sir John Mandeville described himself as a knight from St Albans in England, who set out on the feast of St Michael in 1322, determined to seek adventure as a mercenary (a common enterprise for knights without a quest in that era). His book of travels, simply titled *The Travels of John Mandeville*, first appeared around 1371 and contained many other wonderful accounts as well as a visit to the Kingdom of Prester John.

Spanning more than thirty years, the book is filled with descriptions of exotic places, such as Egypt, Palestine, India and China, and with even more exotic stories. For example, Mandeville described a people the size of pygmies who were forced to suck their food through reed straws, another tribe whose sole nourishment was the smell of apples, and a third with the heads of dogs. Although most of the more accurate content was borrowed from other authors, particularly Franciscan and Dominican missionary explorers but also from broader and classical references, Mandeville is a raconteur of the highest order and his book became an instant bestseller and was very influential—even consulted in great depth by Christopher Columbus in the fifteenth century. Sir John Mandeville has been identified as the pseudonym of Jean de Bourgoigne, a physician of Liège in Belgium who died c. 1372 He had followed this profession for some time in Egypt. Much of his personal story remains quite mysterious.

Monsters from the land of the Merkites, by the Boucicaut Master from the Livre des Merveilles du Monde, *c. 1410–12.*

Prester John described his kingdom as lying three days journey from the biblical Garden of Eden, a land filled with milk and honey in which no poisonous creatures dwelt. Among its many wonders was the Fountain of Youth, which he placed at the foot of Mount Olympus (implying that northern Greece lay within his kingdom). If the waters of the fountain were sipped three times, a man's body would be restored and he would remain thirty years old forever. Within the kingdom was also a great waterless sea which cast up delicious fish, a fountain within a hollow stone that could wash away all sins from devout Christians, a subterranean cavern filled with a river of precious gemstones, which opened occasionally but perilously for those wishing to enter, and a mirror guarded by 3000 men in which he could see events happening throughout his kingdom. His palace was entirely, and predictably, created from ebony, gold, crystal, precious jewels and ivory.

When Prester John left his palace to wage war, he claimed that three (in some versions up to fourteen) jewel-encrusted gold crosses were carried, each leading the way of 10,000 men on horseback and 100,000 foot soldiers. In a less bombastic and more virtuous addendum, Prester John claimed that he made an annual pilgrimage to the tomb of the prophet Daniel near Babylon.

In 1177, Pope Alexander III was said to have sent a letter to Prester John requesting an alliance. Prester John's vaunted but entirely imaginary victory over the Seljuk Turks had inspired hope in the West that such a powerful army from the East might do battle on behalf of the sorely pressed Crusader kingdoms. Alexander was supposed to have entrusted his letter to his emissary and physician Philip, who apparently was never seen again. Just where did Philip plan to deliver the Pope's message?

Even if Alexander's letter to Prester John was a complete fabrication, it is an indication of the extremes to which the Church was forced during the Crusades that many believed the Pope had applied for assistance to a Nestorian priest, no matter how fabulously rich and successful in battle — Nestorianism had been outlawed by the Church of Constantinople after the third Ecumenical Council, held in Ephesus in 431 AD.

The story of Prester John and his kingdom lingered on, refusing to die, although generations failed to see him materialise. The First Crusade had been the only success in a long and brutal series that bled both wealth and men from the West, creating not just a geographical block but a cultural block for centuries. After the disastrous Fifth Crusade (1217–1221), the Bishop of Acre, Jacques de Vitry, brought false but heartening news back to Europe that King David of India, variously described as the son or grandson of Prester John, was marching westward, had already conquered Persia and was en route to Baghdad. Sadly, far from being the hoped-for Nestorian Christian king of the East and their supposed saviour, 'King David', the great warrior was in fact Genghis Khan, and the army he led, the Mongols. The brief flame of hope lit by the bishop was utterly extinguished.

According to the *Epistola*, Prester John's kingdom seemed to encompass vast tracts, but its author's description of the kingdom also revealed the vaguest geographical knowledge. Admittedly few had a reliable grip on geography in the twelfth century. Despite hazy descriptions and unlikely proximities, such as the Garden of Eden, the story of Prester John did provide a few clues.

One was the reference to the River Indus, and a description of what sounds like a complex delta. But the reference is muddied by claims that the river encircled Paradise, of a super abundance of precious stones and a mysterious plant that gave protection from the machinations of evil spirits. The Indus is the longest and most significant river in Pakistan, rising on the Tibetan plateau and emptying into the Arabian Sea near Karachi through a complex delta, the Sapta Sindhu. The Indus Valley was well known in the medieval world, as it had traded extensively with Europe since classical times.

Pakistan borders both Iran and Afghanistan and was crossed by Alexander the Great in the fourth century BC. The story of Alexander and his conquests, together with bravura embellishments added by the *Alexander Romance* of the third century AD, seems to have become interwoven with the Prester John story. Alexander's story certainly lost nothing in its constant retelling. Quite the reverse. By the sixth century it had already been translated into four languages from the original Greek, and from the tenth century Latin version it was retold in all the major European languages. The Syrian version was translated into Arabic, Persian, Hebrew and other Eastern languages. It was an immensely popular narrative in medieval England and a rich vein to mine for a new legend. Alexander was even said to have had a love affair with Thalestris, queen of the Amazons, a tribe Prester John claimed to rule.

Medieval literature is scattered with references to Prester John, all of them generously elaborating on the myths surrounding him. The account of a pilgrimage to Jerusalem by the cleric Johannes Witte de Hese from Utrecht is full of admirable creativity, including his description of a 'visit' to Prester John's kingdom. The ever-unreliable author Sir John Mandeville also provided a detailed account of an imaginative visit to the court of Prester John and his kingdom, which was 'full good and rich'. A modest estimate of Prester John's age at the time would have been 250 years.

As the known world expanded and the extent of the unknown world to the east slowly shrank and became less glamorous, Prester John's kingdom seemed to melt away. The magical land with all its wonders was never found, despite extensive searches. But a true Nestorian kingdom did exist, hidden from the world on a high plateau in ancient Abyssinia (modern Ethiopia). The belief in Prester John flamed back to life in the sixteenth century, just like the phoenix he claimed had lived in his lands.

Europe was aware of Abyssinia, but it had slipped below the radar for centuries. The West was reminded of its existence by occasional visits to the Holy Land by Abyssinian priests and pilgrims, and the kingdom was said to be hidden from the world by towering mountain ranges. It was believed to be the place where the Queen of Sheba had concealed her vast wealth. The shifting geography of Prester John's kingdom was aided by Abyssinia's supposed placement in the 'Indies'. The Roman poet Virgil, writing in the first century BC, and others in the classical world certainly confused India and Ethiopia. The medieval world perpetuated this misconception as a result of the spice trade. Spices from India and further east were first landed on the shores of east Africa before being taken on to Europe. In 1540

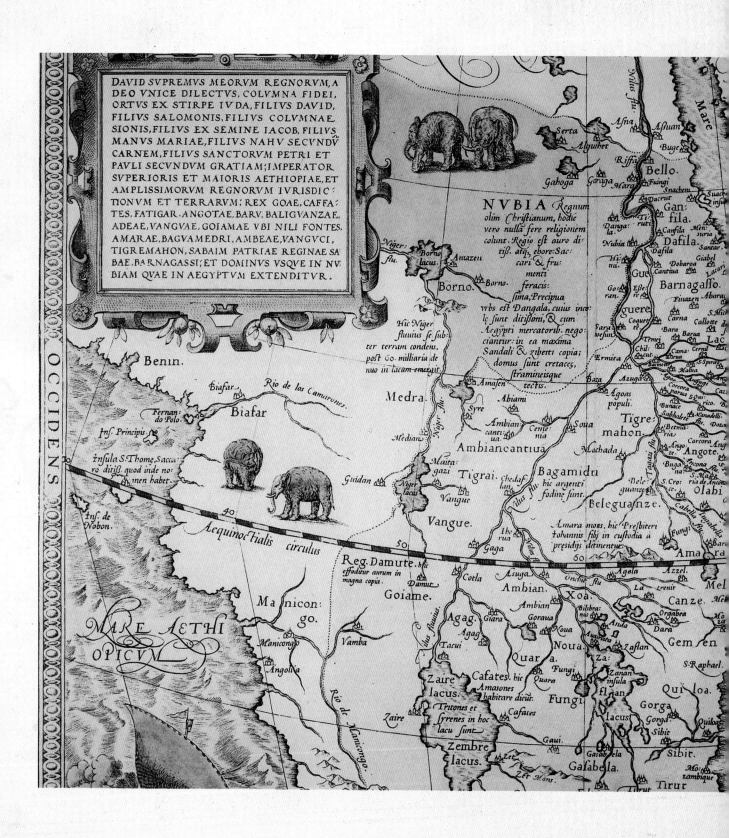

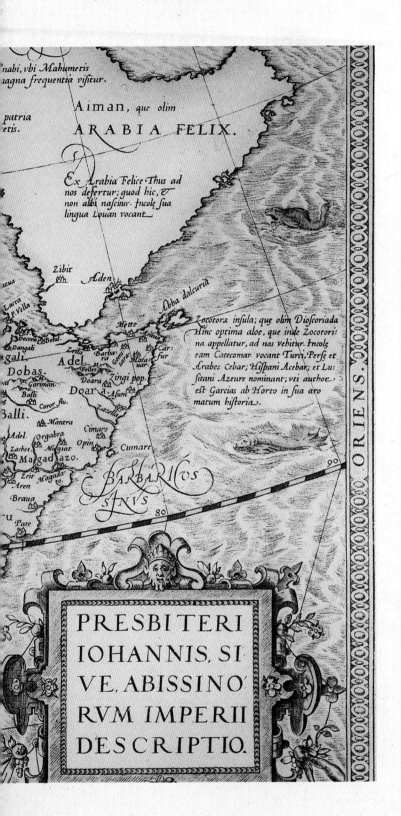

Francisco Alvares, the Portuguese missionary and explorer, wrote a book published in Lisbon about the kingdom of *Preste Joam das Índias*. Alvares acted as the chaplain for a Portuguese diplomatic mission to the court of Ethiopia between 1520 and 1526 and his account was widely translated in Europe during the sixteenth and seventeenth centuries.

In 1557 a Portuguese Jesuit mission was finally sent to the 'kingdom of Prester John', but their plans to convert the Ethiopian Orthodox Church to Catholicism came to nothing. In 1580 Phillip II of Spain gained a second title, becoming Phillip I of Portugal and the Algarves after a constitutional crisis left Portugal with no clear line of succession. Phillip resolved to rekindle the Jesuit mission in Ethiopia and sent out Padre Pedro Pâez from Goa, a man of adventurous spirit and intelligence. Pâez's friendship with the king, his explorations of the lost kingdom and 'discovery' of the source of the Blue Nile added greatly to the West's knowledge of geographical Ethiopia. But the second Jesuit mission ended in terrible civil war between the proponents of the two churches and resulted in the expulsion of the Jesuits.

In 1610, the Dominican friar Luis de Urreta perpetuated the supposed link between Ethiopia and Prester John of the Indies in his *Ecclesiastical, Natural, Ethical and Political History of the Great and Remote Kingdom of Ethiopia*, a work full of wonderful fantasies, such as unicorns dwelling in the Mountains

LEFT: *Abraham Ortelius's 1572 map of Africa includes, in elaborate detail, the Kingdom of Prester John in modern-day Ethiopia, as well as imaginary lakes, rivers and cities. The map is full of legendary and mythical places, including the fabled Mountains of the Moon, located in the centre of the continent.*

of the Moon. It would be pleasant to attribute a vivid imagination to the friar, but he probably borrowed from the account of John Bermudez, who had been sent as an ambassador to the court of Prester John in 1535 and reported seeing unicorns in Abyssinia. As Prester John reputedly supplied various royal courts with an abundance of unicorns (the horn was said to neutralise all poisons, a useful item when death by poisoning was not unknown to royalty), Bermudez's claim is perhaps to be expected. The friar may also have read the account by Marmolius (Marmol Caravaial) in 1573 of pure white unicorns with long smooth ivory horns living among the Mountains of the Moon in High Ethiopia.

But his claim that the Dominicans had long been in the kingdom and should therefore be given precedence over the Jesuits in that land took him into decidedly controversial waters. It was true that a book called *Mirabilia Descriptus*, written by a Dominican missionary called Jordanus c. 1329 makes probably the first definite reference to Prester John as an African, but again Jordanus's flights of imagination were at once highly commendable for their vividness and less than dependable.

Not surprisingly, the Jesuits responded rapidly to Luis de Urreta's claims, none of them more powerfully than Padre Pâez, in his *History of Ethiopia*, c. 1622, which included not only the history of Ethiopia and the role of the Jesuit mission, but also his own adventures and discoveries in that fascinating land.

The book was rewritten by Father Manuel de Almeida c. 1645, largely condensing Pâez's passionate refutation of Urreta, but retaining its historical, geographical and natural history content, and retitled *History of High Ethiopia or Abyssinia*. In 1660 the same book, made barely recognisable as a result of heavy reworking by Father Balthazar Teles, was published under the title *History of Ethiopia or Prester John*.

Prester John may have been the hoped-for Christian ally for the West in their Crusades in the Holy Land, but the quest for his fabled kingdom with its movable location and incredible features lingered into the seventeenth century for the best of all reasons. It was a wonderful fantasy—a dream world infinitely enriched with medieval imagination and creativity, a paradise overflowing with milk and honey, where eternal life might be granted. It was a story far too good to easily let go. By the time the kingdom had disappeared from the maps of the world in the seventeenth century, the curiosity that Prester John aroused had opened the largely fortress mentality of medieval Europe, sending the adventurous far abroad and redrawing the maps of Eurasia and Africa much closer to reality.

BEYOND THE WALLS OF GOG AND MAGOG

The names Gog and Magog recur endlessly in stories told through the centuries, from that of the Kingdom of Prester John and the much embroidered *Alexander Romance* to the prophecies of Nostradamus. But the mystery of who or what they were, and where they are located, only becomes more clouded with time. Both names occur in the Old Testament of the Bible, the first being in the Book of Genesis where Magog is described as the son of Japheth and grandson of Noah (together with Tubal, Meshech, Gomer and Thogoma). Tribal names were assigned according to their founding leader in the time of the Old Testament, and Magog would have been both the name of a tribe and the place they lived. A second mention is found in the book of Ezekiel chapter 38. This reference is taken by many, even today, to be a description of a terrible war which will lay waste to the Middle East, the much foretold Armageddon. The instrument of destruction is said to be Gog and Magog and their allies. Ezekiel is a grim prophet and needs no assistance in creating horrific images:

Thus saith the Lord God; Behold I am against thee,
O Gog, the chief prince of Meshech and Tubal:
and I will turn thee back, and put hooks into thy jaws,
and I will bring thee forth, and all thine army, horses and
horsemen, all of them clothed with all sorts of armour
… thou shalt come from thy place out of the north parts,
thou, and many people with thee, all of them riding upon
horses, a great company, and a mighty army; and
thou shalt come up against my people of Israel, as a
cloud to cover the land …

According to Ezekiel's prophecy, for seven years the cities of Israel would not need to cut firewood, because the weapons of Gog and his great army would fuel their fires. For seven months they would bury the slain to purify the land, and the bodies would be placed in a valley on a route taken by those who travelled eastward to the sea, and it would become known as the Valley of Hamon-gog.

Revelations, the last book in the New Testament, also contains a prophecy regarding Gog and Magog. The book is of mysterious authorship, but it is attributed to St John the Divine, and believed to have been written in a cave on the island of Patmos, offshore from Ephesus on the Turkish mainland. After the fearful vengeance taken against the wicked described in the prophecy, the blessed and holy would dwell in peace and joy and reign with Jesus for a thousand years. Then, 'when the thousand years are expired, Satan shall be loosed out of his prison, and shall go out to deceive the nations which are in the four quarters of the Earth, Gog, and Magog, to

gather them together to battle: the number of whom is as the sand of the sea'.

Islam's holy book, the Qur'an, also tells of Gog and Magog, and describes how the prophet Dhul-Qamayn travelled the world and found a tribe threatened by Gog and Magog, who are described as evil, destructive, and causing great corruption. The tribe offered to pay tribute to Dhul-Qamayn in exchange for protection. He refused their tribute, but helped them by constructing a great wall that Gog and Magog could neither penetrate nor pass over, trapping them until the end of days, when they would be released to descend once again upon the nations of the world. Some have interpreted this ancient story to refer to the exploits of the all-conquering but remarkably just Persian king Cyrus the Great, while others believe that it refers to the reformer and organiser Darius the Great of Persia, who certainly brought peace to his people.

The story also has strong echoes of the *Alexander Romance*, which told of the conquests of Alexander the Great many centuries before. Alexander, who reigned in the fourth century BC and was one of the most successful military commanders in history, was likewise said to have fashioned a barrier that held back the fearful and hostile people of the north, an entirely apocryphal tale. Alexander and his army actually marched in pursuit of the Persian general Bessus through the Caspian Gates, a narrow pass south-east of the Caspian Sea. The more romantically inclined transferred the entire scenario to the Caucasus, where Alexander and his army were said to have passed between two peaks known as the Breasts of the World (a nice touch to enliven the imaginations of readers) and with

Gog and Magog, *1534, by Lucas Cranach the Elder.*

the help of God imprisoned the savage nations of the world, including Gog and Magog, behind huge walls of adamantine or, as some had it, massive gates of iron, so that they could no longer lay waste to the lands in the south.

Explorer Marco Polo's famous, and undoubtedly imaginatively embellished, account of his travels along the Silk Road in the thirteenth century gave rise to another possible identity for Gog and Magog. In keeping with the ideas of his time, Marco Polo suggested that the Cumans were the tribe locked behind the Gates of Alexander. These fierce nomadic warriors of Turkick origin from the steppes of southern Siberia and northern Kazakhstan migrated south to the region of the Volga River before eventually settling west of the Black Sea during the eleventh century. It is believed that the Cumans became the founders of a number of Bulgarian medieval dynasties. The Cumans themselves were defeated in 1238 by the Mongols.

In another part of his travel tales, Marco Polo seems to have placed Gog and Magog beyond the

The adventures of Marco Polo

If Marco Polo had lived in the twenty-first century he would undoubtedly been torn between careers as a professional diplomat, working in a top advertising agency, a bestselling novelist in the Robert Ludlum genre, or perhaps a highly paid travel writer for a top American publication. He certainly had the skills to pursue all these options. He was born in the mid-thirteenth century into a Venetian family of trading merchants with branches of the family business in Constantinople, the Crimea and the East. Together with his father and uncle, he became one of the first Westerners to travel the Silk Road to Cathay (China) where he encountered the Great Khan of the Mongols, the famed Kubla Khan, founder of the Yuan Dynasty and grandson of the feared Genghis Khan, but probably best remembered now for Coleridge's famous opium-induced poem 'Kubla Khan', published in 1816 and beginning: 'In Xanadu did Kubla Khan a stately pleasure-dome decree …' The two older Polos first visited the Mongol court in Kanbaliq (modern-day Beijing) in 1266. The seventeen-year-old Marco accompanied their second visit, reaching Kanbaliq in 1271.

Unfortunately they proved such welcome guests that they were detained at the great Khan's pleasure for the following twenty years, Marco being esteemed for his storytelling abilities, becoming a diplomat for the royal court and travelling throughout the kingdom. Marco was finally allowed to leave in 1291, charged with a final task by Kubla Khan who entrusted him with the safe passage of a Mongol princess to her betrothed in Sumatra. His journey home reputedly took in modern Sri Lanka, various cities in India, and Persia. Marco became a prisoner of war in Genoa for a few months in 1291, and it was during that time that he dictated the book which was to become an instant success, *Il Milione*, which was translated into many European languages, becoming *The Travels of Marco Polo* in English. He ended his days a very rich and very well connected man through the marriage of his three children into some of the noblest Italian families, and not unexpectedly never travelled again.

Did these famous travels ever happen? They are certainly fiercely debated to this day. Some consider them a fictionalised account pieced together from stories Marco heard as a merchant. There are no surviving accounts of his presence in China yet he would certainly have been a novelty and newsworthy. His account has odd gaps, and some critics have pointed out a number of features of China at the time that they feel would have entered a genuine narrative. It certainly didn't help that the original manuscript was lost and translations became dependent on an early Latin version.

He certainly was not the first to enter the court of the Great Khan. Another Italian, Umbrian Giovanni da Pian del Carpine, also known as Friar Johannes de Plano, was one of the first, dispatched in 1245 as part of a well-documented diplomatic mission for Pope Innocent IV to the Great Khan Guyuk in protest over the invasion of Christian lands, to cement alliances (a forlorn hope as they would be detained, then sent packing with the reminder that the Khan was the scourge of God, and a demand that the rulers of Europe should swear their allegiance to him), and not unimportantly carry out a military spy mission. The friar's travels were gruelling beyond belief and he well deserved the archbishopric he was awarded on his return. He wrote two books which in English translation were *History of the Mongols, which we call Tartars* and *Book of the Tartars*, neither of which had the sensational impact of Marco's book.

Marco's book was in the possession of Christopher Columbus and was reputed to be very well thumbed and annotated, and to have been in part his inspiration to reach China via a western passage from Europe. The map which Marco Polo is said to have brought from Cathay is believed to be the basis for the depiction of Cathay in the wonderfully illuminated *mappa mundi* of Fra Mauro c. 1453.

FOLLOWING PAGES: Detail from Fra Mauro's c. 1453 mappa mundi showing Cathay. This map is far more sophisticated than other maps of the time, drawing on the works of Ptolemy, portolan charts, Arabic maps and the journeys of famous explorers such as Marco Polo.

agaz

da questa prouicia scri
ca in golfo tholomeo fa ter
ra ignota

SE

hedificio nobile.

almaror

Pro. serica nel cha
taio
fiume gã

Ausari
mons

Sinu

b. c. n. ctate
nobile soto
nangin.

Saiapsu

cinzu

Iaizu

Lago

Soto
mo d.
gin so
ctade. le

cinzu

nangin

Questa nobel citate
e chome i uno lago
a la qual se po anda
per picola strada
chome apar.

Prouicia de nã
ore. regio

strada

mora

Suzzi

Inquesta citate
se fa grã quatita
de pani doro e seda

Queste insule se dice
esser habundantissime
de ogni metalo.

EANVS CHA TAI
CVS

Quangu

Great Wall of China. In the 1950s and 1960s, at the height of the Cold War, the USSR was cast in the role of Gog and Magog. Today China and the Middle East seem to be under consideration as candidates by some in the West who anticipate an imminent Armageddon.

None of which solves the mystery of just who, what or where the biblical Gog and Magog were. Over the centuries they have been identified with many nations depending on the threat they posed to peace. Some believe the references were to the much-feared tribes living north of the Black Sea who were known to the ancient Greeks as the Scythians. Both Herodotus and Pliny the Elder, many centuries apart, were scathing in their condemnation of the barbaric and cannibalistic ways of these tribes.

Ambrose, a fourth century AD saint and bishop of Milan, wrote in *De Fide* (*Of the Truth*) in 378, 'Gog is the Goth'. For him, the feared southward migration of the Goths, beginning in the fourth century AD, fitted well with the reputation of Gog and Magog. He was by no means the only one to identify Gog and Magog with the Goths. Saint Isidore of Seville, one of the greatest scholars of the early medieval period, who bridged the sixth and seventh century, was equally convinced that the Goths were descended from Gog.

In the none too brief twelve-volume book on the origins, history and deeds of the Getae (Goths), *Getica*, written by Jordanes in 551 AD, Magog was identified both with the Scythians and the Goths. In the eleventh century the historian Adam of Bremen wrote that the Swedes (who were related to the Goths) were the descendants of Gog and Magog, and Queen Christina of Sweden was apparently delighted to consider herself to be a descendant of Magog, albeit hundreds of generations removed.

Some scholars believed that the Mongols had already fulfilled the prophecy of Gog and Magog. Sir John Mandeville not so helpfully echoed the missive of Prester John, identifying the Lost Tribes of Israel as the descendants of Gog and Magog, trapped behind the Gates of Alexander.

It would appear that Gog and Magog became, over time, synonymous with warlike and barbaric invaders. All the apparent contenders among nations for the titles of Gog and Magog have risen, had their moment of glory, power and destruction, and fallen away once more like waves upon the sea. None has proved to be, at least as yet, the prophesied nation. Perhaps Augustine of Hippo in his *City of God*, written soon after the brutal sacking of Rome by the Goths in 410 AD, came closest in identifying Gog and Magog as belonging to no particular place or race but rather as those to be known by their terrible deeds all over the world.

BRITAIN'S GIANTS

Though apparently far from centre stage for the story of Gog and Magog, Britain cannot be overlooked in this curious, ancient and tangled tale. According to one English legend, the third century AD Roman emperor Diocletian had thirty-three daughters each as wicked as the other, who had learned a little too much from their father's persecuting ways. Attempts to curb their activities by marrying them off ended in the mass murder of their husbands by the infuriated sisters under the leadership of the eldest sister, Alba. As punishment, the sisters were cast adrift on the sea, but they were eventually thrown up on the shores of Britain which, as a result, became known as Albion. There they were said to have mated with demons and given rise to a race of giants which included Gog and Magog.

Geoffrey of Monmouth in his *Historia Regum Britanniae* (*History of the Kings of Britain*), written in 1136, wrote of a giant known as Gogmagog, who was thrown over a sea cliff near Plymouth in an exhibition wrestling match by the legendary medieval Cornish hero Corin, super-warrior (he was said to have killed thousands of enemy soldiers with his battle-axe in a single day in Gaul) and well-known slayer of giants.

Somewhat oddly, Gog and Magog are regarded as the protectors of London, and wicker images, and later carved wooden images, of the giants have been carried through the streets in traditional processions since the days of King Henry V in the first part of the fifteenth century. There are even two very ancient oak trees of gigantic girth in Somerset known as Gog and Magog. They are said to be the last remaining trees of a processional avenue leading to Glastonbury Tor and to have been young when Joseph of Arimathea, a secret disciple of Jesus, reputedly landed on English shores with his legendary band of monks. The trees are probably not much more than a thousand years old, though they could be descendants of even earlier plantings.

Just south of Cambridge lie the Gogmagog Hills, where a group of controversial ancient chalk carvings said to represent Gog and Magog, or perhaps the sun and the moon, were discovered in the mid-twentieth century.

PART FOUR

ELUSIVE ISLANDS IN THE SEA OF DARKNESS

~

PENETRATING THE SEA OF DOOM

THE PHANTOM ST BRENDAN'S ISLAND

THE ISLE OF SEVEN CITIES

ST URSULA AND THE ELEVEN THOUSAND VIRGINS

FRISLAND AND OTHER MYSTERIOUS ATLANTIC ISLANDS

OTHER LOST ISLANDS

LEFT: Diego Gutiérrez's wonderfully intricate 1562 map of the New World is decorated with illustrations of sea monsters, cannibals, mermaids and giants. The map trumpeted Spain's explorations in the Americas, and includes real places such as the Virgin Islands as well as the imaginary, including the Isle of Brasile.

FOLLOWING PAGES: Detail from Alejo Fernandez's surreal sixteenth century altarpiece of Spanish caravels journeying to the New World.

PENETRATING THE
SEA OF DOOM

The Atlantic Ocean was more mysterious to the ancient world than Mars is to our world. Beyond the Straits of Gibraltar, known then as the Pillars of Hercules, lay only the eternal question mark. For the Arabs, the Atlantic was the Sea of Gloom or the Sea of Darkness. Some believed the hand of Satan would pluck them from that terrible and confusing sea where, according to the great eleventh century Persian historian and geographer Al-Biruni, the air was eternally dark and the water thick. Others held to a theory that a great fresh-water river called Okeanus encircled the Earth.

Early voyages into the Atlantic by Phoenician sailors were all the more extraordinary given the prevailing beliefs. They established extensive sea-trading routes throughout the Mediterranean from about 1200 to 900 BC onward. According to Strabo, Phoenician traders set up a highly lucrative trade route for tin beyond the Pillars of Hercules to the British Isles. The tin was smelted with copper from Cyprus to make bronze.

A voyage made by Hanno the Navigator, who was sent by Carthage with a fleet of sixty ships in the first half of the sixth century BC through the Straits of Gibraltar, along the west coast of Africa and the Gulf of Guinea to Corisco Bay (modern Gabon) was quite remarkable. According to a Greek translation, his ship finally ran out of supplies at Corisco Bay, where the crew killed and skinned three female gorillas (whose furs, according to Pliny the Elder, were exhibited in the temple of the goddess Tanit until the destruction of Carthage by the Romans), and were then forced to turn back. The brief account of Hanno's journey, called the *Periplus*, was inscribed and hung in the temple of Chronos in Carthage. The *Periplus* mentioned that Hanno had established Carthaginian outposts along the West African coast and revitalised others. Pliny the Elder wrote that 'when Carthage flourished Hanno sailed from Gades [Cadiz in Spain] to Arabia', implying that he circumnavigated Africa from west to east, and that he made public a note of the voyage. In the same period that Hanno set out on his voyage south to explore the African coastline, another Carthaginian, Himlico, had been sent from Gades to explore the outer coasts of Europe and had also published a note of his voyage.

There has certainly been speculation that the Phoenicians pioneered a very early route around Africa, and might even have been trading for gold in south-eastern Africa. Herodotus, writing in the fifth century BC, included an almost throwaway line to the effect that Phoenician sailors, while circumnavigating Africa, 'saw the sun on the right side while sailing westwards', which would indeed be the case if they were hugging the west coast of Africa in the southern hemisphere. Herodotus described a three-year journey Phoenician sailors made from the Red Sea c. 600 BC, circumnavigating Africa from east to west and returning via the Pillars of Hercules.

The Phoenicians mined metals far beyond their original territory. Phoenicia was centred on present-day Lebanon, coastal Syria and parts of Israel, all of which were poorly endowed with the metals they needed. The acquisition of mineral-rich territories was one of the major driving forces behind their colonisation of the Mediterranean and Africa. They established colonies at Carthage in North Africa, on Sicily and on the Iberian Peninsula, which was rich in silver, and on the islands of Cyprus, Corsica and Sardinia. Herodotus described one mining site in which a mountain had literally been overturned in the search for gold. After Phoenicia itself was absorbed by the Achaemenid Persian Empire in 539 BC, the centre of Phoenician civilisation became Carthage, its large outpost in North Africa. The Persian Empire, under the remarkably enlightened rule of Cyrus the Great, would become the largest empire in the world at the time, stretching from modern Turkey and Israel through to Kazakhstan in the north and the Indus River in the east.

Extraordinary though the Phoenicians' voyages undoubtedly were, they involved staying within sight of the mainland as much as possible rather than striking out into unknown waters, even though Phoenician sailors had mastered the art of navigation by the stars. Like all the sailors in the ancient world, they largely hugged the coastline or sailed between coastal reference points. As far as is known, they only lost sight of land on two Mediterranean routes, between the Balearic Islands (including

Ibiza, Mallorca, Menorca and Formentera) off the eastern coast of Spain en route to the Carthaginian mining colony on Sardinia, and from the African coast to the Balearics. Although the Phoenicians were remarkable sailors, they were never recorded as heading far beyond the western shores of Europe and Africa. With manpowered boats, they would have been unwise to try.

Pythias of Marsallia (Marseilles) on the southern coast of France ventured out on one of the first recorded trips into the Atlantic around 330 BC, and wrote of his journey in a long-lost book titled *About the Ocean*. Fortunately the book was quoted by a number of later writers. Pythias certainly visited Cornwall, where he said tin was traded, and possibly Ireland and to the islands of the Hebrides and Orkneys. From there he described a voyage further north to Ultima Thule, which he described as a place lying at the very limit of the world, six days sail beyond Britain. There the night lasted no more than two to three hours. A further day's sailing beyond Thule was the frozen Cronian Sea, where he said the sun never set in summer. By the sixteenth century those frozen waters would be marked on maps as Mare Congelatii, the Frozen Sea. There are various theories about the identity of Pythias's Ultima Thule. Given the sailing times involved and the description, it may well be an early discovery of Iceland or the Shetland Islands. Others think Pythias may have reached Trondheim in Norway. The destination favoured by historians is the Shetlands.

While European exploration of the North Atlantic was very tentative, the Inuit began their exploration of Canada perhaps as much as 80,000 years before. The Norsemen of Norway had colonised Iceland by 874 AD and Erik the Red from Norse Iceland colonised Greenland in 986 AD. Leap-frogging onward, the Norsemen sailed from Greenland to the northeast coast of Canada. The *Vinland Saga*, which began as oral tradition and was finally written down in the twelfth and thirteenth centuries, claimed that c. 985 Bjarni Herjolfsson, a Norse settler in Greenland, was blown off course and sighted a new continent west of Greenland. Around fifteen years later, Leif Ericsson, the son of Erik the Red, voyaged to this new continent.

A number of exploratory journeys followed over the next decade, and the new land was named Vinland, because the explorers found a profusion of grapes growing there. While colonies are believed to have been created, none survived over the long term. The archaeological site at L'Anse aux Meadows in modern-day Newfoundland, declared a World Heritage Site in 1978, is the earliest known European settlement in the New World, a place where Norse ships were repaired for the journey home and a base for overland exploration as far south as the St Lawrence River and New Brunswick.

THE PHANTOM
ST BRENDAN'S
ISLAND

There seems to have been a great deal of carelessness in the medieval and Renaissance periods, as a number of lands and islands were lost, never to be seen again. Phantom islands do exist, often briefly or periodically, as the result of underwater earthquake and volcanic activity. This may be the source of some of the mythology that surrounds many ephemeral islands.

St Brendan's island may fit that category. Ptolemy included in his *Geographia* an island he named Aprositus Nesos, apparently located within the Canary or Fortunate Islands group, which he rather conveniently said 'can never be reached or is not visible' as it was surrounded by mists.

A long Portuguese and Spanish tradition includes an eighth island in the Canary Islands group, which was periodically reported and became known to them as San Borondón. Many of those living on the islands of La Palma, La Gomera and El Hierro who reported seeing San Borondón over the centuries were considered to be reliable witnesses, to

Insulæ Fortunatæ

have seen the island in clear weather, and described it in quite similar terms as being large, forested and mountainous.

In the eleventh century, cartographer San Severo and the Christian writer Father Guanilo (who described San Borondón as Isla Perdida, the lost island) both located San Borondón within the Canaries archipelago. In c. 1280 San Borondón was included on the Hereford *Mappa Mundi* (see page 54). The map placed Jerusalem at the centre of the known world and depicted the island of Crete with a tiny but perfectly drawn labyrinth of Daedalus, together with the major cities and rivers of Europe. On the very edge of the unknown world, gloriously strange and terrible monsters and beasts were depicted. The Canaries archipelago was described on the map as 'The Isles of the Blessed and the Island of St Brendan'. Even at the end of the fifteenth century, Christopher Columbus expressed the hope that he would encounter the island on his journey across the Atlantic in 1492.

ST BRENDAN THE NAVIGATOR

The historic sixth century St Brendan (also known as St Brandanus) belonged to a particularly evangelical period in Irish history, when many monks ventured far beyond their native land. St Brendan is known to have travelled extensively through Wales, reaching Iona off the west coast of Scotland, establishing a number of sees, and founding many churches and two monasteries. One of the monasteries was the once important Benedictine monastery at Clonfert in

LEFT: St Brendan and his monks celebrate Mass on the back of a whale. Colour engraving of a medieval illumination.

THE ATLAS OF LEGENDARY LANDS

County Galway, founded in 557 AD. The monastery is said to have housed an astonishing 3000 monks by the reign of Queen Elizabeth I, when it was proposed as the centre for a university for Ireland, although Trinity College Dublin was finally granted the charter. The monastery flourished for centuries, despite being burned down on three occasions by invading Danes between the ninth and eleventh centuries. The monastery and most of the church were destroyed once more in 1541 and the monastery was not rebuilt. Towards the end of his life, St Brendan established a bishopric at Annaghdown, where he ended his days. He died at the age of ninety-three and was interred at Clonfert. His feast day is still celebrated by many on 16 May.

Known also as St Brendan the Navigator, and revered as the patron saint of sailors and travellers, St Brendan is also famous for a seven-year voyage, said to have been undertaken in search of an earthly Paradise, the Promised Land of the Saints. The story became well known and was often retold, with many moral and apparently fantastic embellishments being added during the medieval period. There is no historic proof of St Brendan's journey, yet the old Irish calendar included provision for a special feast to celebrate it, and at the end of the eighth century St Aengus the Culdee spoke in his litany of the voyage of St Brendan.

The oldest known version of the story is to be found in the anonymous ninth century Latin text *Navigatio Sancti Brendani* (*The Voyage of St Brendan*) — one of the best-known books of the Middle Ages and based on a long oral tradition. The story was eventually translated into other languages, including French, Saxon and Flemish, and in the exquisite little twelfth century cathedral that still stands at Clonfert is a carving of a mermaid combing her hair, a reminder of the sermon St Brendan was said to have preached to the creatures of the sea on his journey.

A PILGRIMAGE TO THE BLESSED LANDS

The tale begins with a Father Barino (Barinthus) coming to Clonfert, claiming that after visiting a fellow monk and hermit he had been taken to an island called the Promised Land of the Saints. Barino described passing through clouds so dense he could scarcely see, before emerging into brilliant light and landing on a verdant and beautiful shore, rich with fruit trees, flowers and precious stones, and with perfumed air. The monks had travelled extensively through this beautiful land, until finally barred by a great river beyond which they were not permitted to pass.

St Brendan was utterly overcome with longing to see this wonderful place. He chose fourteen monks to accompany him. At the foot of Brandon Hill they constructed a vessel made of wicker and covered with hide that had been tanned with oak bark and waterproofed with tar. The ship was supplied with provisions for forty days. Three more monks begged to join the party as they were about to depart, and became part of the group. The monks set forth, but soon the wind dropped and they were forced to row rather than sail. On the fortieth day, exhausted and with their rations used up, they saw a steep, rocky island with great waterfalls.

Three further days sailing around the island's shores brought them to a safe cove where they were

132

led towards a mansion by a dog. A feast had been laid out for them in a hall lined with metal vessels, silver bridle-bits and horns inlaid with silver. This description seems to indicate an encounter with a Viking home. A small black boy was the only servant and St Brendan took him for a demon.

On the next island reached on their voyage, the monks discovered flocks of very large white sheep, and large streams of water filled with fish, flowing from fountains. They celebrated the resurrection of Jesus at Easter with the sacrifice of a spotless lamb, and reprovisioned their boat. Their next landfall was an odd island without sand, trees or grass. They spent the night in prayer, celebrated Mass and prepared a meal in a cauldron. As the cauldron reached the boil, the island began to heave and the monks withdrew, terrified, to their boat. The island immediately sank into the ocean. St Brendan explained to his fellow travellers that God had revealed to him during the night that the island was in fact a gigantic whale called Iasconius. The next island they visited, the Paradise of Birds, was verdant and full of flowers. Moving inland, they encountered a tree completely covered with snow-white birds singing in exquisite unison. One of them explained to St Brendan that the birds had all been taken from grace by the fall of Lucifer. They wandered the Earth, but on the festival days of the Christian calendar they were permitted to take the form of white birds, gathering on the island to sing the praises of the Lord.

The monks reached their next landfall when they were at the point of total exhaustion, discovering a monastery where frugal meals were manifested and lanterns lit dramatically by a flaming arrow. The monks of the monastery claimed to have lived there

for eighty years, since the time of St Patrick and St Ailbe, never ageing or suffering infirmities, never bothered by heat or cold, and wanting for nothing. St Brendan and his fellow monks left the island after the celebration of Epiphany. Next they encountered an island with a fountain of forgetfulness, before taking a northerly, then an easterly course. They discovered that they had completed a great loop that brought them back a year later to the island where they had first celebrated Easter.

Their adventures continued as they witnessed a titanic battle between two huge sea monsters, and encountered the Island of Strong Men where one of St Brendan's men disembarked, bound on a personal pilgrimage. After much suffering, the men reached another island—a paradise with grapevines laden with fruit, abundant vegetables and herbs, watered by six fountains, and with air scented with pomegranates. There they restored their strength for forty days.

It seems they then spent years at sea, always returning to the islands where they had first celebrated Easter and Christmas. At one time they encountered a huge column floating in the sea, made of clearest crystal and hard as marble. They found a hole in the column and sailed through, before being borne north by a favourable wind.

Among their most fearsome experiences was an encounter with an island where the air smelled foul far out to sea, the cliffs were rugged and covered in slag. Thunderous noises of smiths' forges filled the

*FOLLOWING PAGES: 'The Northern Regions',
from Abraham Ortelius's* Theatrum Orbis Terrarum
(Theatre of the World), *1570, includes the islands of
Brasile, St Brendan and Frisland in the North Atlantic.*

air, giant rocks were tossed at them, and smoke rose as if from a fiery furnace. While they watched in awe, the island became a huge glowing mass of fire and the sea boiled around it. St Brendan warned his brethren that they were at the very verge of hell. Later they encountered a high mountain emerging from the ocean, its peak obscured by clouds of smoke, and dramatic coal-black cliffs. After losing one of his men there, St Brendan set sail southwards. As they looked back the monks saw huge flames shooting up into the sky, as if the whole mountain had become a burning pyre.

Thereafter the intrepid band encountered Judas, allowed on Church festivals to be cooled by waves that battered him on a rocky shore, and Paul the Spiritual, a hermit who had lived to at least 140 years, the last sixty without any bodily sustenance.

Seven long years had elapsed since the start of their journey and they were at last to be rewarded. They celebrated Easter once more before the prevailing winds carried them westward until they ran into a great bank of darkness. When they emerged, they found a brilliantly lit shore and attained their goal, the Promised Land of the Saints. This land had no apparent limits—they travelled across it for forty days, and it was thickly forested and filled with fruit trees and precious stones. The light always shone, night and day. Eventually they encountered a wide impassable river, marking the limits of what mortal man was permitted to see. They provisioned their boat, taking with them some of the precious stones, and sailed directly back to their own monastery in Ireland with no further mysterious interventions to lead them in circles.

A TWENTIETH CENTURY ST BRENDAN

In 1979 a man of truly adventurous spirit, Timothy Severin, decided to test the story of St Brendan's odyssey in a practical way that would have earned the praise of the saint himself. In a traditional hide-covered currach, constructed according to the description in the *Navigatio Brendani*, he set sail, following the route that St Brendan would most logically have followed. For all its fragile appearance, a large currach is amazingly seaworthy, capable of withstanding the violent seas off the western islands of Scotland where they were long used. But on a journey across the Atlantic, a currach would have been at the mercy of currents and winds. Severin's boat took him first northwards and then westwards safely across the entire Atlantic Ocean to Newfoundland, which raises the question: did St Brendan and his followers discover North America, and possibly Greenland and Iceland, almost five hundred years before the Vikings, and a thousand years before Columbus? Long before Timothy Severin's trip, the 1497 expedition by Englishman John Cabot in the minuscule ship *Matthew* with eighteen crewmen also set out from Ireland and landed on Newfoundland. It is not impossible that a sixth century St Brendan did the same.

Other evidence of pre-Columban passage to Newfoundland from Britain has also emerged. England had regularly traded with Iceland for salted cod, a trade that was stopped by the King of Denmark in 1475. A royal charter was granted to a group of Bristol merchants in 1479 to replace the supply. Records that emerged in 1955 suggest that they had succeeded in setting up processing facilities for cod in Newfoundland by 1480, and that fishing vessels were regularly setting out from Bristol and crossing the Atlantic to Newfoundland years before Columbus's journey to the Indies.

St Brendan's description of encountering a floating column of crystal certainly sounds like an iceberg. He also described a Coagulated Sea, which would describe the icy slush encountered in the North Atlantic.

The island that stank of rotten eggs, where giants threw burning rocks at the boat as they sailed past and exploded into a globe of fire, sounds remarkably like an erupting volcanic island. The mountain in the sea that spouted fire also sounds volcanic. It is not uncommon for a chain of such eruptions to occur. In 1963 just such an island emerged from under the sea, as a result of volcanic activity in the Westerman Islands off the southern coast of Iceland and located over the Mid-Atlantic Ridge. The island, now known as Surtsey, increased in size over twelve months, with molten rocks, cinders and pumice blown up to 300 metres (1000 feet) into the air for several months, while the column of ash reached 10 kilometres (six miles) into the atmosphere. Other islands appeared temporarily near Surtsey. It is likely that just such an eruption was observed by early medieval sailors off the shores of Iceland.

The description of St Brendan and his men passing through a bank of darkness so great that they could barely see their way before emerging into the great light of their Promised Land of the Saints sounds very much as if the journey ended in the foggiest place on Earth, the Grand Banks off Newfoundland where the Gulf Stream meets the cold Labrador Current. At the ancient Norse settlement largely designed for repairing and re-equipping boats, recently discovered by archaeologists near the town of L'Anse aux Meadows in Newfoundland, a great fog bank rolls in each night to smother the view all the way to the horizon.

Much of the story of St Brendan's seven-year voyage is described as a perilous pilgrimage and acts as a morality tale. But was it based on the journey of a real group of sailors, possibly led by St Brendan himself, that reached Newfoundland and returned to tell the tale? If St Brendan encountered what seem to us now to be frozen seas, active volcanoes, icebergs, Inuit, northern islands and a small monastery, his story suddenly makes perfect sense. In the sixth century, the Irish were already largely Christian converts, deeply committed to their religion with a tradition of monastic life, and many sought a hermit-like existence. It was likely that some monks would travel north and westward in search of places of contemplation; indeed, itinerant Irish monks were already spreading across Europe in remarkable numbers. Another possibility is that the story represents a composite of early Irish seafaring discoveries. By way of corroboration, recent research into the gene pool of the peoples of Northern Ireland, Iceland, the Faroes and further to the north-west has established clear linkages.

Whatever the facts of St Brendan's voyage, a hard cold examination of the medieval story seems to reveal more than a grain of truth. The Irish had certainly reached Iceland by 795 AD. But did monks reach North America centuries before the dates officially attributed to the Norse? We may never know. Hermits leave few traces behind them.

SEARCHING FOR THE
PHANTOM ISLE

Quests to find the phantom St Brendan's Island or San Borondón within the Canary Islands continued long after Columbus made his famous journey, finding North America but certainly not, as he had hoped, St Brendan's Island. In 1570 there was such an outbreak of eyewitness reports of the reappearance of San Borondón in the Canary Islands that the governor of the island of Ferro documented the sightings of a hundred irreproachable witnesses. Similar reports came from Tenerife and Palma, many of them detailed and often made by men of the highest repute. Curiously, some reports came from ships' captains who all told quite similar stories of landing on the shores of the mysterious island with their crews, of a terrible storm building, of the anchor of the ship dragging and their hasty return on board, and then of their ship being blown out to sea while the island disappeared behind them, lost in impenetrable mist. Finally, a new search was launched from Palma for the phantom island, but once again it proved fruitless.

From time to time more sightings were made and in 1720 another frenzy of interest in the lost island resulted in an expedition from Tenerife, commanded by a man history records briefly as being of considerable reliability, Don Gaspar Dominguez, who took with him as ship's chaplains two friars. He returned without success, to the bitter disappointment of the people of Tenerife. In 1759 the island was again sighted by a Franciscan monk from the island of Gomara. He appears to have summoned some forty witnesses and to have examined the island with a telescope.

Mass hysteria may have accounted for some of the spikes in sightings over the centuries, and there is little doubt that some stories were embroidered. Yet it is odd that many apparently sober-minded men were willing to risk their reputation by testifying to San Borondón's reappearance. The island was still located on a French map in 1704 and was included in a scientific treatise by a certain Monsieur Gautier in 1755. Castilian royalty hedged their bets by laying claim to all the Canary Islands, including those that might be discovered in the future.

Perhaps the conclusion reached by the enlightened Spanish Benedictine abbot and scholar Father Feyjóo y Montenegro (1676–64) was correct. He attributed the mysterious disappearing island in the Canaries to an atmospheric illusion, a mirage, similar to that recorded offshore from Marseille, in southern France, and the Fata Morgana, recorded in the Straits of Messina between Sicily and Italy, in which the Sicilian city of Reggia and its surroundings are sometimes reflected out to sea.

THE ISLE OF
SEVEN CITIES

Another phantom island sometimes considered synonymous with St Brendan's Island, although its mythology arises from different sources, was said to lie in the Atlantic Ocean west of the Iberian Peninsula. It was known as the Island of Seven Cities, or Antillia. It may be based on the twin islands described by the first century historian Plutarch (AD 46–c.127) in his biography of the brilliant Roman general and statesman Quintus Sertorius (126–73 BC), sometimes hailed as the 'new Hannibal'.

Having served with the greatest distinction and valour in a number of campaigns and serving in Spain as a military tribune before tasting the bitter politics in which Rome was then embroiled, Sertorius then acted as Hispania's proconsul. Roman politics and factionalism followed him and he became involved in an unsuccessful defence of the province against the forces of Sulla, the man who for whatever reason repeatedly thwarted his ambitions. Twice consul of Rome and then its dictator, Sulla was a brilliant general and politician who initiated the end of the

TERRA SANCTE CRVCIS

SIVE MVNDVS

JAVA MAIOR

JAVA MINOR

CANDYN

MANGI

TEBET

TANGVT

ENLANT

TERRA NOVA

SPAGNOLA

ANTILIA INSVLA

CANIBALOR

REGNVM VAR

SEYLAN INSVLE PARS

PREVIOUS PAGES: Johannes Ruysch's 1507 world map is based on the work of Strabo, but includes the discoveries of Christopher Columbus and John Cabot, with Newfoundland (and Cuba) connected to Asia. Hyperborea and Antillia are two lands from the Atlas of Legendary Lands included on the map.

Roman Republic and was later, not surprisingly, much admired by Machiavelli. Sertorius wisely withdrew to North Africa, capturing Tingis (Tangiers) in his campaign in Mauretania, to the great admiration of the people of Lusitania (modern Portugal). After a rare disastrous campaign, in which he was forced to launch an attack from the sea, Sertorius survived a violent storm to land near the mouth of the River Baetis (now the River Guadalquivir, which runs through Seville in southern Spain). There he encountered sailors who told him that they had just returned from twin Atlantic islands, which lay some 2000 kilometres (1250 miles) off the African coast. The islands were divided from each other by a narrow channel and were known as the Islands of the Blessed. They were a place of moderate rain, rich soil and a great abundance of delicate fruits, produced without labour. The climate was moderate, the air pleasant, the breezes gentle. The sailors claimed that they believed these were the Elysian Fields of Homer.

Battle weary, having survived imminent ship-wreck and betrayal by Rome, Sertorius was for a time obsessed by the thought of these islands. But he was soon distracted by the need to lift the morale of his soldiers, and in the end never set sail for the Islands of the Blessed.

The Isle of Seven Cities is connected to both Portuguese and Spanish legend. It was said that the island was settled by the Archbishop of Porto and six bishops, together with many devout Christians, their livestock and other possessions, when they escaped the invasion of the Iberian Peninsula by the Moors in the eighth century. The refugees were said to have beached and burned their boats to ensure they could never return home and would remain undetected. The archbishop and his bishops each founded a city and the whole island became a peaceful and orderly utopian state. The Blessed Isles of the ancients had morphed into the Island of Seven Cities. Most such legendary places changed their name as old legends became entangled or reconstructed, and with time were also relocated, always elusive, always perilously close to that place on old maps known simply as Terra Incognita.

Antillia, the island's next incarnation and not to be confused with the current Antilles Islands, first appeared on the Francis Pizzigano Chart of 1367 (now in the Biblioteca Nazionale at Parma, in Italy), almost seven centuries after the archbishop's supposed landfall on the island but long before Columbus's voyage to the New World. In the Pizzigano Chart Antillia is indicated by inscription only, but thereafter and through the fifteenth century it appears as a rectangular shape, about the size of Portugal, lying about 320 kilometres (200 miles) west of the Azores (see Bianco map, page 88). On the 1435 chart of the Italian cartographer Battista Beccario, Antillia has acquired mysterious companion islands, called Satanaxio (St Antagio), Royllo and Tanmar, inscribed *insulae de novo repertae*, 'newly discovered islands'. The name Antillia has been said to mean 'island of the sea-dragons' and to be derived from the Arabic words *jezirat al-lin*, or *al-tennyn* (meaning 'dragon's isle'). But it seems more likely that it was derived from the Portuguese *ante ilha*, meaning 'the nearer island'.

Certainly belief in the Island of Seven Cities, under whatever name, remained strong throughout the fifteenth century. In 1414 the crew of a Spanish vessel was said to have sighted the legendary island, a Venetian chart depicted it in 1420, and a Portuguese crew was said to have landed upon it in the 1430s. A Spanish envoy to England, Pedro de Ayala, wrote to King Ferdinand and Queen Isabella in 1498 that, during the previous seven years, the people of Bristol had been equipping two, three or four caravels each year to search for the islands of Brasile, or Hy-Brazil, and the Seven Cities. In later years some Portuguese considered the Island of Seven Cities to have been São Miguel, the largest island of the archipelago of the Azores, known also as the Green Island. It was a major producer of wheat, wine, fruit and cheeses, and had some claim to the paradisical qualities of the legendary island.

Legends tend to mutate to fit their times and the motivations of those who hear them. Antillia advanced westward from its mid-Atlantic position, and before disappearing from the maps of the Atlantic Ocean gave its name to a group of islands in the Caribbean. From the ocean, the mysterious Antillia travelled overland across North America, reverting to a version of its older name and becoming the Seven Cities of Gold located in what would become modern-day New Mexico. In this telling, the archbishop and his companions who escaped from the Moors were said to have found their way to America, where they founded the cities of Cibola and Quivera, cities of unimaginable riches filled with gold and jewels. In very little time, the two cities were transformed by retelling into seven, each a city of gold, one for each of the bishops. The story was further fuelled by the return to New Spain (Mexico) of the shipwrecked survivors of an expedition led by Pánfilo de Narváez to Florida in 1528. Making their way back to Sinaloa on the west coast of Mexico, they described encounters with natives who told them of cities of great riches.

The glitter of gold exerted its usual power and enticed the conquistadors north from Mexico through the waterless trail of the Jornada del Muerto, the 'Journey of the Dead Man', which stretches 160 kilometres (100 miles) from Mexico to northern New Mexico through desert and a vast and ancient lava field. The route is flanked to the east by the Oscura and San Andreas mountains and to the west by the Fra Cristobál Range and the Caballo Mountains. Far from encountering the Seven Cities of Cibola, they found instead the villages of the peaceful agrarian Pueblo People, and instead of golden cities, the beautiful adobe architecture of the region.

Columbus and Antillia

There is more than one link between Columbus and Antillia. The story may be apocryphal, and many historians consider it so, but it was related by the Spanish Dominican monk, sometime Bishop of Chiapa and historian Bartolomé de las Casas, who emigrated to Hispaniola in 1502, and he attested it was well known to those who knew Columbus in Hispaniola. The story claimed that Columbus and his wife had been staying in Madeira when a small, severely battered ship arrived in the harbour, with just six remaining crewmen in desperate condition. Five died soon after arrival, despite Columbus and his wife caring for them. The sixth, the ship's pilot, passed on the story of their misadventures before he too died. The crew of seventeen had set out from a Spanish port, but when well out to sea had encountered severe gales, forcing them westward for twenty-eight days, far beyond charted waters into the area marked on maps as *vile sea*. They had made landfall on an island where they were able to renew their water supplies. The return journey, with the winds at last in their favour, was nevertheless terrible with their provisions failing and one man after another dying. The pilot had taken some bearings and described the island's inhabitants as naked, but the remainder of his information appears lost to history.

Did this incident happen? Did it provide Columbus with further indirect evidence that a journey west from Europe might lead him to new lands rather than oblivion? If the story is true, did the ill-fated seamen make landfall in the Indies before he did? Columbus certainly believed in the existence of Antillia and planned to make it a stopping place in 1492.

RIGHT: Christopher Columbus landing at Hispaniola, 5 December 1492, from his De insulis nuper in mari Indico repertis, inventis epistola, *woodcut in Carlo Verardi,* Historia baetica, *Basel, 1494.*

ST URSULA AND
THE ELEVEN
THOUSAND VIRGINS

Rather sadly, St Ursula was removed from the Roman Catholic canon of saints and her cult suppressed by Pope Paul VI in the revision carried out in 1969, but her story lives on. According to legend, Ursula was a beautiful fourth century Romano-British princess, the daughter of King Donaut of Dumnonia in south-west Britain (sometimes referred to as King Dionotus of Cornwall).

Ursula was promised in marriage by her father to a pagan, Conan Meriadoc, the governor of Armorica (Brittany). Conan was a great warrior who had helped the Roman Magnus Maximus to become the Emperor Maximus (also known as Maximianus and, according to Geoffrey of Monmouth, Maximian) and sole ruler of the west. Conan applied to King Donaut not only for his daughter's hand but also, in the name of his men-at-arms, for a group of Cornish virgins to be sent to Brittany as brides. (According to Geoffrey of Monmouth's entertaining but partly fictionalised *Historia Regum Britanniae*, Conan's men married local women from Brittany rather than Britain, but not before cutting out their tongues to maintain the purity of the language.) Ursula had devoted her life to God and wanted nothing to do with the marriage. Nevertheless she was sent by ship to Armorica together with eleven other virgins. With retelling of the story, by the ninth century this number had swelled to a most unlikely 11,000 noble-born virgins and another 60,000 virginal young women.

A miracle occurred—a great wind blew up, forcing the ships to make port elsewhere on the coast of Gaul. After giving thanks for her deliverance, Ursula swore she would not proceed with the marriage until she and her companions had made a pilgrimage to see the Pope in Rome.

In some versions of the story, the trip took three years and involved many terrifying but no doubt edifying experiences, rather in the style of St Brendan's adventurous seven-year sea journey. On arriving in Rome, Ursula persuaded Pope Cyriacus (of whom there are no records) and Sulpicius, Bishop of Ravenna, to travel with them to Cologne, which was then under siege by the Huns. Various other volunteers were said to have joined the group, including Pantalus, the first bishop of Basel (Basle) and a fourth century martyr, Jacques, Bishop of Liège (another dubious addition, as the first bishop of Liège was appointed in the seventh century), King Ethereus from Britain and even Conan Meriadoc himself, who was said to have been married to Ursula by the Pope.

Geoffrey of Monmouth, uncharacteristically, told a much shorter tale. He claimed that some of the boats sank, while others, including the one with Ursula onboard, were blown off course onto islands in the mouth of a river in Germany, where the women were slaughtered by the Huns and the Picts.

Ursula is in some ways a prototype of St Joan, Maid of Orléans, leading her band of maidens, volunteers and church leaders to the aid of the besieged city of Cologne. Unlike Joan, Ursula did not participate in the fighting, and her first campaign was to be her last. Some say she attracted the attention of one of the chieftains of the Huns, who massacred her and the 11,000 virgins after Ursula refused to marry him. An alternative story claims that the Huns beheaded all the virgins in a terrible massacre, while the chieftain shot Ursula with an arrow through the heart.

Belief in Ursula continued for centuries and her cult was widespread. Hildegard of Bingen composed chants in her honour, and in 1535 the Order of the Ursuline nuns, devoted to the education of young girls, was founded by St Angela de Merici and subsequently spread around the world. Even if Ursula never existed, perhaps the virtues she represented should still be celebrated: courage, strength, honour and moral determination.

Only in a purely apocryphal sense do Ursula and her 11,000 virgins belong in this story of the invisible atlas. If the story of Ursula might just possibly be true, at least in part, what is absolutely impossible is the idea that she and her companions crossed the Atlantic Ocean. Yet not one but two groups of islands off America were named for them. Christopher Columbus encountered a group of small islands clustered around a larger island in the Caribbean. He named the large island Santa Ursela and the smaller islands Las Once Mil Virgines (The Eleven Thousand Virgins). They are collectively known now as the Virgin Islands.

In 1521 the northern Portuguese explorer and ship owner Juão Álvares Faguendes named another group of islands, just off the southern coast of Newfoundland in honour of the martyred 11,000 virgins. This time the name did not survive, and the islands became the French territory of Saint-Pierre and Miquelon. Ferdinand Magellan also celebrated the story of the virgins during his circumnavigation of the world. In 1520, when he rounded a cape at the south-eastern tip of South America and saw before him what must have been a truly blessed sight, the Straits of Magellan, on Ursula's feast day, 21 October, he named the cape Cape Virgenes.

The Martyrdom of Saint Ursula and Her Ten Thousand Virgins, *early sixteenth century. The virgins numbers had not yet reached 11,000.*

FRISLAND AND
OTHER MYSTERIOUS
ATLANTIC ISLANDS

In 1558 a book called *De I Commentarii del Viaggio* was published in Venice. It claimed to contain a series of letters and a map relating to the North Atlantic travels of two brothers, Nicolo and Antonio Zeno, in the late fourteenth century. The letters and maps had purportedly been discovered by a descendant, also named Nicolo Zeno. If the book was true, it was historical dynamite, showing that America had been discovered a century before the voyage of Columbus. The story was not entirely impossible, although

obviously much embroidered, but most historians now consider it a hoax.

Nicolo and Antonio were historical figures, members of an important Venetian family, and noted navigators. Their brother Carlo was a famous Venetian naval hero. The first section of the book contains letters said to have been written to Antonio by Nicolo, and there is some evidence that the first voyage described in the letters did take place, and that Nicolo returned to Venice in 1385. Nicolo was said to have sailed from Venice for England and

Flanders in 1380, but to have been caught in a gale and blown off course. He was shipwrecked on an island lying somewhere between Britain and Iceland and was rescued by Zichmni, ruler of the duchy of Sorant located in 'Frisland', an island described as being larger than Ireland. Zichmni was described as the owner of a group of islands called Porlanda. He has been identified by some as Henry I St Clair, Earl of Orkney. Nicolo was made admiral of Zichmni's fleet. After conquering the Shetlands, the two ventured into the North Atlantic, attempting an invasion of Iceland, which was repelled.

Thereafter the manuscript sinks into fiction, with a claim that they then attacked several islands called Bres, Broas, Damberc, Iscant, Mimant, Talas and Trans. Nicolo then supposedly voyaged on to Greenland where, in a story reminiscent of that told about St Brendan, he discovered a miraculously heated monastery. On returning to Frisland he died. The danger of weaving fiction around reality is that reality has an annoying way of spoiling a good yarn. Far from dying in Frisland in 1394, the historical Nicolo was back in Venice standing trial for embezzlement carried out while holding the position of military governor in Greece from 1390 to 1392. He died in Venice in 1400.

The letters in the second batch were purportedly sent from Antonio to Carlo. We are told that, after Nicolo's alleged death in Frisland, Antonio became admiral of Zichmni's fleet. A group of fishermen apparently landed in Frisland, telling a remarkable story of a twenty-five-year voyage in which they travelled westward and encountered two strange lands, Estotiland, said to be 1600 kilometres (1000 miles) west of Frisland, whose inhabitants traded with Greenland, and Drogeo. The men described encounters with terrifying sea monsters and cannibals. Somewhat oddly, this immediately inspired Zichmni and Antonio to head out into these terrible waters, travelling west in search of the two mysterious lands. They encountered a land called Icaria, whose inhabitants were none too fond of strangers, and continued westward, landing on a promontory at the southern end of Engrouelanda. Zichmni was so impressed with the favourable character of the place he resolved to stay there and create a settlement but Antonio, far less impressed, returned to Frisland.

PRESERVED BY THE MAP MAKERS

All this would be no more than an entertaining story if it were not for the very deceptive map that accompanied the letters. A second version of the map was published in 1561 in Venice by Giordano Ruscelli. This was followed soon after, in 1569, by Gerard Mercator's map of the known world, which included the Zeno brothers' supposed discoveries. Worse, the fictitious lands were included by the Flemish scholar and cartographer, Abraham Ortelius, in his 1570 *Theatrum Orbis Terrarum* (*Theatre of the World*), an atlas of fifty-three maps, which was to remain in print for more than forty years. What was paper to the cartographer was dangerous sea, bitter cold and gales to the navigator, and Martin Frobisher's sixteenth century explorations to Canada were endangered by Mercator's map. When Frobisher encountered Greenland, he believed he had discovered Frisland, and when he encountered Baffin Island, he believed that he had found Greenland. The mysterious Frisland continued to appear on maps into the eighteenth century.

And what of Henry I St Clair? That is where a true mystery begins. Around the arch in the stained-glass window of Rosslyn Chapel, built by Henry's grandson, the first Earl of Caithness, and commenced in 1446, are large carvings of plants that closely resemble maize—a plant unknown in Europe when the carvings were made. Some historians, who most certainly were not botanists, have derided this interpretation and identified the plants as wheat or strawberries. If the plants are not corn, then either the carver was so surfeited with whisky that he wildly distorted images of wheat and strawberries, or created purely decorative, imaginary but surprisingly accurate images of maize. The carvings are certainly neither of wheat nor of strawberries. The Clan Sinclair celebrated the 600th anniversary of Henry's journey to America in 1998. Were there grains of historical truth tucked away in the story of Zichmni, just as there may well have been in the story of St Brendan?

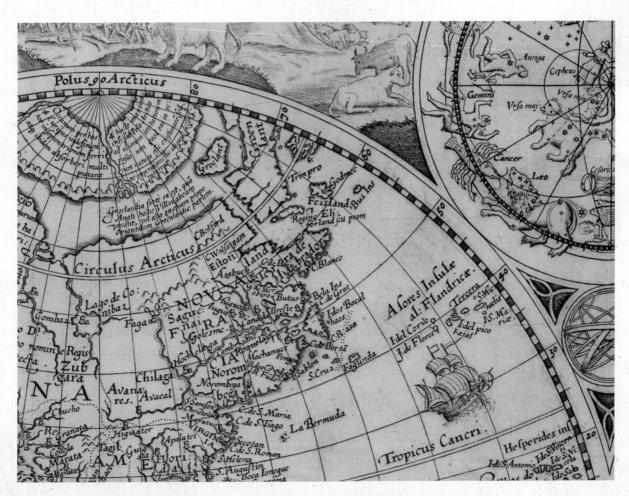

Detail from Orbis terrarum typus de integro multis in locis emendatus, *by Jan Huyghen van Linschoten in 1594, showing Frisland and Bus (Buss) Island.*

OTHER LOST
ISLANDS

A number of other strange and mysterious islands appeared on maps of the Atlantic at the same time that Frisland was being drawn. The Isle of Brasile, or Hy-Brazil, was one of the most persistent, appearing on maps for five centuries and not being completely dismissed until the 1870s. It was usually represented as a donut shape with islands lying within, or as twin islands separated by a narrow channel. It seems never to have quite decided where to call home. In earlier centuries it was located west of Ireland but, possibly shy of increasingly known waters, it later retreated in the direction of America. Clearly ambivalent about its location, it appeared twice on the 1367 Pizzigano map.

The Isles of Demons had a shorter map life. Supposedly, off the coast of Newfoundland, they were said to be terrifying places, full of unimaginably fierce monsters and demons. Fortunately no such islands lie off Newfoundland, but they were depicted on the 1507 Ruysch map (see pages 140–1), and later in the maps of both Mercator and Ortelius (see pages 134–5) in the 1560s and 1570s.

Buss Island was rather different. In 1578 Frobisher was on his third Arctic expedition, in an attempt to find the North-west Passage to China, when one of his vessels ran into trouble and was forced to return to England. The crew reported encountering a large, verdant and fruitful land which was not represented on any existing map. The name given to the land came from the type of vessel which the crew sailed, a *busse*.

Almost a century later, in 1671, Captain Thomas Shepherd claimed to have rediscovered the island and mapped it. Other reports of sightings were made but, like the Isle of Brasile, Buss Island became shy as more ships ventured into its vicinity. Yet it continued to appear on many maps.

A 1745 Dutch map was inscribed with its location and the proposition that it had sunk. As a result the island was rechristened the Sunken Land of Buss. Soundings taken in the area of the Dogger Bank, part of a submerged land bridge between Britain and Europe in the eighteenth century did indicate quite a shallow sea in one place which was thought to support the existence of the Sunken Land of Buss. However, Doggerland, as the sunken region is more properly known, disappeared some time after the last Ice Age, not in the last few hundred years.

RUPES NIGRA AND THE FOUR ISLANDS

Some ideas have a life of their own. As adventurous explorers gradually shrank the size of Terra Incognita, the northern polar region remained one of the great uncertainties, a place ripe for exercising the imagination.

In the fourteenth century a Franciscan monk in Oxford wrote a book purporting to record his discoveries in the North Atlantic. The book, called *Inventio Fortunata (Fortunate Discovery)*, was lost within a century, although a copy had been presented to the English King Edward III in 1360. Nevertheless, while it existed the book excited the imagination of many, including cartographers such as Martin Behaim, who later included its ideas on his globe of 1492, and Johannes Ruysch, who made a marginal notation derived from the book in his 1507 map (see pages 140–1). *Inventio Fortunata* created an exciting if entirely imaginary geography of the North Pole.

A second travel book, called the *Itinerarium* and also destined to be lost, was written in 1364 by Jacobus Cnoyen of the Netherlands. It included a summary of the ideas in *Inventio Fortunata*, as related to the author in Norway by another travelling Franciscan monk.

This imaginary polar world would have appealed to the fourteenth century mind, with its sense of symmetry and wonder. At the North Pole was said to be a giant glistening black magnetic rock with high cliffs called the Rupes Nigra, 53 kilometres (33 miles) wide, which was responsible for attracting the compass needles of ships. The rock stood within the polar sea and the whole was encircled by four large islands, each the size of Greenland or greater, almost interlocking, but separated by wide oceanic rivers, through which poured the waters of the four surrounding seas, sucked into a great whirlpool at the top of the world where they plunged, endlessly swirling, down into the bowels of the Earth.

It is understandable that this image might have attracted the public imagination. But it was also

accepted by some of the greatest intellects of the day. The notion was still current in 1577, when the great Flemish cartographer Gerard Mercator wrote about it to his close friend John Dee in England. Dee was sometimes known as the Elizabethan Magus, a brilliant mathematician who walked a fine line between science, Hermetic philosophy and alchemy. In a letter now held in the British Museum, Mercator described the polar region in exactly the same terms as the *Inventio Fortunata*, with four huge islands, four seas that divided the north, and the great indrawing of the waters of those seas into a huge central whirlpool that sucked the seas into the Earth. Mercator's map of the North Pole region, the 'Septentrionalium Terrarum', is exquisitely beautiful, but incredibly wrong.

What were these two great men thinking of? Columbus had 'discovered' America eighty-five years before. The terrible Greek fear of ships tumbling over a great oceanic waterfall at the edge of the world and plunging down into the bowels of the Earth had long been put to rest. Yet Mercator and Dee apparently accepted this complicated and unlikely theory of the geography of the polar region. If only they had applied the maxim of Ockham's Razor, ironically developed by yet another fourteenth century Franciscan monk-scholar of Oxford, William of Ockham, to their complicated concept: 'The simplest explanation is more likely to be the correct one'.

LEFT: *Gerard Mercator's world map of 1578 was arguably the most accurate of the period, and based on meticulous research, and yet this, his 1598 polar map, was uniquely wrong, even for the time. At the centre of the map looms Rupes Nigra, a huge magnetic mountain, and the cause of the Earth's magnetic field, surrounded by four huge islands.*

The mysterious floating islands

The natural phenomenon of floating islands is fairly well known. They are generally associated with marshlands, lakes and river systems, and begin life as a tangled mass of aquatic plants, such as reeds and sedges, extending ever outward from the shoreline, accumulating mud and rotting vegetation, and gradually growing. They can reach several square kilometres in size before breaking away from land and floating free, buoyed by gases from decomposition, until their lives are finally ended by storm fragmentation or encounters with the shore. Sometimes they re-attach to solid land — and so seem to mysteriously disappear. The great Sudd region of the Nile River, which proved such an impassable barrier to the Emperor Nero's army, is filled with such floating islands. In some lakes, as in Florida, they can be a great nuisance to home and boat owners, swamping properties when driven ashore by the wind, and are regularly chopped up and cleared.

The mythical island of Loycha, said to float on a lake in Ireland and to have a wonderful flora of many herbs capable of curing all the ills of humankind, was described in the *Speculum Regale* (*The King's Mirror*) written in old Norwegian in the late Middle Ages c. 1250. It was said that only one person could land on this island at a time, and that the island had a life of just seven years. After that it would attach to the shore and a new island would be born. It was a classic description of a floating island, with the slight addition of a magical flora.

In the seventeenth century a thermal lake near Tivoli in Italy that had been the focus of a popular bathing establishment, contained sixteen floating islands, known as *le sedici barchette* ('the sixteen boats'), which were described by more than one author. The islands are now gone and the lake is shrinking owing to mineral deposition. The place is currently called Lago della Regina, but has been known variously as La Solfatara, Lago delle Isole Natanti and, in Roman times, Lacus Albuleus.

RIGHT: This 1572 map of Mexico City by Georg Braun and Frans Hogenberg presents an idyllic scene far removed from reality. The city was built on top of the Aztec capital of Tenochtitlán after the Spanish conquistadors razed its buildings and slaughtered its citizens.

MEXICO.

The mysterious floating islands

In 1795, the viceroy of New Spain (Mexico) described another such large thermal pool, called Zacoton, which still has fifteen circular floating islands of reeds.

For many centuries, the Uros people of Lake Titicaca in the Peruvian Andes have lived in their own water world, building artificial floating islands based on pontoons of reeds, living in reed houses and fishing the lake for food so that their communities could live safe from fears of invasion by Inca and Collas tribes.

When the Aztecs migrated south through Mexico, they followed the instructions of their god and protector, Huitzilopochtli. In the fourteenth century their chieftain was told that their new city would be built on the island in Lake Texcoco. They were to look for a sign to mark the exact place, an eagle eating a snake and perched on a cactus growing from a rock surrounded by water. The Aztecs found their unlikely sign and built a great city called Tenochtitlán, beginning in 1325 AD.

When the population increased, the island could no longer provide enough food and the Aztecs devised a brilliant agricultural system based on floating gardens or *chinampas*. Even today this wonderfully effective agricultural system can be seen. The floating islands, enriched by silt dredged from the canals, always well watered, and with a microclimate created by the stored daytime heat of the sun re-radiated at night to raise the temperature by a vital few degrees, resulted in flourishing vegetation. Tree roots gradually anchored the productive islands, bearing their crops of corn, vegetables and fruits and even supported houses. The causeways the Aztecs built to connect the original island to the shore also protected the *chinampas* from damage. At its peak, Tenochtitlán was a city of well over 250,000 people, criss-crossed by canals, with a huge market place, gardens and fountains. In the sacred precinct of the city, magnificent palaces, pyramids, a massive plaza, aqueduct and temples were built. In 1521 Hernán Cortés and his Spanish army invaded a city more splendid than they had ever seen.

But half a millennium later, almost nothing survives of that once magnificent city. In an act of extreme but righteous vandalism in the name of his religion, Cortés destroyed virtually all of imperial Tenochtitlán, and built a Spanish city over the top of it. Even stones engraved by the Aztecs were recarved with Spanish symbols, obliterating the signs of Aztec occupation. Cortés built his own residence over the razed palace of the Emperor Montezuma, and the Catholic cathedral was built over the Aztec temple. Much of what was left of the arts of the Aztecs was destroyed following a battle in 1692, and their finely wrought gold jewellery was melted down into ingots for transport to Spain.

Tenochtitlán was buried under developing Mexico City. In 1978 excavations led to the discovery of the seven layers of the magnificent Templo Mayor, also known as the Pyramid of Huitzilopochtli, the religious centre of Tenochtitlán. It was just one short city block away from the huge Zocalo Plaza in the heart of Mexico City and the Catholic cathedral.

The floating islands that fed the people of Tenochtitlán have also survived. Today they produce gloriously colourful tropical flowers and roses destined for florists' markets, and the canals between the long-anchored islands are filled with colourful boats, mariachi bands and Mexicans enjoying a day's outing from the city.

Other floating islands are not so easily explained as either natural or built phenomena. The fifth century BC Greek historian Herodotus was a highly observant traveller and sceptic, not easily impressed with wild stories. Yet he described an island he visited in Egypt called Chemnis, in the middle of a large deep lake. It had an abundance of palms and fruit trees, and a large temple to Apollo with three altars. He was told it was a floating island, although he recorded that he never saw it move. The Egyptians told him that the island had at first been fixed and motionless. The goddess Leto, one of the eight original deities, had been entrusted with Apollo by Isis, and she saved the child by hiding him on the island. Typhon hunted everywhere for this son of Osiris, and so the island was given the ability to float to save Apollo from discovery. Did the island really float? Could the island float with the weight of a temple on board? Was the story purely a legend? The description is just possible.

The floating agricultural islands of Tenochtitlán were eventually anchored by the roots of the trees growing on the islands. A naturally formed floating island in an area protected from storms and the possible resulting damage might do the same over time, and the islands of Tenochtitlán certainly supported houses. Pomponius Mela, a southern Spaniard who wrote a rather dry and certainly small Latin geography c. 40 AD described the island Chemnis in similar terms to Herodotus, although he was convinced that it did indeed float.

FRANCISCA

Corterati

C. Britonum

Exteriores

Terra florida

Oceanus occidentalis

Panuco · Inf. Tortucarū

amaho

Fortun

Iucatana

CVBA

Hispaniola

Inf. Hesperidum

niftitan

S. Paul

Sci una

Antille

Iamica

Dominica

S. Iacobi

Beragna

PARIA fabundat
auro & margaritis

Canibali

Nouus   orbis

Insula Atlantica quam uo/
cant Brasilij & Americam.

Catigara

Die Nüw

Welt

Regio Gigantum

7. infulę Mar
gueritarū

Mare pacificum

Fretum Magaliani

REAL BUT VERY WRONG

LEFT: Sebastian Münster's 1540 map of America was the first major European map to correctly show the New World as a separate landmass to the Old. North America, however, is shown as a narrow strip of land with a bite out of the top, reflecting the belief that the continent was only a small barrier to Asia.

FOLLOWING PAGES: Christopher Columbus disembarking in America. Engraving from Historia Americae *(History of America), 1602, by Theodore de Bry.*

9

EARLY LANDINGS
IN THE
NEW WORLD

It has often been said that history is written by the winners. Historians work to redress the balance and reveal the truth of the past, but the historical viewpoint of the early era of exploration in the New World was very much that of the dominant seafaring nations of fifteenth and sixteenth century Europe. It was as if history had begun with their explorations.

There is every reason, for instance, to believe that there were other 'discoveries' of North America, even before John Cabot, to whom the official credit is given, and possibly also of the West Indies before Columbus found them. They were in turn preceded by the original discoverers and occupiers of those lands. It would be wonderful to time travel and solve some of the questions historians may only ever be able to debate because of the lack of surviving evidence.

One of those questions was whether the Irish reached Greenland centuries before the Norse, and America nine centuries before Columbus (see the voyage of St Brendan, page 129). Strip away the medieval trappings of magic and miracles and moral tales and there is evidence that long before the Norse began leap-frogging westward from island mass to island mass in the far North Atlantic, the Irish seem to have had quite a grasp on the geography of the region.

Despite the possibility that the Irish made landfall in North America well before the first millennium, the Norse explorer Leif Ericsson is credited with being the first European to have landed in North America and to have established the colony of Vinland (possibly at L'Anse aux Meadows). Few dispute that he established Vinland, but it is doubtful that he was the first Norseman to sight North America. That feat appears to have been achieved accidentally by Bjarni Herjolfsson who was sailing from Iceland to Greenland on a visit to his parents in the summer of either 985 or 986 AD and was blown off course by a severe storm. He recorded encountering a low-lying forested land to the west that looked hospitable. His ship was not equipped for exploration and Herjolfsson and his crew were anxious to resume their journey to Greenland, so they turned back, managed to get their bearings, and reached their destination. Herjolfsson reported his observations in both Norway and Greenland but no exploratory party was sent out to follow this lead.

Leif Ericsson was intrigued by the story, and ten years later he bought Herjolfsson's boat, hired a crew and sighted the land described by Bjarni, where he later founded Vinland.

There were almost certainly many voyages to the shores of eastern Canada before Cabot and those who followed. Fishermen from the Basque coast, which extended down the Bay of Biscay,

as well as from Brittany and Galicia, reportedly went there to take advantage of Newfoundland's abundant codfish. But they were not armed with Royal Charters like Cabot and therefore landfall was unofficial and unrecorded.

MYSTERY HILL

The authenticity of the Norse colony at L'Anse aux Meadows, dated to c. 1000, is now generally accepted by archaeologists. Other places of possible earlier European settlement remain contentious, but are difficult to explain away. Mystery Hill near Salem in New Hampshire (not the town on the coast associated with the Salem witch trials) is one such site, located about 40 kilometres (25 miles) from the coast, where the remains of apparently ancient structures have been found. To those familiar with Celtic sites in Europe, Mystery Hill is well named. Sometimes, but far less justifiably, it is called America's Stonehenge.

The hill is quite a gentle one, and it is covered in open deciduous woodland which can be hauntingly beautiful wreathed in early autumn mists. The activities of white settlers over the centuries have made the history of the site more difficult to unravel. In 1936 it was finally fenced for protection. The then owner believed that a group of Irish monks (the Culdees) had settled on the site, suggesting a period between the eighth and twelfth centuries, but there is no evidence to support that theory. There is, however, evidence of much older occupation at the site.

Walls, tunnels, dolmens, standing monoliths and buildings are spread over about 17 hectares (40 acres); it is estimated that as much as 40 per cent of the stone originally on the site was removed

Sua er v pundara ᴢ meli S mælt at engi maðr skal hafa ranga pundara eða með keruoldu. En sa er rette pundari at xx. uetr sei fiordung hui ok megi at uega s at uisi at fion dungi ok æ meira at uega en uær ex fiordunga veit s at er annar pundari er heit handpundari. sa er uisa at hælfri ꝍ. ok æ meira at uega en hælfan annan fiordung þ sk uera tungu pundari. Suka sk giera .ij. almar slikar sem uir hafa. En þessi sko va með kolto til bu myniar ok fra luta er i koll dum sk mela. er fiau fyrst buskio ka er liggr hælfr annar fiordum gr. þa er fiordungr er giorer an ua ag xx. merkr rugar ᴢ vista þ sꝰ i kecalloi ᴢ dwaga weyis. kuen ar kav fiol i fiordung. hælfr ann an kuen askr ᴢ kariask. Sko þes ser pundarar ok með kolto ligg ia a tig uelli und logmanᴢ sæti. Skal þar eft hur systu madr retta sina pundara stuku ᴢ med kolto en bende eft fra með kollouin þuær systu. En hur sem eithu ert i þessari grein heer rangt sekr ꝍ. uid kg es hu at ok hafi

ꝼ mætt eft systu mætᴢ þunda rum marka. En æ eru aller bo nið skyltð með kolto at hafa.
her kergi punðon lut holia ok her þarri bullr ᴢ sug þyrir kijalkom
ſ øikalor
ſpaumu
Ver ein toglig þar tekia ein engi smii er i þiond sk taka

styur mæti eða hs loggligum v ꝼloðs mænni ᴢ nefna uttni uið tuau eða fleari ok segi ſ t aðaf nar er þar toku. en hm t lægu burðar er skip bijgg. En eꝥ þa sk isæ vm kaup mala sitt. þa hafi sa sitt mæl er uttni gylg ok þa ſk sua ᴢ suia at ū heyrm oð ykkr beggia ok sꝥ vorud ſa ſaritð ᴢ samkaupa v þar tek ꝍ ᴢ ſ vm lest ok leigu. þa er ſ uttni loglega biort ᴢ at log sullu þar tekit eft uærū þarm lögū.

S kip þ er hurðskim þ er e sausa þars fry suar æ .ij. dagrum þ er alt þært i and incorporated into local buildings, such as churches and houses, used as kerbing stones, or in the construction of the Lawrence Dam. Some of the stones moved away have been found to carry apparently ancient inscriptions.

A number of massive, monolithic standing stones, weighing up to 10 tonnes each and bearing a close resemblance to those on sites in Great Britain, form various astronomical alignments. One structure, which has been called an Oracle Chamber, closely resembles a dolmen or Neolithic burial chamber, and a number of artificial caves have also been found. A farmer who owned the site in the first half of the nineteenth century used one of the caves as a cellar and built his house directly over several of the ancient structures. Also on the site is a very large, centrally located flat stone positioned over four supporting stones with a central channelled groove which has been described as a sacrificial altar.

The entire area has a number of mysterious, unexplained stoneworks, including the remarkable Upton Chamber, which consists of a 1.8 metre

LEFT: Historiated initial from the beginning of a chapter on seafaring and trade, from a copy of an original fourteenth century law collection 'Jonsbok' (vellum), Icelandic School.

(6 feet) high and 4.2 metre (14 feet) wide tunnel leading into an inner chamber measuring 3.6 metres (12 feet) in diameter and 3.3 metres (11 feet) in height, surmounted by a number of stones weighing several tonnes. Certainly the many structures found in New England are not the work of one or more farmers with too much time on their hands.

Once seen, the complex is not easily forgotten … or explained. Astronomers and researchers who have made calculations based on the alignments of the monoliths believe they were erected between approximately 2500 BC and 1900 BC, which would date the complex to around the most conservative date for the great megalithic monuments of Avebury in Wiltshire. Carbon testing of artefacts in undisturbed strata and tree roots penetrating some chambers gave dates from around 2000 BC and 1500 BC respectively.

Other artefacts dated to around 1000 BC would indicate long occupation of the site. Over the last quarter century researchers have become even more interested in this enigma. Mystery Hill is far from being the only possible megalithic site in North America. The New England region is rife with such mysterious structures.

The Vinland Map: one of the greatest frauds or a fabulous find?

The world of science is far from the dispassionate, coldly logical arena imagined by many. In truth, it is a battlefield of ideas and opposing theories fiercely debated and defended. And when the reputations of experts, the world of antiques and forgery, and very big money come into conjunction, gauntlets are hurled down with even greater force. And that is exactly what happened in the fascinating case of the famous Vinland Map, which takes its name from the land lying to the west of Greenland where, according to Norse sagas, a Viking colony was founded a millennium ago. If the experts who contend it is authentic are right, the map is the oldest known cartographic depiction of North America, predating Columbus by about sixty years. If, on the other hand, it is a fake, the most recently published valuation, a not so small fortune of US$25 million, would make it one of the most successful forgeries ever perpetrated.

The map first turned up in the hands of an Italian bookseller in the 1950s. It consisted of a two-page spread bound into a pair of fifteenth century works, the codex *Historia Tartarorum* and *Speculum Historiale*. The map had no provenance — an authenticated traceable history — that most useful multiplier of value in the world of antiques. It was then purchased in 1957 by an antiquarian book dealer in New Haven, Connecticut for US$3600. The map was said to represent the accumulated knowledge of Norse seafarers depicting, in a remarkably accurate way for the period, the British Isles, France, the Iberian Peninsula, Mediterranean Europe and Scandinavia, what appears to be the Azores Islands located in the mid-Atlantic off the west coast of France and Spain, and to the west of Scandinavia, shown in sequence, Iceland, Greenland, and a part of present-day Canada known to have been explored and settled by Vikings. Both Hudson Bay and the Gulf of St Lawrence appear to be represented. The map was subsequently purchased at a vastly increased price, reputedly around US$1 million by a benefactor of Yale University for its Beinecke Rare Book and Manuscript Library.

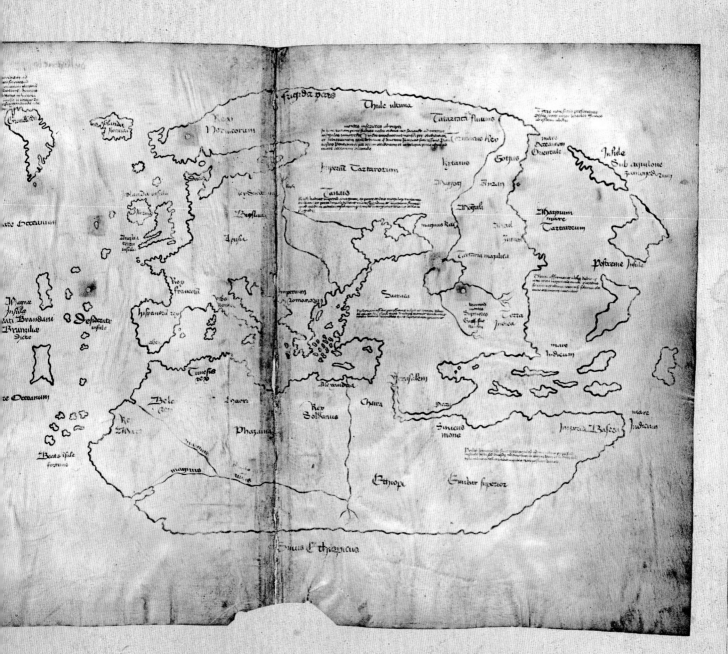

Discovered in the 1950s and purporting to date from the mid-fourteenth century, the legendary Vinland Map is generally considered to be a forgery.

The map became the subject of an immediately controversial book called *The Vinland Map and the Tartar Relation*, which included mention that it had been authenticated after several years of study. The publication led to an international conference in the following year at the Smithsonian Institute which ended in sharply divided opinions and a recommendation that scientific evaluation be carried out on the Vinland Map.

In the face of continuing debate, in 1974 the map was analysed using polarised light microscopy which revealed that the ink used on it contained a form of anatase (titanium oxide) which was not used before 1923. As a result, the Yale Library announced that 'the famous Vinland Map may be a forgery'. Since then the map has become a perennial and oddly irresolvable topic of academic dissention.

A second research paper, also based on analysis of the map's ink, but using a different technique involving particle-induced X-ray emission, was published in 1987 and, while anatase was found, it was said to be present in only trace amounts. This questioned the 1974 findings. A subsequent study in 1993 confused the issue yet again by presenting complex reasons for the possible presence of anatase in medieval iron-gall ink. However, as that ink had not been demonstrated on the map, the paper was something of a red herring.

Research involving radiocarbon dating of the parchment used in making the map, published in 2002, established that it was genuinely old, from c. 1425 plus or minus eleven years.

The positions of wormholes in the map are said to match those in the remaining pages of the book in which it was found, although this too has been challenged. The watermarks on the map's parchment appear to match those of adjacent pages in the works and were dated to c. 1430 with considerable certainty using radiocarbon dating. This combined evidence may seem to indicate a genuine medieval document. But such results could also be explained if the map were drawn by a twentieth-century forger on blank pages in the book.

Those who are familiar with antiques forgeries know that very old paper stocks have been used to fool carbon-dating techniques for everything from letters and diaries supposedly associated with famous figures of the past to maps and period watercolour paintings. In the same way, genuinely old but relatively worthless oil paintings are cleaned off and canvases repainted with works 'in the manner of' valued artists of the past using pigments authentic to the period. It can be a devious world for even experts to negotiate. Carbon dating on its own can be misleading. Unfortunately, the removal of sufficient ink for radiocarbon dating purposes would require more than is now present on the entire map.

Medieval inks were usually made from soot (Indian ink) or from the galls on the oak trees *Quercus ruber* (iron-gall ink) containing gallotannate, and combinations of the two. The inks age in characteristic ways. Indian ink remains stable but iron-gall ink fades and leaches a characteristic yellow to brown stain into the parchment. Iron-gall ink is also destructive over time, making the parchment brittle, resulting in holes developing along the lines of ink.

A 2001 analysis by Raman spectroscopy showed Indian ink overlying a persistent yellow pigmentation which was not from iron-gall ink but the modern form of anatase. This confirmed the 1974 findings. The investigators found no evidence of medieval iron-gall ink or of the characteristic long-term damage caused by iron-gall ink. The conclusion was that the map was a very clever and painstaking fake, using Indian ink over yellow pigment in the form of synthetic anatase, probably forged in the twentieth century on genuine fifteenth century parchment, some time after 1923.

The German Jesuit priest Father Josef Fischer, an expert on mid-fifteenth century maps and a collector of old maps, who died in 1944, has been identified as the most likely forger, his motivation a complex plot of revenge against the Nazis, who had persecuted the Jesuits in 1938 and forced the sale of the college where he taught. Fischer is also credited with the discovery of the legendary Waldseemüller world map created in 1507 (see pages 42–3).

The debate on the authenticity of the Vinland map continues to rage, however. As recently as July 2007 a group of Danish cartographic experts who had studied the map for five years, announced their conviction that the map was real, attributing the controversial anatase to the use of sand in drying wet ink during the medieval period. Thus the debate continues, perhaps never to be decided one way or the other.

COLUMBUS DISORIENTED

For cartographers during the Age of Exploration, mapping was very much like putting together a jigsaw puzzle with half the instructions missing and no frame. Without the ability to calculate longitude, and with navigators exploring only fragments of coastline, many map makers filled in the missing sections with their imagination and flawed logic. Some maps could only be described as fantastic speculation.

Interpretation is everything in mapping, as the exploration of the Americas would prove. Probably nowhere were more incorrect guesses made. What had been assumed to be empty ocean, known on the old *mappae mundi* as the Ocean Sea and supposedly the only barrier between Europe and Asia, had become filled with confusing segments of a new coastline that refused to conform with that of China.

Further exploration only added to the confusion, with the segments linking together to become an impossibly long and impassable barrier to those seeking a shorter route to the spices of the East Indies and riches of China. Even more confusingly, supposed islands became peninsulas and peninsulas landmasses.

North America, confidently expected by early explorers to be a slim strip of land easily traversed in a few days, disobligingly widened into a continent that defied overland travel. The space on the globe that early cartographers had filled with an over-expansive Asia and the Ocean Sea proved to contain a huge double continent and an ocean that would outrival the Atlantic. Yet for a while at least, many early navigators saw the New World as a kind of annoying roadblock in their search for fame and fortune in Asia, not the wonderfully diverse land it would prove to be.

Columbus was certainly confused about where he was during that famous voyage in 1492. When he stumbled upon Cuba, he was convinced he was somewhere along the shores of mainland China. On 1 November 1492 he recorded in his log: 'I am certain that this is the mainland and that I am before Zayto and Quinsay, 300 miles distant, more or less'. (Zayto is modern-day Zhao'an, while Quinsay is Hangzhou.) Columbus first reckoned Cuba to be an island, with mainland China and India lying to the west. Shortly afterward he decided Cuba was the Mangi Peninsula, a mysterious and imagined large peninsula shown jutting southward from Cathay on medieval *mappae mundi*. Columbus's confusion simply grew. When he encountered the island of Española on 6 December, he recorded it as Japan, despite the fact that the local people called it Cibao (the name of a lush valley in the present-day Dominican Republic). It was all extremely confusing and would remain so for many years.

The Alberto Cantino *Mappa Mundi*, created in 1502 and based on Portuguese explorations (see page 174), showed that Europeans were still very much confused by discoveries in the Americas, ten years after Columbus's first voyage. While many of the islands of the West Indies were quite accurately depicted, the Mangi Peninsula was still shown north-west of Cuba in order to conform to the supposed coastline of China. The Florida Peninsula to the northeast is nowhere to be seen, its discovery still lay in the future, supposedly in the year 1513.

The famous map of the world created by the Flemish astronomer, explorer, cartographer, and secular priest Johannes Ruysch (see pages 140–1) produced in 1507, still clearly shows Cathay with various islands of the West Indies offshore, together with the legendary island of Antillia. There appeared to be no understanding that an entirely new continent lay between the West Indies and Asia. The map is still remarkably rooted in past cartography, depicting the ever-persistent lands of Gog and Magog north of Cathay, and Scythia to the north of Moscow. India and East Asia remain confused and in some sections almost entirely imaginary. The mysterious Mangi Peninsula is depicted south of Cathay, with Quinsay located on the coast to the north. Not until the 1530s would the mythical Mangi Peninsula finally disappear from its supposed location north-west of Cuba, and it would be halfway through the sixteenth century before cartographers accepted that the New World was a separate entity rather than an extension of Asia.

If this seems strange in the light of our knowledge, neither Columbus nor the early map makers could be blamed for the errors they made.

Occanus
occidetalis

Terra del Rey de portugall

Has antilhas del Rey de castella:

Este he o mar o antre castella e portugall

a esta terra he descobrta y madado del Rey de castella

Linha equinocialis:

Mare occeanu

Tropicus capricorni.

Pollus antarticus:

Instrumentation for measuring longitude accurately over extended distances was still no more than a dream. But the most significant reason for continued error was their reliance on Ptolemy's miscalculation of the size of the Earth and its known landmasses. Although Ptolemy's *Geographia* had been written more than a thousand years before, it remained the absolute authority when Columbus made his first journey. On Ptolemy's *mappa mundi* (see pages 32–3), the Mediterranean—then the centre of the Western world—was exaggerated by about 30 per cent. Asia was also exaggerated, and the circumference of the Earth underestimated.

Columbus also put his faith in the calculations made by the Phoenician geographer Marinus of Tyre in the second century AD, which underestimated the distance between Asia and Europe. Columbus's own calculations were additionally victim to the many quite different measurements represented by the 'mile' in various parts of Europe. Columbus had concluded that only 2400 nautical miles (4445 kilometres) of sea lay between the most westerly point of Spain and Cathay, a distance that he believed was achievable if good fortune accompanied him. In reality it is approximately 9500 nautical miles (17,600 kilometres). Little wonder that early explorers and cartographers of the New World fully expected the Americas to lie close to Asia.

Even so, it is worth noting that Columbus's proposal to find Asia by travelling westward was rebuffed on more than one occasion by experts

LEFT: This section of Alberto Cantino's 1502 world map is quite accurate in its depiction of the West Indies, but the landmass to the north reflects Columbus's theory that he had reached the Mangi Peninsula, and Florida is nowhere to be seen.

advising the royal court of King John II of Portugal, and later the royal court of Ferdinand II of Aragon and Isabella I of Castile, on the basis that he had underestimated the distance he would need to travel. Isabella cleverly gave Columbus an annual stipend until a final decision was arrived at so that other countries would not be able to fund his plans. Both Genoa and Venice had initially refused to equip his proposed voyage before Columbus approached Isabella, and she was shrewd enough to ensure they would not be in a position to change their minds.

Despite all the problems involved, the misunderstandings, the great secrecy in which both Spain and Portugal kept their early maps of the New World, and the still primitive apparatus of navigation, the 1570 map (see pages 208–9) showing the Americas produced by Abraham Ortelius, the Belgian geographer, cartographer and creator of the first modern atlas, *Theatrum Orbis Terrarum* (Theatre of the World), just eighty-two years after Columbus made landfall, is a work of genius, remarkably close to actuality and equally remarkably detailed with regard both to the coastline and interior geography of the Americas. It also succeeded in depicting the true immensity of the Pacific Ocean and the coasts of Nova Guinea and Terra Australis, admittedly joined together rather than separated by a narrow strait, but recognisable two centuries before James Cook would 'discover' Australia. Terra Australis on the Ortelius map merges in the south into Terra Incognita. The very beautiful map of the New World produced in 1596 by Theodore de Bry at Frankfurt-am-Main also depicted the east coast of what was marked as the continent of Terra Australis.

THE FLOWERY
ISLAND
OF FLORIDA

I t would be many years before Europeans transformed their maps of Florida, with its long peninsula extending southward from the North American mainland and necklace of exquisite low sandy cays reaching into tropical waters, from an island to part of the mainland. But long before Columbus, Spain's great sea rival Portugal laid claims to reaching the New World and unquestionably discovered Florida. Andrea Bianco's 1436 world map (see page 88) appears to show the peninsula of Florida on Antillia far

off the coast of Portugal. The so-called 'Cantino map' (see page 174) passed into the hands of the powerful Este family in Italy in 1502, a copy of a secret Portuguese map, obtained in Lisbon by a spy. The Cantino *Mappa Mundi* differs from Bianco's map in depicting Florida at approximately the correct distance and in relatively proportionate size to Europe.

Columbus might have been, in fact should have been, the first to discover Florida on his first journey to the New World in 1492. On 13 October, when still at his first landfall on Cuba he noted in his diary: 'The natives here have indicated to me that not only is there land in the south and southwest, but also in the north-west. Furthermore, if I understand correctly, it is from the northwest that strangers come to fight and capture the people here'. It was a very large hint that a significant landmass lay both to the north and south, so why did he fail to follow such an important lead?

Columbus became the first of a seemingly endless line of those who would be seduced into plundering these new lands for their treasure. His encounter on 13 October included observations of the local people, whom he described as 'all young and of fine shapes, very handsome … straight-limbed without exception, and not with prominent bellies but handsomely shaped'. He described their canoes, which were large enough to contain 'forty or forty-five men', which the locals paddled out to trade 'balls of cotton, parrots, javelins and other things too numerous to mention'.

Unsurprisingly, Columbus described himself as being 'very attentive to them'. He said he:

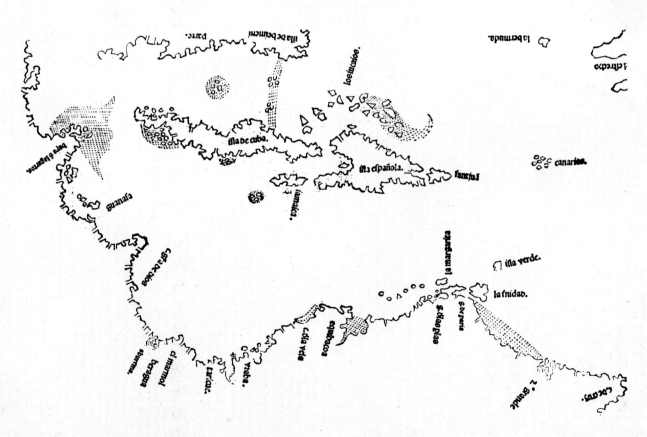

Florida is presented correctly for the first time, but unlabelled, as a peninsula attached to North America north of Cuba, on Andrés Morales's 1511 map of the Caribbean.

... strove to learn if they had any gold. Seeing some of them with little bits of this metal hanging at their noses, I gathered from them by signs that by going southward or steering round the island in that direction, there would be found a king who possessed large vessels of gold and in great quantities. I endeavoured to procure them to lead the way thither, but found they were unacquainted with the route.

One sometimes wonders whether these explorers ever realised the limitations of sign language—that was a remarkably complex conversation. Although Columbus's stated purpose was to find the Asian coast, a possibly fortuitous wind blowing from the wrong direction combined, as he admitted in his ship's log, with a desire to seek gold saw him subsequently plot a course to the south-west away from Cuba rather than northward, where he would have discovered present-day Florida.

In 1601 Bartolomé de las Casas's *Historia de las Indias* was posthumously published. It contained a charming account of the discovery of Florida by Juan Ponce de León and his crew after they departed from the Bahamas. 'They left, sailing to the north-west. On Sunday, 27 March ... they saw an island ... and they called it La Florida, because it presented a beautiful vision of many blossoming trees and was low and fair, and also because they discovered it during the time of Pascua Florida (flowery Easter).' It is a pleasant story, and it seems a pity to take the honour of discovering Florida from Ponce de León, but he certainly wasn't the first European to discover it. Florida was first depicted on a map by Spanish cartographer Andrés Morales in 1511 (see page 177), and Ponce de León did not discover the 'island' of Florida until 1513.

PONCE DE LEÓN'S EXPLORATIONS AND EXPLOITATIONS

Ponce de León was a conquistador who had accompanied Columbus on his second voyage to the Americas in 1493—a voyage that was focused largely on colonisation and consisted of seventeen ships and around 1500 men. The island they discovered and settled on this voyage was originally named San Juan Bautista, but almost immediately became Puerto Rico. As Columbus's lieutenant, the highly ambitious Ponce de León founded the first Spanish settlement at Caparra on Puerto Rico in 1493, and went on to become the first governor. Ponce de León's time there can scarcely be considered honourable, as he and his fellow conquistadors enslaved the local Tainos people, forcing them to work in mines or in construction. The death rate among the Tainos from both hardship and introduced diseases was horrific, but Ponce de León became a very wealthy man as a result of his time on Puerto Rico.

Christopher Columbus tactfully wrote in his log, which was to be presented on his return to Queen Isabella, a reminder to their majesties that as a result of his deeds he:

... might entitle himself High Admiral of the Ocean Sea and Viceroy and perpetual Governor of all the islands and continental land that he might discover and acquire, as well as any other future discoveries in the Ocean Sea. Further, that his eldest son should succeed to the same position, and so from generation to generation forever after.

It was, therefore, rightly assumed that the title of military commander would pass to his son Diego when Columbus died in 1506. The Spanish authorities chose to revoke those rights and it was only after a court case in Madrid that Diego was allowed to assume the title. In the meantime Ponce de León had been given the governorship of Puerto Rico, a title he lost in 1512 as a result of Diego's successful courtroom battle. Probably by way of compensation, Ponce de León was granted the right to explore areas north of Cuba. He used his considerable wealth to equip three ships and set out in search of conquest in 1513.

He made landfall somewhere in the northeast of present-day Florida, and he claimed La Florida for Spain. He then sailed south, charting the coastline, passing around the Florida Keys and mapping the gulf coast of Florida to Cape Romano. From there he sailed to Havana in Cuba before returning once more to the east coast of Florida, where the crews stopped off at what is now Biscayne Bay and the city of Miami, before sailing back to Puerto Rico. Ponce de León returned to Spain in 1514 and in 1515 was commissioned to undertake an expedition to Guadeloupe, which ended in failure, and he returned to Puerto Rico once again.

In 1521 he planned to set up a colony in Florida. He took just two ships, which must have been crowded, as they carried a company of about two hundred, including farmers, soldiers, artisans and priests, together with the necessary goods and chattels, and farm animals. They made landfall in south-western Florida, somewhere near the estuary of the Caloosahatchee River, which drains the northern Everglades. It was not an auspicious choice, for soon after landing they were attacked by Calusa Indians, and Ponce de León was hit in the shoulder with a poisoned arrow. The surviving colonists re-embarked and sailed to Havana, where Ponce de León died of his wound.

POLITICAL ESPIONAGE AND THE GRAB FOR LAND

The truth was that the discovery of the Americas, no matter under what name or geographical misapprehension, was like opening Pandora's Box. There was no way of officially controlling its exploration, whatever the intentions of the great seafaring nations. In addition to official public explorations, there were also any number of clandestine and opportunistic enterprises. New discoveries led to a land grab by European nations anxious to stake a claim in the New World. The belief that new sources of wealth were there for the taking and rumours of cities of gold and mountains of diamonds fuelled the search, and also the need for discretion.

Portugal in particular was careful not to advertise its explorations of the South American eastern coastline—and with good reason, since informants infiltrated the country, eager to earn rewards for passing secret information to its rivals. Portugal in turn paid spies in other countries, including England. Spain was equally careful to keep its explorations in Mexico and California under tight wraps. Both countries considered that all expeditions required the sanction of the state, and

FOLLOWING PAGES: The beautifully ornate Virginae item et Floridae *(Virginia and Florida)* was included in Jodocus Hondius's 1606 edition of Gerard Mercator's atlas. It is based upon accounts of early English colonists and shows Indian and early European settlements.

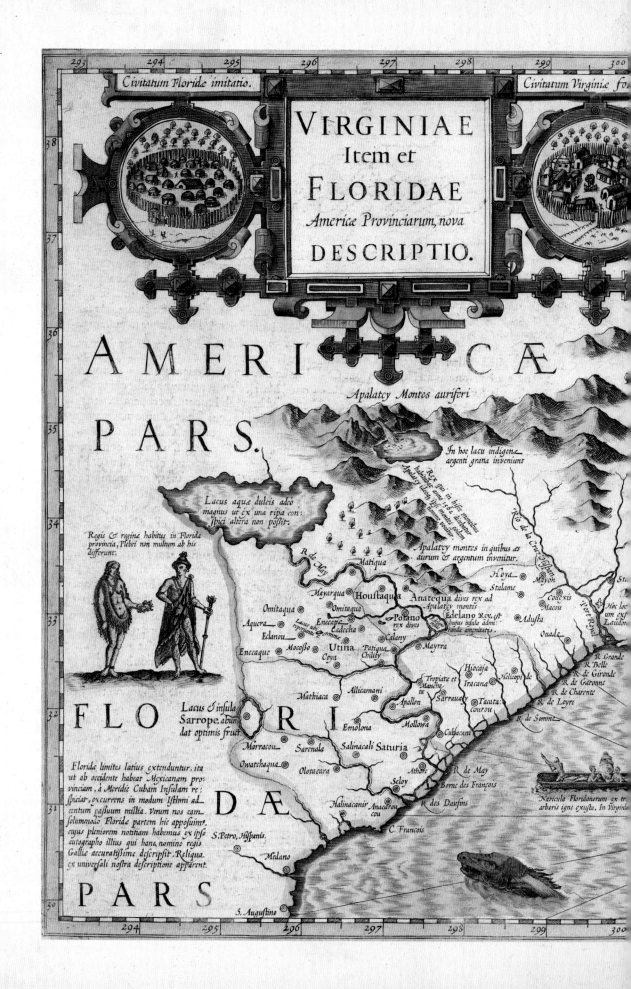

THE ATLAS OF LEGENDARY LANDS

they treated the information gathered by explorers as state secrets. Revealing those secrets was an act of treason punishable by death.

Adventurers and pirates soon joined in the plunder. Some made accidental and for that matter, unwanted discoveries, by being shipwrecked or lost, blown by hurricanes or up-ended by waterspouts, to be tossed onto shores never before seen by Europeans. Many voyages must also have been reported verbally by returning sailors. The New World was leaking its secrets like a sieve.

For that reason, we will probably never know how information about the Florida Peninsula returned to Europe, but return it did and Florida (unnamed but unmistakably located) appeared on a 1511 map by the cartographer Andrés Morales (see page 177), depicting Spain's discoveries within the Ocean Sea—two years before Ponce de León's 'discovery'. On the Morales map, Florida was depicted northeast of Cuba, which is labelled, and as part of the mainland of North America. It could not have been placed on the map as a result of confusion with the shores of the mysterious Mangi Peninsula in Asia, which even Columbus knew had to lie somewhere west of Cuba.

The Morales map appeared in some editions of Italian Peter Martyr's *Opera*, an important historical account of newly made discoveries in the New World. Martyr created many significant literary works centred on the exploration of the Americas, often under the instruction of the Catholic Church in Spain, and was the first to identify the importance of the newly discovered Gulf Stream. He commented on the map produced by his cartographer Morales, 'At the north [of

Cuba] there have been discovered marvellous countries and lands'.

The Morales map is confirmed by an account supplied by Bartolomé de las Casas, sometimes called the Apostle of the Indies, in his sixteenth century three-volume *Historia de las Indias* (*History of the Indies*). Las Casas was born in Seville in 1474, the son of a foot soldier on Columbus's first expedition who subsequently acquired a great fortune in the Indies. Bartolomé was a young man in the crowd that welcomed Columbus and his fellow voyagers home after the 1492 journey, and he was fired with admiration for the great navigator. As a result of the fortune that his father had accumulated, Bartolomé was sent to study divinity and law at the prestigious University of Salamanca, completing his studies in 1498. Four years later he accompanied the conquistador Gonzalo Fernández to the New World and settled in Hispaniola, the Spanish foothold in the Caribbean.

In 1510, the year Spain began its massive extraction of gold from the New World, las Casas became the first man to enter the priesthood in the New World. He was ordained in Santo Domingo, the capital of Hispaniola, and left there the following year as part of the 1511 expedition sent to conquer and occupy Cuba.

Las Casas transcribed Columbus's log and at least twice in his *History* made it clear that he had access to the long-lost map Columbus made of his discoveries on the first voyage. The original log was presented to Queen Isabella, who instructed that a copy be made for Columbus, but this has been lost. Without las Casas's transcription, no contemporary account of Columbus's great voyages would have survived. Las Casas was a learned man, unlikely to misreport an incident. His report of those early years in the New World is a historical cornerstone, and it includes what sounds like an only too likely story of the real first European discovery of Florida.

According to las Casas, a Spanish consortium was brought together in the West Indies to fit out several ships with the intention of capturing Indians in the Bahamas (then called the Lucayos). The ships sailed from Puerto Plata in today's Dominican Republic, but on searching the islands of the Bahamas they were unsuccessful. Unwilling to return empty handed, and facing considerable financial loss, not to mention embarrassment, they decided to journey north in search of better fortune while their supplies held out. They discovered land. Las Casas emphatically stated: 'It is certain that this was the land and coastline that we now call Florida'.

According to Las Casas the crew finally made port in Santo Domingo with a cargo of Indian slaves. It seems that Florida was discovered by a dubious group of slave traders rather than Ponce de León. To further confuse the issue, Ponce de León himself recorded encountering a Spanish-speaking Indian in Florida in 1513. However, one honour cannot be denied to Ponce de León—he was the first to name a state in what was to become the United States.

The map created by the great cartographer Gerard Mercator with the Dutch map maker Jodocus Hondius, *Virginae Item et Floridae* (*Virginia and Florida*) published in Amsterdam in 1606, continued to distort Florida but did show many geographic features of the coastline and inland, from south of St Augustine to north of Chesapeake Bay (see pages 180–1). This map remained influential for another century. In the interior of the Florida Panhandle are a particularly alluring Eve-like figure, together with what may be a tribal chieftain, an early representation of the native turkey and what appear to be native elk, which once ranged freely through Florida. The Appalachians are also indicated. In the sea to the south and north lurk fearful monsters which have a definite resemblance to giant marine iguanas.

CALIFORNIA: THE ISLAND OF AMAZONS

I f Florida was to be mistaken for an island and even a cartographers' flight of fantasy lying somewhere south of China, then California would fare even worse. In 1510 a Spanish novel of romance and chivalry, *Las Sergas de Esplandian* (*The Exploits of Esplandian*), was published. Based on an earlier book by Portuguese writer Vasco de Lobeira, *Esplandian* was written by Garci Rodriguez Ordóñez de Montalvo and filled with improbable but stirring adventures. It described an island inhabited by black Amazons said to be located on the west coast of the New World:

Know ye that on the right hand of the Indies there is an island called California, very close to the side of the Terrestrial Paradise and inhabited by black women without a single man among them and living in the manner of Amazons. They are robust of body, strong and passionate in heart, and of great virtue. Their island is one of the wildest in the world with bold rocks and crags. Their arms are all of gold, as are the harnesses of the wild beasts which, after taming, they ride. The island everywhere abounds with gold and precious stones. In all the island there is no other metal.

This magical island was ruled by the goddess-like Queen Califia, who also commanded a fighting force of five hundred griffins, terrifyingly strong creatures, half eagle, half lion, that were trained to keep the islands free of men. Califia was described as:

… a queen of majestic proportions, more beautiful than all others, and in the very vigour of her womanhood. She was desirous of accomplishing great deeds. She was valiant and courageous and ardent with a brave heart and had ambitions to execute nobler actions than had been achieved by any other ruler.

The combination of beautiful dusky Amazons and gold was irresistible to the Spanish explorers in New Spain (Mexico). It is ironic that California, centre of the dream factory of the world, should be named for a story that might have been hatched in the heart of Hollywood. The book, or at least its contents, must have come to the notice of the conquistador Hernán Cortés, infamous in history for his brutal overthrow and destruction of the Aztec Empire in Mexico, and governor of New Spain, who said in 1524 that he expected to find the island of the Amazons on the north-west coast of Mexico. Like Columbus, who had a preconception that the islands of the West Indies lay off the coast of Cathay, the idea of an island filled with Amazons influenced early explorers' perceptions of the geographical reality of the Californian coastline.

Supposedly in the name of God and Spain, but most certainly also in the name of gold, Cortés financed exploratory voyages north from Acapulco on the Pacific coast of Mexico between 1533 and 1535, and in 1536 led a third voyage himself, landing near present-day La Paz near the southern end of the 1250 kilometre (775 mile) Baja California Peninsula, which extends south parallel to the mainland. Cortés created a short-lived settlement there and believed, at least for a while, that the peninsula was an island, which he named California. The name would one day apply to a far larger area and include much of what the Spanish designated Alta California. Surprisingly, Cortés was only the second Spanish explorer after Ponce de León to name an American state.

Later expeditions appeared to conclusively prove that the 'island' of California was a peninsula. In 1539, under Cortés's instructions, the navigator Francisco de Ulloa was sent along both the Pacific and Gulf coasts of Baja California. He named the gulf waters the Sea of Cortés, a name still used today. At the northern end of the gulf he reached the mouth of the Colorado River and could find no further sea passage, seemingly proving beyond doubt that the Baja California was not an island, and that the gulf was not the hoped-for Northwest Passage to the Orient, known by the Spanish as the Strait of Anián.

But there was no spoiling a good yarn. The story of the island of California was revived by Juan de Fuca's entirely fictitious claim to have discovered the long-sought Northwest Passage. Fuca, a Greek navigator sailing under the Spanish flag (and a Spanish name as he was born Apostolo Valerianos) sailed up the west coast of Mexico northward

HAVAN *port* **S. DOMINGO** **CARTAGENA** **MEXICO** *cv sc*

GROENLANDian

VIRGINIAN

K. of FLORIDA

W.O: of MEXICO

K. of newe ENGLAND

Newe land *Part of Euro:*

Groenlandia

Baffins Bay

dia

Frisland

Icacia Ile *Bus Ile*

The Northerely part of America
seeing that it could not bee contained which in the compasse of
this Mape, unlesse we should have
discribed the said country in a
lesser forme, wee have there fore or-
dayned this litle Carde above drawne
within wch ye North pole is included.

Y streight of Davi:

Hudson straigh

Hudsons
bay

NEWE BRITTAINE

THE NOR THERNE

Canada

PART OF AMERICA *AL*
BI

New England

C. Codd

Capischi *Calicuas*

THE NOR THERNE

NEWE
GRA
NADA

VIRGI

FLORI
DA

THE BAY
OF MEXICO

NEWE
SPAINE

THE

SOUTH

220 *230* *240* **THE EQUINOCTIAL CIRCLE** *250* *260* *270* *280* *290*

THE PERUVIANE

SEA

OCEAN

the Tropicke of Capricorne

THE PACIFICKE

SEA

Y streight of Magellanic

The Streight of le Mai:

AMERICA
*with those known parts in
that unknowne worlde
both people and manner
of buildings Discribed
and inlarged by I.S. Ano. 1626.*

Are to be sold by Thomas
Basset in Fleet-street, and
by Richard Chiswell in St
Pauls Churchyard.

THE UNKNOWNE WORLD

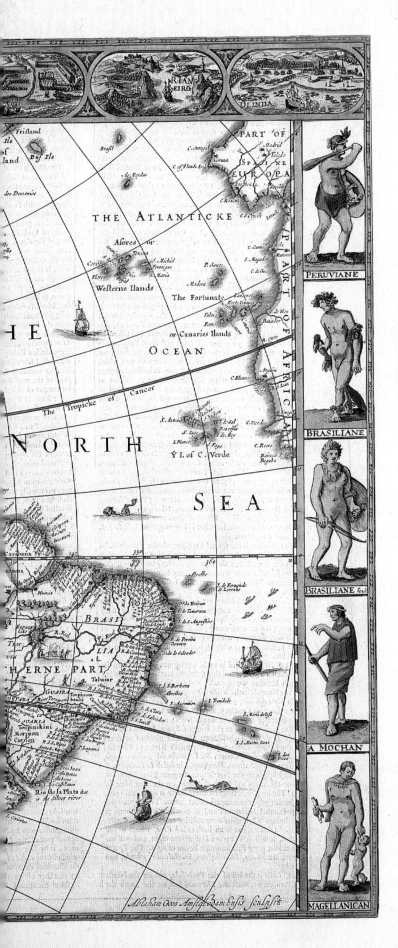

to Vancouver Island through the strait that now bears his name, later reporting he had found the route to Cathay.

More misinformation that seemed to confirm that California was an island was supplied by Juan de Oñate, governor of New Spain, who led an expedition that travelled down the Colorado River in 1604–5. He was genuinely convinced that the Gulf of California continued northward and out to sea, making California an island. The always forcefully expressed opinions of the Carmelite friar Antonio de la Ascensión also supported the island theory. In 1602, he sailed up the western coast of California with Sebastián Vizcaino, keeping a journal of the voyage in which he claimed the 'island of California' was separated from the mainland by 'the Mediterranean sea of California'.

It was left to another man of the cloth, the Jesuit cartographer and missionary priest Eusebio Francisco Kino, perhaps better known simply as Father Kino, to prove once and for all to any who would listen that Baja California was indeed a peninsula. Kino's expeditions, made partly to find suitable overland routes between the missions being established in the (then combined) Sonora and Baja regions of New Spain, were also to solve the question of the island of California, which had intrigued him long before he left Europe. Between 1698 and 1706 his expeditions from Sonoran California led him to explore the Gila and Colorado rivers, which flowed into the Gulf of California. Kino was convinced

LEFT: John Speed's 1627 map of the Americas was one of the first maps to present California as an island. The border is decorated with illustrations of Native Americans from different parts of America.

that he had resolved all debate and had proved conclusively that California was not an island. His map was printed in Paris in 1705, and most Jesuits agreed with his findings, but at least one who had accompanied him on expeditions did not believe the peninsula theory. Other Jesuit missionary explorers in the region settled the question beyond any doubt during the eighteenth century, more than two hundred years after the great debate should have been settled by Francisco de Ulloa.

Both of the maps of North America created by the cartographers Mercator and Ortelius correctly showed what is now known as the Baja California Peninsula. But the legend of the island of Amazons and the continual doubts raised about the peninsula theory combined to influence cartographers far into the eighteenth century. A 1622 map drawn by Michael Colijn of Amsterdam, showing the island of California, was the first, but by no means the last, to restore island status to Baja California.

John Speed's famous, ornamental map, published in London in 1627 in his *A Prospect of the*

Most Famous Parts of the World (see pages 186–7), was perhaps the most effective in reinforcing the notion of California as an island, which made this one of the most famous of all maps of the Americas. It depicted much of South and Central America with some accuracy, as well as the eastern coast of North America, including Chesapeake Bay, Delaware Bay and Hudson Bay. Delightful sea monsters, ships and flying fish decorate both the Atlantic and Pacific oceans. But it continues to be best remembered for the great Baja mistake. Jan Jansson's 1636 map *America Septentrionalis* (*North America*) followed—the first map by an influential Dutch cartographer to show the island of California.

The Island of California remains perhaps the single greatest cartographic error in history, though in fairness there is intense rivalry for that title. Perhaps after another million or so years of tectonic activity, the 'pro-island' theorists will finally be proven right when the Baja Peninsula becomes completely isolated from the coast.

THE INCREDIBLE
SHRINKING
CONTINENT

Columbus was not the only one to make serious errors in mapping the New World as a result of Ptolemy's miscalculation of the Earth's circumference. A map created in London in 1651 by John Farrer entitled *A Mapp of Virginia Discovered to ye Hills* (see page 190) reflects not only faith in Ptolemy, but also the triumph of hope and greed over reality.

John Farrer was born in London, and became a successful merchant who was caught up early in the excitement of the new colony in Virginia, after its faltering beginnings in the reign of Elizabeth I. He was a member of the Royal Council of the Virginia Company, which acted under royal charter to exploit the new colony for its natural wealth and establish industries but proved to be a disastrous failure for investors. Farrer was an active investor, personally establishing a silkworm industry in the new colony — an unlikely endeavour until it is seen in the context of the Western obsession with reaching Cathay.

In 1649 Farrer wrote a treatise modestly entitled *A Perfect Description of Virginia*, which was subsequently published in London. There is no doubt that his passion for the new colony was a driving force in his life. He even named his daughter Virginia after his beloved colony, writing that anyone 'speaking unto her, looking upon her, or hearing others call her by name, he might think upon both at once'. She was intended, no doubt in the nicest possible way, to be a walking billboard for

the young colony. Virginia went on to continue her father's silk business in the colony.

Farrer's treatise was incorporated into a larger book entitled *Virgo Triumphans: or, Virginia richly and truly valued*, written by Edward Williams and published in London in 1650. In the third edition of the book, printed in 1651, a map was finally included. It revealed a misconception of far greater

A Mapp of Virginia Discovered to ye Hills *by John Farrer, 1651. Farrer's map is oriented with west at the top of a narrow North American continent with a narrow band of water, the longed-for Northwest Passage, on the right.*

magnitude, if shorter lived, than the famous California Island debacle.

The Farrer map portrayed a remarkably skinny North American continent with the Pacific Ocean ('The Sea of China and the Indies') located virtually on the other side of the Blue Ridge Mountains. It was no cartographic accident. Farrer himself wrote that beyond the 'falls' at the head of the James River in Virginia 'will be found like rivers issuing into a south sea or a west sea, on the other side of those hills, as there is on this side, where they run from the west down to the east sea after a course of one hundred and fifty miles'. The legend he provided advised that a mere ten days march westward from the head of the James River would bring a traveller to the west-flowing rivers, and from there to the Sea of China and the Indies.

Farrer claimed to have based his map on that created in 1625 by the English cartographer Henry Briggs. Briggs holds the dubious honour of not only creating the incredible shrinking American continent, but also of being one of the first to include the 'island' of California on a map. The Briggs map contains the note: 'California sometimes supposed to be a part of ye western continent but since by a Spanish Charte taken by ye Hollanders it is found to be a goodly Ilande'.

Farrer's map of then-known areas of Virginia and Maryland was distorted, but it contained a number of geographical reference points and named a number of places for the first time, including the Dutch and Swedish settlements to the north of Virginia. On the far right is a very odd geographic feature, something that would be sought in vain, the Northwest Passage. A later version of the map, revised by Virginia Farrer around 1652, blocked this impossible feature at its western extremity, and the 'falls' on the James River was retitled 'hills'.

If anything, the map created by Nicholas Sanson of California and produced five years after Farrer's map takes the prize for pure fantasy. It depicts an elegantly elaborated but imaginary Californian coastline, and a Lake Taos overflowing into the River del Norte (the Rio Grande), which exits into the Gulf of California. It is assumed that he created this rather wild concept by underestimating the size of the North American continent, as did many others, and becoming thoroughly confused by the route of the Rio Grande, which opens into the Gulf of Mexico.

THE FALSE
SEA OF
VERRAZANO

One factor that contributed to the misinterpretation of North America made by Henry Briggs and others was a persistent belief in the mysterious False Sea of Verrazano as depicted on the famous Münster map of the Americas (see page 160). But even as the extraordinary length of the combined landmasses of the Americas became apparent with exploration, and the possibility of bypassing the new continents to reach Cathay and the East Indies became more doubtful, the dream of finding a quick route through did not recede. Everyone expected that sooner or later a way would be found, perhaps like the Straits of Magellan but located more conveniently in North America, or perhaps a narrow isthmus that could be easily traversed before resuming a sea journey westward. Such an isthmus had been discovered in Panama by Vasco Núñez de Balboa (see page 236), but it was far south of the desired latitude and increasingly under Spanish domination. Explorers were ripe to be tricked by wishful thinking, and Giovanni da Verrazano would be the one in 1524 to offer that false hope, which would persist for well over a century.

Verrazano was a nobly born Florentine and master navigator who had made a number of voyages to the eastern Mediterranean and Newfoundland. He was engaged by the French King Francis I to discover the much-desired passage through North America. Francis was a remarkable man—a humanist, passionate, intelligent and honourable, a valiant knight in battle, a patron of the arts and a peacemaker who is sometimes referred to as France's first 'Renaissance King'. Verrazano could have had no better sponsor. But once again, wishful thinking would distort an explorer's perception of reality.

Verrazano was a meticulous map maker and was the first European to explore the Atlantic coast of North America from South Carolina to Nova Scotia. His chart of the coastline is the most recognisable of the time, and his logbook was amazingly detailed. On his 1524 expedition he made landfall at Cape Fear, in present-day South Carolina, and sailed south for a short while, before heading north. His landfalls included what is now New York Harbor, although he seems to have missed the Hudson River. He returned to France via Narragansett Bay, following the coastline of Maine.

His long, descriptive and in many parts exciting and entertaining letter to Francis I summarised this voyage, which almost ended before it began when huge damage was incurred in gales, which caused two of his boats to founder, and the remaining two to put into port in Brittany for repairs. Verrazano was left with just one boat, the *Dauphine*, to make the journey to the New World. His letter is at times disturbingly forensic in its attitude. It is impossible not to be appalled by his casual taking of an Indian boy from his grandmother, much as he might have collected a specimen of a new species, followed by the throwaway line that they would have taken a twenty-year-old girl 'who was very beautiful and tall' but she was screaming too loudly for them to safely carry her through several woods on their way back to the sea. The undefended girl and the old lady had been caring for six children between them and had become isolated from their people when they fled from the strangers. There seems to be not the slightest comprehension of the agony their actions caused. Yet this same man would describe with sensitivity the beauty of the region and detail the lushness of the grapevines they encountered in more northerly latitudes, 'the wild roses, violets and lilies, and many kinds of herbs and flowers'. Verrazano named all the lands they saw in eastern North America Francesca in honour of Francis, a name that can be found on some old maps.

Because sailing boats were quite limited technologically, it was not possible to simply sail along the coastline mapping every feature. Instead, Verrazano was forced to sail away from the coast and tack back towards it, a technique that was unavoidable but also caused him to miss some obvious geographical features, including Chesapeake Bay and the Delaware River. With every tack landwards he must have hoped to see a passage opening up before him that would lead directly to Asia. And with every tack his frustration must have grown.

At last Verrazano found what he firmly believed to be the magical passage. He wrote in his letter to Francis:

We called it 'Annunciato' from the day of arrival, where was found an isthmus a mile in width and about 200 long, in which from the ship, was seen the oriental sea between the west and north. Which is one, without doubt, which goes about the extremity of India, China and Cathay. We navigated along the said isthmus with the continual hope of finding some strait or true promontory at which the land would end toward the north in order to be able to penetrate to those blessed shores of Cathay.

In reality the 'blessed shores of Cathay' were as far away as ever.

It is generally believed that what he mistook for the Pacific Ocean was Pimlico Sound and Albemarle Sound and the string of sandy barrier islands that constitute the Outer Banks of the modern state of North Carolina.

The Outer Banks were also where, between 1585 and 1587, England would attempt to establish its first foothold in the New World under the direction of Sir Walter Raleigh. Fort Raleigh would be the birthplace of the first English child to be born in the New World, Virginia Dare. That attempt ended in terrible failure and the unsolved mystery of the Lost Colony of Roanoke. All 116 men, women and children who had settled a village called Roanoke simply disappeared from the face of the Earth. But there is evidence that the timing of the settlement was appalling, during the worst drought in eight centuries.

When Verrazano returned to France, his 'discovery' was included in two manuscript maps, one by Visconti Maggiolo in 1527, who inscribed the sea as Mare Indicum, the other by Giovanni's brother Giralamo da Verrazano in 1529. The latter included a legend which read, 'from this eastern sea you may behold the western sea and there are six miles of land between them'. Both maps showed North America with a huge 'bite' taken out of its eastern side, leaving a thin strip of land to the south and west. The 'bite' became known as the Sea of Verrazano.

Verrazano made two further trips to the New World, the first to the coast of Brazil, the second, on which he died, to Florida and the West Indies. There are mixed reports about the manner of his death at the early age of forty-three. The consensus is that he was killed by Indians, some say at the hands of cannibals, but quite where he died remains contentious, with the Lesser Antilles, the Bahamas and Florida, which he explored on his last voyage in 1528, all possible locations. His brother witnessed the terrible scene from the ship anchored out to sea, but was unable to come to his help in time.

Verrazano may have died, but his false sea had taken on a life of its own and was still being represented on maps long after his death, the most important being the German cartographer Sebastian Münster's famous and very influential map 'Novae Insulae (New Islands), XXVII Nova Tabula' of 1540, the first printed map devoted entirely to the New World. The Sea of Verrazano was also shown on Münster's very popular 1540 edition of Ptolemy's *Geography*, and later in his masterwork *Cosmographia* (*Cosmography* or *Geographis Thought*) in 1544.

If there were significant errors in Münster's 1540 map, it nevertheless remains the first to show North and South America as twinned continents, rather than North America connected to Asia in various ways.

JOHN CABOT
AND EXPLORATIONS
IN THE NORTH

In the light of Irish and Norse achievements (see pages 164) it is ironic that the English claimed that John Cabot discovered North America, or even claimed him as one of their own, although he is thought to have settled in England around 1494.

John Cabot was born Giovanni Caboto, near Naples c. 1450. His father was a merchant trading in spices and as a young boy Giovanni seems to have spent some time in the great seaport of Genoa. By 1461 he was living in Venice, which lay at the crossroads of Byzantium and Italy. The latter had become a great maritime nation and super power by the fifteenth century, eventually controlling the Adriatic and enriched by centuries of trade, particularly in spices. Venice had also taken advantage of several crusades, particularly the Fourth Crusade.

When Cabot moved to Venice, the state had assumed the title of Most Serene Republic, and there were few better places in all Europe for an expert mariner and spice trader to be. Cabot married a

John Cabot and His Three Sons *by G. Ramusio and F. Grisellini, 1762.*

Venetian lady with whom he subsequently had three sons, all of whom would sail with him.

But the centre of action and wealth had shifted to the countries of Spain and Portugal, both of which were trying to break the Italian monopoly on spices by pioneering sea routes to the East Indies and India. Portugal achieved its objective when Bartolomeu Dias succeeded in rounding the Cape of Good Hope and Vasco da Gama later successfully pioneered a route around Africa to India. Columbus achieved equally exciting economic returns for Spain with his discovery of the West Indies, even though the longed-for western route to Cathay had not been found.

For an expert navigator, the explorations being undertaken by those two countries were an irresistible lure, so Cabot moved his family to Valencia in Spain. Cabot believed he could achieve what Columbus had not, and reach China by taking a far more northerly approach. But neither Portugal nor Spain wanted his services. His background in the Italian spice trade could not have been helpful.

The merchants of Bristol, the second largest port in England, regularly formed consortiums to support exploration and trade, and they listened to Cabot's ideas when Portugal and Spain would not. They had already funded several expeditions in an effort to locate the legendary island of Hy-Brazil. At the time England was like a sleeping giant, only beginning to stir after centuries of internal strife while her Iberian rivals began their economic and imperialistic rise. Henry VIII would not be born until the year before Columbus's first voyage to the Americas, and Elizabeth I would not be crowned until 1559, when England would, under her shrewd

reign, finally become a great maritime power. But even so, Bristol mariners and fishermen were already very active. They had almost certainly made trips to Newfoundland and Labrador before Cabot landed there. There is good evidence that they had set up a cod processing plant and had also sent a number of probes into the North Atlantic in search of trade opportunities. But these were unofficial journeys.

In 1496 Henry VII issued letters authorising John Cabot and his sons to go with:

… full and free authority, leave, and power, to sail to all parts, countries, and seas, of the East, of the West, and of the North, under our banners and ensigns, with five ships … to seek out, discover, and find whatsoever islands, countries, regions or provinces of heathens and infidels, whatsoever they be, which before this time have been unknown to all Christians.

It would be nice to believe that, misguided though the king might have been by modern standards, he was motivated by the well-intentioned aim to convert to Christianity all peoples encountered by Cabot as well as by considerations of financial gain in the Orient and West Indies. Slave trading had already begun, very rewardingly, in the West Indies, and it may be that the king also had in mind the pope's ruling that Christians could not be made slaves. The ruling had certainly not escaped the Spanish conquistadors, who were often none too willing to make conversions.

Cabot's first expedition in 1496 was a failure, although we know of it only through a letter sent to Columbus in 1497 by John Day, a British merchant and spy for the Spanish Inquisition. He reported that arguments had broken out on board Cabot's ship, supplies had run short and Cabot had run into very heavy seas, eventually being forced to turn back after reaching Greenland.

Cabot's next voyage in May 1497 took him to Newfoundland, but he was confident that he had reached Asia. His actual landfall was probably Cape Bonavista. As Columbus did not actually land on mainland North America until 1498, Cabot is given credit for being the first European to set foot on North America after the Norse. In 1498 Cabot again set out for the New World, and this time the misfortune that had dogged him on his first journey overcame him. Four of his five ships went missing in terrible weather off Ireland and were presumed lost with all hands. A fifth ship finally made it back to Ireland to report the losses, which included Cabot.

Sebastian Cabot, one of John's three sons, followed in his father's footsteps, searching for the elusive Northwest Passage in 1508 in the employ of Spain. After various aborted return journeys to North America, in 1525 he would become the victim of gold fever, like so many in the New World. He began a voyage intended to emulate Magellan's but, seduced by the rumour of a silver mountain when he reached the Rio de la Plata in Argentina, he instead sought its riches.

The expedition ended in disaster and his exile to Africa when he returned to the Spanish court empty handed. Three years after his release he became Pilot Major of Spain, then to the annoyance of the Spanish king accepted an appointment as Great Pilot in England. Unlike many adventurers he died of old age, reaching his eighty-second year.

JACQUES CARTIER'S SEARCH FOR THE NORTHWEST PASSAGE

Like John Cabot, Jacques Cartier was convinced that China and the great wealth of Asia lay somewhere west of Newfoundland, and that he would be able to discover the Northwest Passage. Cartier was a highly respected mariner from Saint-Malo, the ancient fortified seaport on the coast of Brittany, who had already proved his abilities on voyages to Brazil and to Newfoundland. In 1532, when Brittany formally joined France, Cartier was brought to the attention of King Francis I of France, who had earlier sponsored Verrazano's exploration of the east coast of North America (see page 192). The meeting took place at the Manoir de Brion and resulted in a commission that was nothing if not forthright in its intent, stating that Cartier was to 'discover certain islands and lands where it is said that a great quantity of gold and other precious things are to be found'.

Cartier set sail in May 1534 and explored Newfoundland, the area now designated the Canadian Atlantic Provinces and the Gulf of St Lawrence, where he found the mouth of the St Lawrence River. It was not a time when environmental issues were exactly uppermost in European minds and Pliny, who had preached environmental conservation thirteen centuries before, would rightly have been appalled, for at the Island of Birds, Isles-aux-Oiseaux, his crew reportedly killed 1000 great auks, now an extinct species. The great auk, or garefowl, was a stately, flightless bird larger than a goose, around 90 centimetres (36 inches) long, with short wings, black feathers, red-rimmed eyes, a long, sharp, spear-shaped beak, and a large white spot between the beak and the eyes. They laid only one large egg a year, some 15 centimetres (6 inches) long—a reproductive rate that made them particularly vulnerable. Great auks were found only in remote places such as islands where their inability to fly had not put them at a disadvantage. Until humans encountered them. If ever there was an island that corresponded with St Brendan's Paradise of Birds (see page 129), the Isles-aux-Oiseaux, with its colonies of magnificent great auks, would be it. If St Brendan and his men had reached the Newfoundland Banks, it is possible that their Island of Birds was based on reaching just such an island.

Cartier's account of his 1534 voyage found favour with the king and he was granted considerable powers to commission and equip a second expedition. Cartier's second voyage set sail three days after Pentecost in May of 1535. Once again, they visited the Isles-aux-Oiseaux which sadly, in the light of the future extinction of great auks, Cartier described as, 'So full of birds it was that all the ships in France might be loaded with them, and yet it would not seem that any were taken away'. Feeding from the immensely fish-rich seas off Newfoundland, the auks must once have been present in huge populations. Now even the cod they fed on are dwindling in number.

Cartier's second journey did not proceed as smoothly as the first. Huge gales in the Atlantic separated his ship from the other two vessels of the expedition, and they became lost in huge fog banks. Cartier had foreseen the possibility and arranged a rendezvous at Blanc Sablon, where the three ships were reunited. Nevertheless, the expedition was a journey of great significance. They travelled up river from the entrance of the St Lawrence as far

as Hochelaga (now Montreal), then an important Iroquois settlement. From the summit of Mount Royal he was able to survey the vast and magnificent panorama of woods and mountains further inland, beyond the junction of the St Lawrence and Ottawa rivers, and his guides told him of great lakes that lay still further inland (Lake Ontario and Lake Huron). Ironically, Cartier apparently hoped, at least initially, that the St Lawrence was the much-desired Northwest Passage. A party that he sent ahead to explore with boats proved that the great river created a fresh-water outpouring almost 5 kilometres (3 miles) from shore.

The expedition overstayed their time and the winter closed in by mid-October. The crew were forced to over-winter rather than return to France. Cartier sought suitable shelter for the boats and a place to make camp by sailing up the St Lawrence. He described being surrounded at one point by a great company of white whales, which he described as 'white as snow, and were never before of any man seen or known'. He also recorded that, during the terrible winter that followed, the water froze to a depth of more than a fathom (1.8 metres/6 feet) and snow was piled 1.2 metres (4 feet) high. Cartier's men strengthened their defences against the weather, hunted and salted away food supplies. But scurvy, caused by a lack of vitamin C in their diet, was the greatest danger. Cartier recorded in his log that not ten of his men were well enough to tend the other one hundred. They were saved by Domagaya, the son of

FOLLOWING PAGES: Jacques Cartier on his third voyage to Canada with would-be colonists, from Nicolas Vallard's 1542 portolan atlas. The map is of eastern North America and is oriented with north at the bottom.

son of an Iroquois chief, who they had taken with them to France on their previous voyage. He showed them how to prepare a remedy for scurvy using the foliage and bark of arbor vitae (Tree of Life or White Cedar, *Thuya occidentalis*). Although forty of the eighty-five men still alive were extremely ill, all eighty-five recovered and would live to see through the bitter winter. Cartier wrote, 'All the doctors in Europe could not have done as much in a year as this tree did in one week'. He took specimens back to France on his return, where it received the name Tree of Life, and became one of the first North American tree species to be planted in Europe.

THE KINGDOM OF SAGUENAY

During Cartier's second voyage of exploration of Northern Canada in 1535, again under the auspices of the French king, yet another mysterious place was added to the imaginary atlas of the world. Cartier was told by the Haudenosaunee or Iroquois of the mysterious Kingdom of Saguenay, which lay further to the north and was apparently an El Dorado, full of gold, precious jewels and other treasures. Cartier decided to take the Iroquois chief Donnacona back to France to lend maximum weight to his claims about the mysterious kingdom.

Cartier returned to France with quite detailed knowledge of the geography of north-eastern Canada and a shrewd estimate of its great potential for settlement and future wealth. While his behaviour towards the Iroquois had not been blameless, he had certainly not created the level of antagonism that had followed Spanish invasion in the south, and the potential for a more peaceful coexistence had been established. But kings have a way of wanting tangible returns for their speculative outlays, and Cartier was wise enough to know that Francis I, who had been sorely pressed in a series of wars against the Holy Roman Emperor Charles V would expect a fairly immediate prospect of riches at the end of the second voyage, which had lasted for fourteen months.

Francis I was impressed by Donnacona's account of the Kingdom of Saguenay, and a third expedition was organised, but this time Cartier was made captain general, or second in command, while the expedition was to be led by a Huguenot courtier, Jean-François de la Rocque de Roberval, who gave his gracious permission for Cartier to depart ahead of him. Cartier set sail with five ships from Saint-Malo in May 1541. There was no mention now of pioneering a route through the Northwest Passage. There were supposedly riches closer to hand. The plan was to set up a permanent French colony on the St Lawrence River and find the Kingdom of Saguenay. Cartier's ships reached Stadecona on the St Lawrence in August, but the welcome they were given was less than warm, so he continued upstream, eventually choosing Cap-Rouge, now part of Quebec City, to establish the settlement. There they offloaded convicts to carry out much of the necessary construction and tend to livestock that had survived the voyage. The settlers then began digging vitally important vegetable gardens, and built fortifications, and erected an additional fort above the settlement, which had been named Charlesbourg-Royal. The ground was covered in 'gold' and 'diamonds', and great quantities were gathered to be loaded onto two ships, which were dispatched back to France.

With the season closing in, on 7 September 1541 Cartier took some longboats further upstream on a reconnaissance for Saguenay. Rapids upstream proved too great a barrier to his travelling up the Ottawa River and he turned back, to find the settlement in deep trouble. For whatever reason, the previously cordial relationship with the Iroquois had soured and thirty-five settlers had been massacred before the fortifications could be defended. The settlement struggled through the long deep winter, at least free of scurvy owing to the use of arbor vitae. But Cartier was hampered by reduced manpower and the need for greater protection.

It was impossible to both search for Saguenay and defend the settlement, and in early June 1542 Cartier departed with his ship carrying a load of 'precious stones' from around the settlement. On reaching the Newfoundland coast he encountered Roberval, who had finally left France with his cargo of artillery and supplies for the colony. Cartier, a man of considerable civility, must nevertheless have used some well-chosen salty language in dealing with Roberval, who insisted Cartier turn back and continue to search for Saguenay. Cartier left Roberval to his own devices, departing under cover of darkness and sailing on to France.

It is a pity the third expedition had not been supplied with a metallurgist. The gold turned out to be 'fool's gold' (iron pyrites), and the diamonds, quartz crystals.

Cartier retired to Saint-Malo and his estate, with the enviable record of not losing a single ship on his three voyages, dying there at the age of sixty-five during an epidemic in 1557. An island, a river, a bridge, a state park and at least one important street have been named for him in Canada as a tribute to his great contribution to exploration. As for Roberval, conditions continued to deteriorate at Charlesbourg-Royal. Disease, hostile Iroquois and extreme weather conditions took their toll until the settlement was abandoned, a year after Cartier left. No further settlements were made in New France until the founding of Quebec City in 1608.

The mystery of the Kingdom of Saguenay would never be solved. The story derived from a legend of the Algonquin people centred around the present-day areas of Quebec and Ontario, which told of a race of tall, blonde, white-skinned men living in a land rich in furs and gold. Was it all a misunderstanding? Chief Donnacona certainly believed in the story. Could it have described a Norse settlement in pre-Columbian Canada? Nothing was ever found of the kingdom, but the riches of the area did indeed lie in furs. Initially the French crown recouped some of its outlay dealing in furs, followed by the Hudson Bay Trading Company (Compagnie de la Baie d'Hudson), the oldest commercial corporation in North America, which was established in 1670.

PEPYS ISLAND

In 1699 a book entitled *Collection of Original Voyages* was published in London by James Knapton. Written by William Hacke, it described a voyage made in 1684 by the English buccaneer William Cowley. It created a mystery that would eventually even involve James Cook.

Cowley described a journey south along the coast of Brazil in which they encountered at a latitude of about 40 degrees south sea as red as blood (the colour of which was attributed to great shoals of shrimps). Cowley also described a company of vast numbers of seals that barked like dogs, as well as an abundance of large whales, one hundred times more numerous than in the northern hemisphere. At 47 degrees south, Cowley encountered an island, which he named Pepys Island (although in the quaint illustration provided in the book it is called Peypses Island—it was a period of flexible spelling). The island was named in honour of Samuel Pepys, the famous diarist, member of parliament and at that time Chief Secretary to the Admiralty. Cowley recounted that the island had a large bay where it was estimated a thousand ships might anchor. In addition, good supplies of timber and water were available, as well as abundant fowl and fish. Altogether it seemed a most satisfactory island.

Between 1764 and 1766 Commander Patrick Mouat and Captain John Byron, on the *Tamar* and *Dolphin*, were circumnavigating the globe with secret instructions to chart and survey what would become known as the Falkland Islands. When they set sail from Rio de Janeiro they determined to find Cowley's island and sailed parallel courses as they approached 47 degrees south, far enough apart to ensure they would see the island. The island failed to appear and the two boats continued south, rounding Cape Virgines before entering the Straits of Magellan, from which they proceeded to a group of islands discovered by the English explorer Captain John Davis in 1592. Byron took possession of them in the name of King George III of England in 1765 and named them the Falkland Islands. East Falkland Island had two significant bays, Port Egmont where Byron established a vegetable garden, and Berkeley Sound. The island was 3 degrees further south in latitude than Pepys Island but they considered the two islands might well be the same. (It is probable that the Sanson Islands, recorded on charts by the Spanish in 1522, and at approximately the same time on charts by the great Turkish admiral Piri Reis, were the same as the Falkland Islands.)

The strategic value of the Falklands was obvious from the time of their discovery in 1592 and Spain, France and England became locked in rivalry for their possession. Lord Anson, later the first Lord of the Admiralty, had first planned to locate Pepys Island and explore the Falklands in 1740, but a still powerful

Spain objected to the establishment of a British base in the area. For the British it was a temporary setback. Following Byron's annexation of the islands, Captain John McBride established a garrison at Port Egmont in 1766. Probably totally unknown to the British, in 1764 the French navigator Louis-Antoine de Bougainville had already established a settlement at Port Louis on East Falkland. Having objected to Britain's plans for settlement in the Falklands, the Spanish could hardly allow the French to colonise inside what they called their 'zone of influence', and that same year they offered to buy the island from France. France formally renounced its claim in 1766 and Bougainville was duly compensated, in turn renouncing his claim to any rights in the settlement in 1767. In the meantime the British had discovered the French settlement, and demanded that its occupants be evicted forthwith. Something of a Mexican standoff followed in 1769, when Spanish and British ships encountered each other in the Falklands and strongly worded 'letters' were exchanged. The Spanish expelled the British from Port Egmont in 1770. But the British star had achieved ascendancy and the greatest empire the world would ever see was in the making. Threatened with war as a result of their actions, the Spanish withdrew their claim on the Falklands, restoring Port Egmont to the British in 1771. What remained of the Spanish presence was fully and formally withdrawn by 1811.

It is probable that Mouat and Byron were correct in their assessment, and that Pepys Island was one of the Falklands, and that Cowley had incorrectly calculated the latitude. Perhaps that latitude has an odd effect on sailors. In 1762 a Spanish ship reported a group of three islands to the east of Cape Horn, lying between the Falklands and Georgia, and named them the Aurora Islands. They were next sighted in 1794 by a ship sent out to locate them precisely. The Auroras were last sighted in 1856, but they continued to appear on maps until the 1870s.

On his voyage to Tahiti in the *Endeavour* made between 1768 and 1771, Captain James Cook also looked for the mysterious Pepys Island. Sir Joseph Banks, a botanist appointed to the voyage, described how a midshipman at the mast saw something very like an island when they were at a latitude of 47 degrees, but that it grew no larger after some time spent travelling towards it and, as Banks put it, 'we were convinced that we were in chase of Cape fly away as the seamen call it'. Cook was not the only one not to find the mysterious Pepys Island.

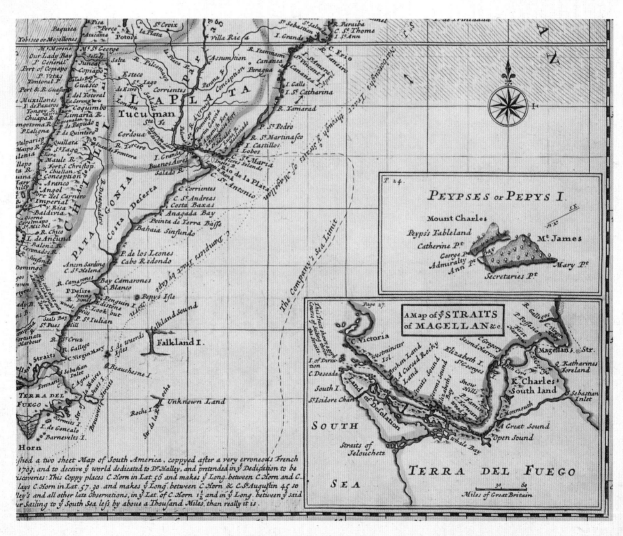

Herman Moll's map of southern South America, published in 1736, included an inset of Pepys Island with various promontories and bays labelled, despite its non-existence.

TERRA AUSTRALIS,
THE GREAT THEORY

Terra Australis Incognita, meaning 'unknown land of the south', was an idea long before it became a reality, just like California. The theory, formulated by the ancient Greek philosopher Aristotle, described a land on the underside of the world that would act as a counterweight to the continents in the northern hemisphere. Ptolemy elaborated on this idea, saying that the great South Land bounded the Indian Ocean to the south. Many cartographers depicted a vastly enlarged version of Antarctica extending northward as far as New Guinea, although some were better than others at narrowing down the possible location of Terra Australis. Nevertheless it remained the great question mark on world maps, and for a long time would be known only as islands and small coastal segments, rather than the continent it was.

Driven by the obsession with gold and spices, the search for faster routes to the Moluccas, or Spice Islands as they were known, and the possibility of a great south land filled with unimaginable riches, both Spanish and Portuguese expeditions sailed close to Australia. Spain used its papally ordained dominance of the New World set out in the 1404 Treaty of Tordesillas, and followed a route around Cape Horn in South America to the Philippines, which they had colonised in 1565, and discovered the Marquesas, the Solomons and a number of islands in the Carolines during the sixteenth century. Portugal used its ordained right to the other half of the world to approach the East via the Cape of Good Hope at the tip of southern Africa. Portugal explored the East Indies in the early sixteenth century, and discovered New Guinea. The Dutch ousted the Portuguese from the Moluccas at the beginning of the seventeenth century, and in 1605 a Dutch survey ship was sent out to explore the north coast of the south land. Others would follow.

DUTCH EXPLORATION

The first authenticated deliberate voyage to New Guinea and Australia was made by William Janszoon in a tiny ship called the *Duyfken* (*Little Dove*) in 1606, sent out with the aim of searching 'south and east lands' for gold.

Even more significant was the 1611 journey of Dutch sea captain, Hendrik Brouwer who travelled form Europe, rounded the southern tip of Africa, then headed directly eastward into the Indian Ocean. It was a feat the equal of that of Columbus. Like Columbus he took advantage of prevailing

RIGHT: In 1570 the first modern atlas, Ortelius's Theatrum Orbis Terrarum, *was published. Along with fifty-two regional and country maps the atlas included a world map depicting a gigantic continent covering much of the uncharted southern hemisphere.*

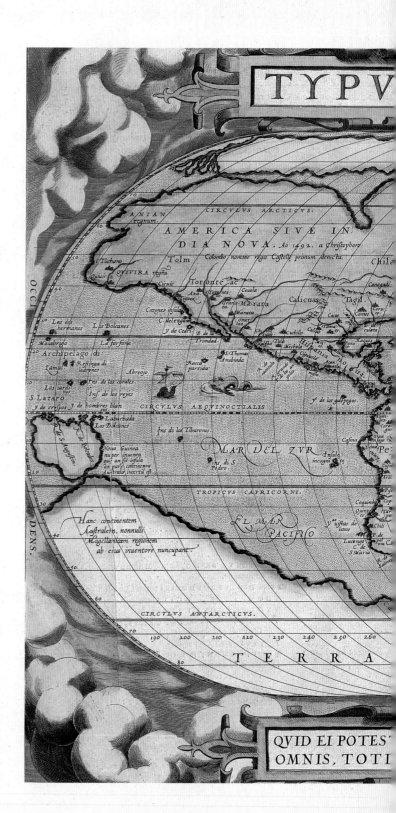

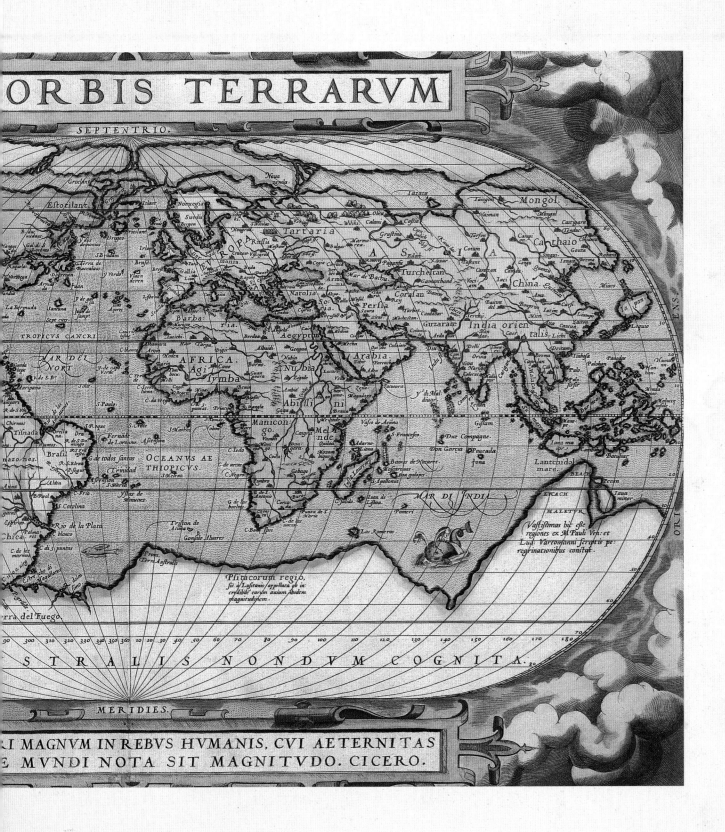

winds and currents. Not until after more than 7000 kilometres (4350 miles) did he change course and head northward to Batavia (present-day Jakarta). In a feat that would have required nerves of steel, he cut as much as twelve months off the established route.

In 1616 Dirk Hartog on the *Eendracht*, a 200-tonne Dutch East India ship with a complement of two hundred on board, led the second expedition known to have landed on the shores of Australia. Using the route established by Brouwer, but sailing further east, he encountered a group of islands off the western coast of Australia, the largest of which he named Dirk Hartog Island. He left behind a pewter plate nailed to a tree, the only evidence of his discovery. The plate was found eighty-one years later by William de Vlamingh, another Dutch East India captain, who returned it to the Netherlands. Today it is in the Rijksmuseum in Amsterdam.

In 1642–43 another remarkable journey of exploration was undertaken by the Dutch navigator Abel Tasman, who sailed south of the continent, discovering both Tasmania and New Zealand.

That great gift to all serendipitous discovery by sailors, being blown off course, had given a number of vessels engaged in the spice trade the chance to see and chart parts of Australia's western coastline. Some of these journeys also ended in tragedy, including the wreck of the Dutch ship *Batavia* on its way to Indonesia, and the subsequent horrendous mutiny of her crew in 1629–30 on the islands of Houtman's Abrolhos, also off the western Australian coast.

BRITISH AND FRENCH EXPLORATION

In 1688 the British buccaneer, sea captain and scientist (an odd mixture but true) William Dampier explored parts of northern western Australia around King Sound, as well as Southeast Asia, and the Bismarck Archipelago off the northeastern coast of New Guinea. Dampier is considered the first man to have circumnavigated the globe three times.

With the eighteenth century power shift from Spain and Portugal to Britain and France, it was the latter two countries that would increasingly explore the Pacific region. Great French explorers such as Louis-Antoine de Bougainville, the naval officer Jean-François de Galaup, the Comte de La Pérouse and Antoine-Raymond-Joseph de Bruni d'Entrecasteaux would become famed for their exploits. The last two are remembered in place names in New South Wales and Tasmania.

La Pérouse was given the broadest directives by King Louis XVI and was destined to land in Botany Bay in Australia just five days after Captain Arthur Phillip had arrived with the First Fleet and run up the British flag on Australian shores. La Pérouse headed to the Solomons, with his ships *L'Astrolabe* and *La Boussole* taking water and in need of repair. Both ships foundered in a storm off the Solomons and sank with almost all hands. Most of the survivors were subsequently killed when they made land on the Solomons. Bruni d'Entrecastreaux was sent out in 1791 to find La Pérouse and reached the Solomons, but La Pérouse and his men were already dead. Both wrecks have been located and have been explored underwater. The story may be apocryphal but it is said that as Louis XVI was led away to the guillotine he inquired, 'Have we got news from Monsieur de la Pérouse?'

New Zealand, visited by the Dutch navigator Abel Tasman, was considered to be part of Terra

Australis, and it was not until Captain James Cook, after observing the transit of Venus on Tahiti in June 1769, circumnavigated New Zealand later that year and accurately charted the coastline, that its island nature was discovered. On Cook's second journey of discovery in 1772–75 he sailed through the high latitudes towards the southern polar circle, proving once and for all that there was no huge counterweight in the southern hemisphere. It is thought quite probable that he sighted Antarctica.

CIRCUMNAVIGATION OF AUSTRALIA

Only when Matthew Flinders circumnavigated the Great South Land in 1801–3 was the shape of Australia finally established. Flinders also proved that known parts of the north-western coastline and the eastern coast were all part of the same landmass. Australia was at last revealed as a separate continental mass, with neither New Guinea nor New Zealand attached.

Flinders was a Royal Navy commander who had already established a remarkable reputation as a sailor and navigator. He joined the Royal Navy at fifteen, entranced by the story of Robinson Crusoe. He sailed as a midshipman on HMS *Bellerophon* before transferring to HMS *Providence* under the notorious Captain Bligh, transporting breadfruit trees to Tahiti from Jamaica. He sailed to Australia in HMS *Reliance*. His first explorations of the coast in 1795 were with his good friend George Bass, a ship's surgeon, sailing south of Sydney in the pitifully small open boat named, with good reason, *Tom Thumb*. In a subsequent journey made in 1798 in the *Norfolk*, again accompanied by George Bass, he circumnavigated Tasmania. Bass Strait, named

for his friend, between the Australian mainland and Tasmania is recognised as one of the most dangerous places in the world for smaller ships. In his next journey, made in 1799 and again in the *Norfolk* but now without Bass, Flinders charted southern Queensland waters, exploring Moreton Bay and naming Redcliff, now a coastal suburb of Brisbane.

After these short surveys, Flinders returned to England in 1801 to petition for the funding of his great dream—to circumnavigate and map the entire Australian coastline. Sir Joseph Banks, who had accompanied Cook on his first Pacific voyage, supported Flinders's cause. He received the backing he required and, like Cook, outfitted a colliery boat, noted for their seaworthiness and capacity, which was named the *Investigator*. He also obtained the total support of Ann Chapelle, who would become his great love and his wife before he returned to Australia, although the Admiralty refused to allow her to accompany her husband on the voyage.

Flinders first explored the entire southern coastline of mainland Australia, then circled the continent in an anti-clockwise direction, charting the coast as he progressed. He safely navigated the Great Barrier Reef, which had cost Cook dearly when he had to stop to repair the *Endeavour* in North Queensland, establishing the route through the reef still known as Flinders Passage.

His journey was full of incident, and at Cape Catastrophe the ship's boat was lost with eight crew, including Flinders's close friend John Thistle, and near Timor more crew were lost to dysentery. The *Investigator* finally limped back to Sydney, its hull deteriorating, in 1803. In the way of armchair critics, some have said that Flinders failed to

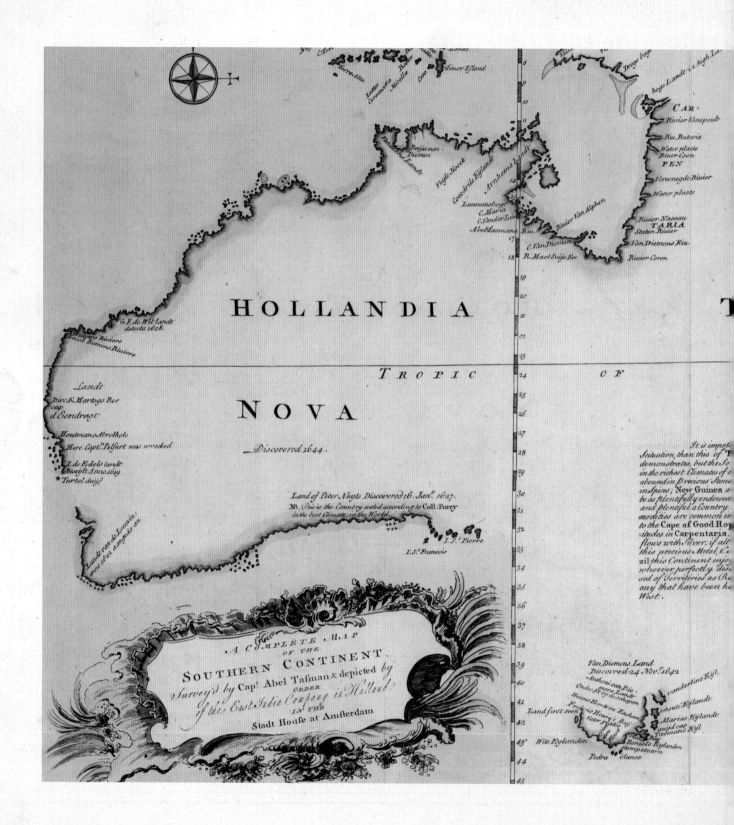

the Dutch Names have been preserved that if hereafter any Discoveries should ever be Attempted all the places mentioned may be readily found in the Dutch Charts which must be procured for such a Voyage. The Reader is desired to observe that nothing is marked here but what has has been Actually discovered which is the reason of the white Space between New Holland and New Zealand, and again between New Zeland and New Guinea which make the South and East sides of Terra Australis; It is also requisite to observe, that the Country discovered by Ferdinand de Quiros lies according to his description on the East Side of this Continent directly Opposite to Carpentaria which if Attentively considered will add no small weight to the Credit of what he has written about that Country and which has been very rashly as well as very unjustly treated by some Critical Writers as a Fiction; whereas it Appears from this Map of Actual Discoveries, that there is a Country where Ferdinand de Quiros says he found one; And if so why may not that Country be such a one as he describes? In Tasmans Voyage we have shewn why he did not make this Matter more plain.

RRA AUSTRALIS
Discovered A.D. 1644.

PRICORN

a Country that promises fairer from its
is no longer incognita, as this Map
nt Discovered. It lies Precisely
e Islands of Sumatra, Java & Borneo,
luable Commodities; and the Moluccas
behind it must by a parity of Reason
the Island of Madagascar is so Noble
peak it; and Gold, Ivory, and other Com
part of Africa from Melinda down
ain to C. Gonsalez; here are 9. same Lat.
, and New Zealand; If Peru over
s of Chili are filled with Gold, and
more precious, are y product of Bra
of the same position and therefore
it will become infalliably posses
. & as capable of Improvement, as
out, either in the East Indies, or the

detect and explore a number of major rivers, but the miracle was that he accomplished so much in such gruelling conditions.

After Flinders's return to Sydney, he departed as a passenger for England in the *Porpoise*, which was wrecked on an uncharted reef off the Queensland coast. In a heroic feat of seamanship rarely equalled in the history of seafaring, Flinders organised the survivors and brought the ship's cutter back to Sydney, an extraordinary and perilous journey of 1130 kilometres (700 miles).

Once again he set out for London, this time on the schooner *Cumberland*, again with dreams of seeing his wife. He was ill fated as a passenger. The *Cumberland* was in poor condition and forced to make repairs in Mauritius, a French colony. There Flinders was taken prisoner and held as a British spy under harsh conditions for seven years. When he finally reached England in 1810 he was in poor health.

Although Flinders was promoted, he received no recognition for his achievements. He died in poverty at the age of forty in 1814 after a long illness, on the same day that his important book, *A Voyage to Terra Australis*, was published. His wife Ann and daughter Anne were left in dire circumstances, and it was decades later, and after Ann's death, that compensation was offered to their daughter by the colonies of Victoria and New South Wales. (Matthew Flinders's grandson, Professor Sir William

LEFT: A 1744 map by John Harris based on the surveys made by Abel Tasman. The west coast of Australia is extensively charted, but the east coast, coastlines to the north and south, and most of New Zealand remain unknown.

Matthew Flinders Petrie was the famous Egyptian archaeologist who pioneered a systematic approach to the investigation of archaeological sites.)

It was Matthew Flinders who named the new country 'Australia', a name which was officially adopted in 1824. Flinders's maps of the Australian coastline would prove so accurate that they were still in use long after his death.

His companion in early exploratory trips, George Bass, also died young, disappearing under mysterious circumstances in the Pacific.

THE OTTOMAN MAP OF ANTARCTICA?

Australia was not the only 'counterweight' to the northern hemisphere. The continent of Antarctica lay at the South Pole. It was not fully mapped until the twentieth century, but a great cartographic mystery surrounds its discovery.

The Piri Reis map, which was discovered in 1929, is attributed to the famous Admiral Piri Reis of the Turkish Fleet and dated to 1513. It is drawn on gazelle skin and has been expertly authenticated. Piri Reis is known to have copied a number of useful maps held in the Imperial Library in Constantinople—he

made no attempt to disguise the fact that they were copied and made notations on them to that effect. He noted in the margins that the original of this map dated to around 330 BC, the time of Alexander the Great, and he had added information from several other charts. Most of his source maps were dated to the fourth century AD, though some may well, in their turn, have been copies of earlier maps.

This is the world's most controversial map. It depicts the west coast of Africa, the east coast of South America and, to the south, the coast of Antarctica, in detail. Not only would this have been extraordinary in 1513 but, far more importantly, he drew the coastline as it would have been if it were free of ice. The last time the coastline could have been viewed like that was 4000 BC …

The Piri Reis map is also remarkably accurate in terms of latitude and projection.

RIGHT: The 1513 Piri Reis map, based on ancient sources, is one of the most accurate maps of the 1500s, charting the Atlantic Ocean and the continents that flank it to the east and west. Controversially, however, the coastline extends below South America to link up with Antarctica as it appeared in 4000 BC.

THE MOUNTAINS
OF THE MOON

Of all the places mentioned in Ptolemy's *Geographia* (c. 150 AD), none aroused more speculation and fascination, then and for centuries afterwards, than the origin of the great Nile River and the identity of the Mountains of the Moon from which the Nile was said to rise. In the fifth century BC the Greek writer Herodotus had described his visit to Egypt and his travels up the Nile River as far as Elephantine. There he met a priest who was convinced that he knew the secret source of the Nile. The priest confidently described two mountains, called Crophi and Mophi, each containing a huge bottomless fountain whose waters mingled to become the source of the Nile. Herodotus, who was nobody's fool and was remarkably adept at detecting the flaws in many of the more creative stories he heard, expressed characteristic and perfectly reasonable doubts about the Egyptian priest's ideas.

Nevertheless, six centuries later, Ptolemy included a version of the priest's story in *Geographia*.

He was partly influenced by some rather persuasive corroborative evidence provided by a merchant named Diogenes, who reported that he had made a journey inland from Rhapta, a now lost ancient trading port on the coast of East Africa. Rhapta was regarded at the time as being on the edge of the known world. To the south, ships travelled into a region around the equator known as the Doldrums, where the monsoonal winds of the north and the trade winds of the south seem to cancel each other out, and sailing ships can be entirely becalmed for weeks.

Diogenes recounted how he had undertaken a twenty-five day trek inland, which had led him to the source of the Nile. He described the Nile River as flowing from a group of very high mountains covered with snow into two great lakes. Experts argue about the identity of the place Diogenes saw, suggesting that it was Mount Kilimanjaro, or even claim that his entire story was a fabrication. But it is possible that he was the first Westerner to see the source of the White Nile, and his description is remarkably accurate.

Ptolemy finally wrote in *Geographia*, 'Around this bay the Aethiopian Anthropophagi dwell, and from these toward the west are the Mountains of the Moon, from which the lakes of the Nile receive snow water'. Ptolemy could not resist the interesting addition of cannibalistic Africans (Aethiopian Anthropophagi), and in following passages he adds descriptions of some unlikely animals to be found in the lands bordering Libya, where all elephants were born white, and mysterious rhinocerosopusses prowled.

Both Alexander the Great and Julius Caesar were lured by stories of the fabled Mountains of the Moon and contemplated sending expeditions. The emperor Nero did send expeditionary centurions, but they failed to pass the great barrier of the Sudd—the vast swamp in southern Sudan with its endlessly changing channels, dense expanses of papyrus and reeds, floating islands of matted plants, fever-carrying mosquitoes, crocodiles and wallowing hippopotami. In major wet seasons, the Sudd can extend over 130,000 square kilometres (50,200 square miles).

The earliest known map to show the entire African continent, albeit much distorted, appeared with some variations in Sebastian Münster's works *Geographia* (1540) and *Cosmographia* (1544). Münster was the most influential cartographer of his day, and his African map included Ptolemy's two lakes fed by waters from the Montes Lunae, or Mountains of the Moon (see pages 218–19).

In 1570, Ortelius created a map of Africa far better proportioned than Münster's. Ptolemy's two lakes were still included, although they were located further south. In 1630 the Dutch cartographer William Janszoon produced a map of greater accuracy, ornamented with beautiful, detailed graphics, which again showed Ptolemy's twin lakes as the source of the Nile.

By the late eighteenth century, doubts were being cast on Ptolemy's Mountains of the Moon, but Abbé Clouet's map, studied by all good French schoolchildren after its publication in 1787, continued to show them as the source of the Nile. John Cary's 1805 map—of exemplary layout and up-to-date geographical information—still showed the Blue Nile and the White Nile emerging from the Mountains of the Moon, although the latter were depicted as an extension of the Mountains of Kong stretching all the way from West Africa. Fortunately for future exploration and trade, no such continuous barrier existed.

SEEKING THE WHITE NILE

The Mountains of the Moon were destined to remain cloaked in mystery for many centuries, and were increasingly regarded as a myth. Then in the nineteenth century, that Victorian age of great exploratory expeditions and quixotic endeavours, a British Army officer, John Speke, finally succeeded in discovering both Lake Victoria and the source of the Nile.

John Hanning Speke served in the army in India, where he took part in several battles. He spent his leave exploring and game hunting in the Himalayas and entered the then remote kingdom of Tibet. On taking furlough from the 46th Regiment of the Bengal Native Infantry in 1854 after completing ten years' army service he resolved to explore and hunt game in Africa. In Aden, he met the famous swashbuckling explorer, linguist and writer Richard Francis Burton, who had recently become the first modern European to enter the Islamic holy city of Mecca. Burton was planning a hunting trip combined with a trek into East Africa, with the goal of locating Ptolemy's Mountains of the Moon and perhaps the source of the White Nile. Speke was invited to join the party when one of its members unexpectedly died. After preliminary separate explorations in Somalia (Burton to repeat his earlier feat by travelling to what is now modern Ethiopia and entering the ancient walled Islamic city-state of Hârer, becoming the first known European to survive the attempt, and Speke to explore the Wadi Nogal)

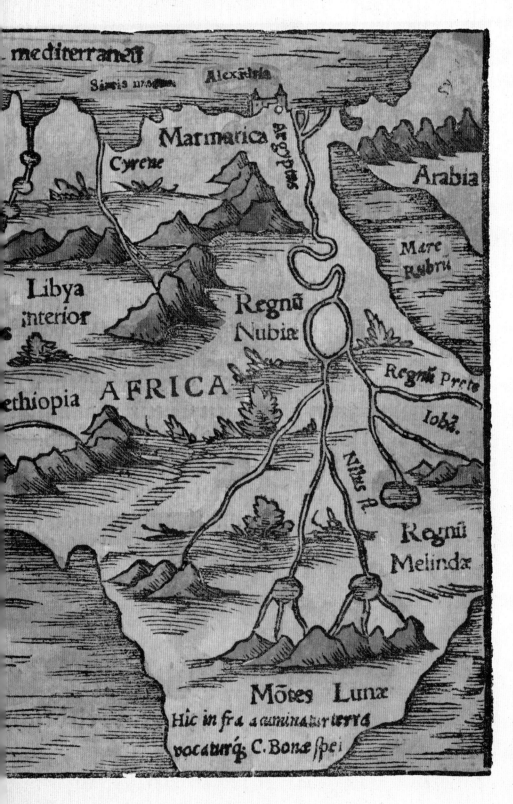

LEFT: The earliest known map of the African continent, by Sebastian Münster, 1540, with the Mountains of the Moon in southern Africa clearly depicted as the source of the Nile.

they rejoined forces. Their camp was attacked by Somali tribesmen near Berberah, bringing their first exploration to a disastrous end, with one member of the expedition killed. Speke sustained several severe spear wounds before escaping and Burton was speared through both cheeks. Burton wrote about this terrible experience in *First Footsteps in East Africa*, published in 1856. He went on to non-combatant duties for the British army while Speke went on to serve in the Crimean War.

The siren call of African adventure soon came again. Burton was commissioned by the British Royal Geographical Society to discover the source of the Nile and invited Speke to join him in searching for a great lake called Tanganyika, said to lie in the heart of the continent, which might prove to be the source of the White Nile. This was destined to become a journey to hell, beginning in 1857 and lasting until the spring of 1859. The route had been closed off by Arabs, and after considerable delays Speke and Burton chose to enter central Africa through Zanzibar. Both men suffered appallingly from tropical diseases and parasites, and Speke became temporarily both deaf and semi-blind. The expedition was under-funded and suffered from desertions. Nevertheless, Burton and Speke became the first Westerners to see Lake Tanganyika (which is now bordered by four countries, Tanzania, Burundi, Zambia, and the Democratic Republic of Congo), and known to be both the second-largest by volume and second-deepest fresh-water lake in the world. They stayed long enough to explore a section of the shoreline. On the northern side, high mountains enclosed the lake, and Speke hopefully marked these on their map as the Mountains of the

Moon, although they had disproved Burton's theory that Lake Tanganyika was the source of the Nile.

Speke and Burton then turned back towards the coast to rest at Tabora, in present-day Tanzania, where they were told of a vast lake that lay to the north. By then Burton was too weak to continue, so Speke went on alone, making what he called a 'flying trip' and discovering and naming Lake Victoria (Victoria Nyanza). Based on its immense size he was convinced it would prove to be the source of the Nile. Burton disagreed. According to Burton's journal, 'We had scarcely, however, breakfasted, before he announced to me the startling fact that he had discovered the sources of the Nile … he felt at once no doubt but that the "lake at his feet gave birth to that interesting river which has been the subject of so much speculation and the object of so many explorers"'.

Speke returned to England ahead of Burton and created an irreversible, very public, and famous rift with his companion in exploration. It was the age when huge prestige attached to successful exploration and the Royal Geographical Society, founded in 1830, reigned supreme. (Though it might have been a little exaggerated, the depiction of the Reform Club in the film *Around the World in Eighty Days* (1956), set in 1872, was not far from the reality of the Royal Geographical Society of the time.) Despite what was supposedly a gentlemen's agreement to make a joint presentation of a paper about their discoveries, for whatever reason Speke went ahead and presented a paper on his own on 8 May 1859, in which he truthfully laid claim to having discovered Lake Victoria and expressed his belief that it was the source of the Nile. Just thirteen days later Burton arrived back in England to hear that the paper had already been presented. Burton and Speke finally presented a joint paper in June.

Before Burton had even reached England, however, Speke had persuaded the president of the Royal Geographical Society, Sir Roderick Murchison, to fund another expedition to confirm his belief in Lake Victoria as the source of the Nile. The rift between Burton and Speke only expanded when Speke chose the inexperienced Captain James Augustus Grant, whom he had known in India, to accompany him on what was to be his third and final journey into the interior of Africa in 1860. The men set off from Zanzibar and reached Lake Victoria in 1861. Speke and Grant mapped part of the shoreline before Speke went off on his own to find the source of the Nile, arranging to meet Grant downstream.

Speke finally reached the northern shore in 1862, after being detained for months by his involvement in the internal power struggles affecting the newly installed young Kabaka, Muteesa, of the old kingdom of Buganda, who was destined to be the last in the dynastic line of more than thirty kings. Buganda, on the northern shore of Lake Victoria, is today part of modern Uganda. Here Speke at last found the falls that marked the place where Lake Victoria gave birth to the Nile. He had solved the mystery that had haunted adventurous spirits since the days of Herodotus.

He named the waterfall the Ripon Falls in honour of George Robinson, First Marquess of Ripon. In 1954 the construction of the Owen Falls Dam would submerge the Ripon Falls and the source of the Nile forever.

Speke and Grant had been told of yet another lake lying northeast of Lake Victoria and planned to explore it, but they were refused access to the lake by Buganda's neighbour Bunyoro, a country occupying almost the entire eastern shore of what would later be named Lake Albert. Warfare in the area also prevented them from following the course of the Nile, which had been their intention, but they followed it as closely as they could, gaining permission to at least travel north through Bunyoro. They then moved on to Gondokoro in Sudan, about 1200 kilometres (750 miles) from Khartoum, established as a trading outpost by John Petherick, the British consul and merchant after they set out for Zanzibar. Two and a half years later Speke and Grant reached Gondokoro, exhausted and very lean.

Petherick had gone game hunting, but they were welcomed with a thoroughly British cup of tea (though possibly hoping for something even more bracing) by Samuel White Baker and Baker's beautiful and much younger unofficial second wife, Florence. Florence was said to have been born Barbara Maria Szász in Transylvania and captured by white slave traders. She was held for some time in a harem in the Ottoman Empire before being offered for sale. Apparently Baker purchased (or rescued) her from a slave market at Vidin on the southern bank of the Danube.

Baker was one of those extraordinary, larger than life characters who seemed to epitomise the unstoppable empire-building of Great Britain in the nineteenth century—a rugged, wealthy, adventure loving, enormously charming man of great strength, legendary energy and considerable intellect who seemed to pack several lifetimes of achievement into one. Like Burton and Speke, Baker had dreamed of discovering the source of the Nile.

THE ILLUSTRATED LONDON NEWS

No. 1211.—VOL. XLIII.   SATURDAY, JULY 4, 1863   WITH A SUPPLEMENT, FIVEPENCE

WAR WITH JAPAN.

IF a sarcastic enemy of this country were asked to define what was meant by the advancement of civilisation by England, he would probably reply the opening of new markets for trade at the point of the bayonet. Although, as good patriots, we may reject the sneer, as men of common sense we must accept the fact. Passing by other and less important, though, so far as the theory is concerned, not less significant instances, take that of China. For how many years did we offer civilisation in the shape of bales of goods for sale to a country so benighted as not to understand the symbol; and how long was it that we were kept on the threshold of a land, the exclusiveness of which gave it an air of enchantment to our eyes? But the urgency of our

peculiar principle of civilising the barbarian was not to be denied; and, after a protracted series of mistakes in ravaging the coasts and destroying provincial peasants, who were of less account in the estimation of the ruling powers than so many pigs of the Emperor's own breed, in the course of a third or fourth Chinese war we found ourselves in Pekin; and at last we were understood. It was discovered at the fountain head of Chinese policy that the armed Englishman was only the precursor of the enterprising trader; and, so far as things have yet gone, there is every reason to believe that the Celestial Empire is at length opened to the commerce of Europe, with special advantages attaching to that of England. On the abstract question of general policy involved in the system of

the invasion by the sword to make way for the invasion of commerce it is useless now to dilate; but, in reference to the conduct of the details of that policy, a useful lesson has been learnt from the course of events in our successive operations in China. It has been clearly demonstrated that little wars, even with Asiatics so unwarlike as the Chinese, are mistakes. When we left off something like buccaneering on the seaboard of China, and waged war as between Queen and Emperor, the difficulties were found to be less, and the results actual. As it has been with China, so it seems that it is likely to be with Japan. The latest accounts inform us that, ere this, war has been distinctly declared against Japan by England, France, and Holland, and the question arises how

RECEPTION OF CAPTAINS SPEKE AND GRANT BY THE ROYAL GEOGRAPHICAL SOCIETY.—SEE PAGE 17.

Departing from Cairo in 1861 with what must have been one of the most luxuriously equipped of all African expeditions (the food was said to have been supplied by Fortnum and Mason), he and Florence arrived in Khartoum a year later, where he received a request from the Royal Geographical Society to find Grant and Speke. How odd that in such a huge continent and in such vast wilderness, not only did Stanley calmly encounter Livingstone, but that Baker should arrive in Gondoroko in Sudan followed by Speke and Grant a fortnight later. Baker had successfully explored some of the tributaries of the Nile.

When Speke told him of his great success, Baker was understandably depressed that his dream of being the first to discover the source of the Nile had been snatched from him. However, with a remarkable generosity of spirit that went quite unappreciated later in London, Speke and Grant, according to Baker, 'with characteristic candour and generosity gave me the map of their route, showing that they had been unable to complete the actual exploration of the Nile and that a most important portion remained to be demonstrated'. Speke and Grant were also generous enough to offer well-substantiated information about Lake Albert, on which they had expended so much time and fruitless effort.

Baker's explorations led to the discovery and naming of Lake Albert in 1864. He wrote, 'I rushed into the lake, and thirsty with heat and fatigue, and with a heart full of gratitude I drank

LEFT: Cover of the Illustrated London News *from 4 July, 1863 commemorating the reception of Captains Speke and Grant at the Royal Geographical Society.*

from the source of the Nile'. Unfortunately it wasn't. But he did establish where the Nile again emerged from Lake Albert. His explorations led to honours, including a gold medal bestowed by the Royal Geographical Society and soon afterward a knighthood. The two very popular books based on his travels, and a novel, sold exceptionally well. Baker also travelled through Egypt as a companion to the decidedly rakish Prince of Wales and future King Edward VII. But Baker failed to endear himself to Queen Victoria as a result of his irregular lifestyle. Between his purchasing his wife from a slave bazaar and absent-mindedly forgetting to marry her throughout their entire exhausting time in Africa, Her Majesty was not amused.

Sir Samuel and Lady Baker discreetly married after this African adventure, and together with 1700 Egyptian troops undertook a military expedition into the Upper Nile to suppress the activities of slave traders. For four years Sir Samuel was the Governor-General of the territory of the Equatorial Provinces, and pasha and major general in the Ottoman army, before handing the reins to the man the world would remember as Gordon of Khartoum. Against all odds Baker lived to seventy-two. After further travels, through North America and Japan, and the publication of more books, he died on his estate in south Devon and lies buried in Brompton Cemetery in London.

Speke would follow a very different life path. Leaving Baker and his wife at Gondoroko, he travelled down to Khartoum, where he cabled the Royal Geographical Society in London with one of the most momentous messages ever recorded: 'The Nile is settled'. It would be the high point of his life and the last truly happy one. Returning to London, he discovered that in Burton's eyes the Nile was very much not settled. Speke had not followed the river all the way downstream, which left room for doubt. Nor had he circumnavigated Lake Victoria to establish that he had indeed explored the same lake that he had discovered in 1858. Speke published *Journal of the Discovery of the Source of the Nile* in 1863. Members of the Royal Geographical Society were split in their convictions for Lake Victoria as the source of the Nile, some supporting Burton, others Speke.

In 1864 Burton and a co-author, geographer James McQueen, published *The Nile Basin*, which refuted Speke's claims and even, quite incomprehensibly, reverted to the theory that Lake Tanganyika was the source of the Nile.

The Royal Geographical Society arranged a debate between the two explorers, to be held in Bath in September 1864. The day before the debate Speke died of a self-inflicted gunshot wound while hunting partridge. It was never entirely decided whether he committed suicide or had died as the result of a simple accident. There were even rumours at the time hinting that he and Burton had been lovers. He was buried in Somerset—a sadly short life of just thirty-seven years for such an extraordinary man. Mount Speke in the Rwenzori Mountains of Uganda are named for him.

Was there any truth in the rumours that he and Burton had been lovers? After all, Burton was made of the stuff that modern tabloids would love to get their hands on, ripe with possibilities, and his disdain for the prurience of Victorian society had been well aired. No one will ever know, because on his death in 1890 in Trieste his wife burned all her husband's journals—a strange act for someone who had shared many of his later travels, but perhaps in obedience to his last instructions. (Elizabeth Arundel had become engaged to Burton just before he left to discover the Nile and finally married him in 1861, becoming undoubtedly his greatest supporter.)

Burton was an immensely complex man, intense and irascible, an obsessive game hunter, a brilliant intellectual who found himself expelled from Oxford University (his interests in Asian languages, philosophy and esoteric studies lay well outside the prescribed undergraduate program), a poet and author, soldier, explorer, inveterate traveller, linguist (he was fluent in a number of languages, including Hindi, Swahili, Arabic, Persian and Turkish), and a great student of Asian cultures. Burton was the author of forty-three books, and created the definitive translation of the *Arabian Nights*, entitled *The Thousand Nights and a Night*, and *The Perfumed Garden*. He made a great deal of money from a private publication through the Karma-Shastra Society of his translation of the *Kama Sutra of Vatsyayana* (printing through a publisher would have been a recipe for prosecution and imprisonment for both Burton and the publisher). He was hungry for erotic experiences and had a lurid reputation as a libertine, which in the end apparently saw the Church of England refuse him burial in Westminster Abbey.

The poet Wilfrid Scawen Blunt was less than complimentary, describing Burton's face as 'dark, cruel, treacherous, with eyes like a wild beast'. He was certainly a contrast with the puritanical Speke, who might have provided the model for nineteenth century muscular Christianity with a colonial arrogance that was not unusual in his day. It was certainly destined to be a difficult partnership—Speke easily offended and Burton easily offending.

THE 'RAINMAKER' UNVEILED

As for the great debate that never was, the Welsh-born and American by adoption Henry Morton Stanley settled the question once and for all by circumnavigating Lake Victoria in 1874, three years after he found Dr Livingstone in Tanganyika. This proved that Speke had been quite correct in identifying Lake Victoria as the source of the Nile.

Despite his success in discovering Lake Albert, Sir Samuel Baker failed to discover the Mountains of the Moon, yet he was so very close. The great Italian explorer Romolo Gessi, a member of General Charles George Gordon's administration in the Egyptian Sudan, was the first European to circumnavigate Lake Albert, but he also failed to see the Mountains of the Moon. That prize was left to Henry Stanley on his last expedition in 1889, which lasted a gruelling 987 days and covered more than 9650 kilometres (6000 miles).

While Stanley was on the shores of Lake Albert, a rare event occurred. The clouds parted, revealing the brilliantly white peaks and glaciers of a range now known as Rwenzori, making him the first Western European to see what are still referred to as the Mountains of the Moon. They lie just north of the equator between Lake Albert and Lake Edward. The mystery of the origins of the White Nile and the Mountains of the Moon had finally been resolved. An age of heroic adventure in Africa and a quest that had lasted more than 2500 years had ended. And the answer proved not to be simple.

The Nile was initially fed by the streams and rivers flowing into Lake Victoria. At the northern rim of Lake Victoria the waters of the lake spilled over the now lost Ripon Falls to form the river that would be known at this point as the Victoria Nile. It began its complex journey through intermediate lakes including, most importantly, Lake Albert, which was also charged with the waters of the smaller Lake Edward via the Semliki River in the Western Rift Valley. Spilling out of Lake Albert at its far northern end, the river resumed its northward journey as the Albert Nile, later becoming the White Nile.

On reaching Khartoum it joined the Blue Nile to become the mighty Nile River that watered the land of Egypt and controlled the lives of all who lived there for millennia. The source of the Blue Nile had been sighted at Lake Tana in Ethiopia by the Spanish Jesuit missionary Padre Pedro Påez in 1618.

Ptolemy's two great lakes that created the White Nile can reasonably be assumed to be Victoria and Albert. The fabled Mountains of the Moon, the massively looming range of Rwenzori, were not the ultimate source of the Nile, as once believed, but they were certainly located within the complex of rivers and lakes that feeds the emerging Nile. The great watershed of Rwenzori feeds into the Semliki River, which then flows into Lake Albert.

The mountains retain their mystery to this day. Located on the Uganda–Congo border, they are often shrouded in cloud, giving them their well-earned name among the local people of Rwenzori, the 'rainmaker'. But when the clouds clear another of its names, Gambaragara ('my eyes pain'), becomes obvious, as the awesome range is snow capped and contains brilliantly reflective white glaciers. The mountain chain is 120 kilometres (75 miles) long, with six major peaks—Mount Stanley, Mount Speke, Mount Baker, Mount Emin, Mount Gessi and Mount Luigi di Savoia. Its seventh and tallest peak, Mount Margherita, reaches 5120 metres (16,800 feet), making Rwenzori the highest mountain range in Africa, and Mount Margherita the third-highest mountain after freestanding Mount Kenya (first discovered by Europeans in 1849) and Mount Kilimanjaro (discovered in 1848). Unlike Kenya and Kilimanjaro, which are both of volcanic origin, the great peaks of Rwenzori were created by the massive underlying forces in the Earth's crust that formed the Great Rift Valley between three and four million years ago. There are many beautiful glacial lakes in the range—could these have been the Egyptian priest's depthless fountains inside the mountains as described to Herodotus?

Rwenzori is extraordinary for its luxuriant plant life, much of it on a gargantuan scale, at least partly due to the incessant rain, which falls 350 days of the year. This must have added to the mythical reputation of these mountains. Rwenzori has been described as the most remarkable tropical biosphere on Earth and was gazetted as a World Heritage site in 1994, with giant moss-covered heath trees reaching a height of 12 metres (40 feet), enormous senecios and lobelias up to 6 metres (20 feet) tall. The range is also the home of vulnerable mountain gorillas, which the American primatologist Dian Fossey researched and eventually died trying to save from poachers, together with elephants, chimpanzees, leopards, antelopes, giant forest hogs and Rwenzori colobus monkeys. Because of heavy hunting and poaching, particularly in the 1970s and 1980s, none of these animals exist in the numbers encountered by nineteenth century explorers, and many larger species are rarely seen now. How much less believable would Ptolemy's Mountains of the Moon have been if he had also written of giant plants, mountain gorillas, rain that never ends and massive glaciers in the tropics!

RIGHT: A German version of Speke and Grant's explorations in central Africa, 1860–64, to Lake Victoria and, ultimately, the source of the Nile.

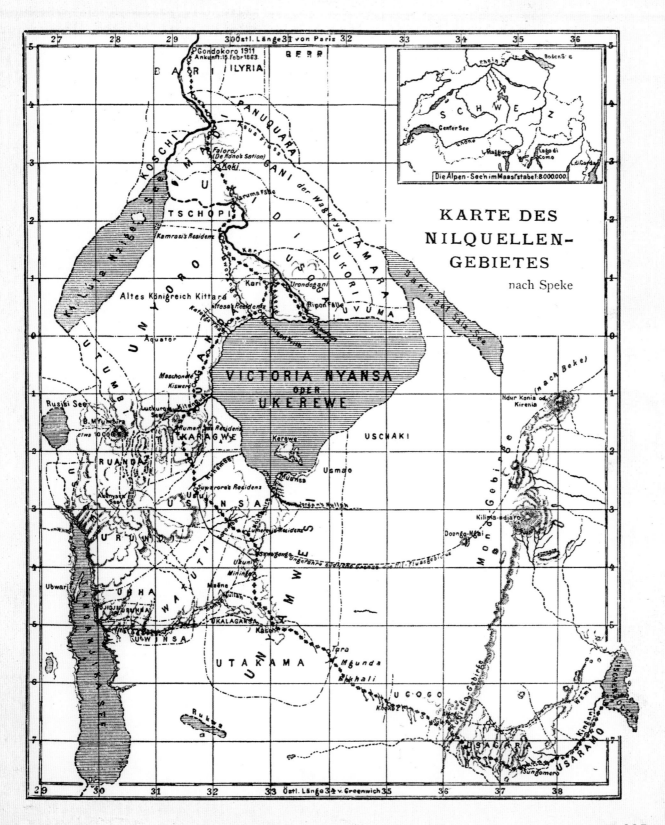

KARTE DES
NILQUELLEN-
GEBIETES

nach Speke

Maslen's new Amazon

It would be reasonable to assume that the nineteenth century would be a time when mythological locations would be subject to intense scrutiny, but in Australia a belief in a huge inland sea drew one expedition after another, all determined to locate it. The long inland river systems that explorers encountered and mapped west of the Great Dividing Range during this period of exploration included the Darling, Bogan, Murrumbidgee, Murray, Namoi, Gwydir and McIntyre rivers. Their discoverers were convinced that many of those rivers must eventually empty into a vast inland sea, or that they were tributaries of some great rival to the Amazon River.

Apparently no one took into serious account Australia's already obvious aridity, severe droughts, high evaporation rates and the resulting lack of water needed to create such a vast body. Some of these rivers could be reduced to little more than a string of waterholes in droughts that could last several years.

The wonderfully creative map of Australia created by Thomas J. Maslen, a former officer of the East India Company, did nothing to suppress such wild hopes. His map shows the continent's coastline reasonably accurately, although the Great Australian Bight reveals considerable guesswork.

Published in 1827 in his book *The Friend of Australia* and designed to promote exploration, the map reveals a river system that the Great South Land could only dream of, and at least as grand as the Amazon. At its heart, and straddling the Queensland–Northern Territory border, is a huge inland sea fed by numerous broad, long rivers flowing westward from the Great Dividing Range, including the Macquarie and Castlereagh rivers. Flowing westward from the inland sea, which he labelled Delta of Australia, an extraordinarily wide river twists its way to the northern coast of Western Australia, a journey of thousands of kilometres, opening into a huge island-dotted delta. The massive river effectively separated most of northern and southern Australia, which he labelled respectively Australindia and Anglicania. An equally imaginative second river system drained the deserts inland from the southern coast of Western Australia and South Australia, reaching the sea in a huge estuary west of Adelaide.

In 1844 explorer Charles Sturt, still driven by his faith in an inland sea, set out on his last attempt to find it. Instead he encountered the vast, waterless Simpson Desert, and the dream was finally put to rest. At the heart of the continent lay a desert more than 900 kilometres (560 miles) wide that would be the last place in Australia to be mapped. More than a hundred parallel dunes, up to 200 kilometres (125 miles) long and reaching to 35 metres (115 feet) high, characterised a landscape ironically described as a 'frozen sea'.

A new quest replaced the search for an inland sea, as explorers took on two of the greatest tests of endurance on the planet—traversing the Great South Land, the driest continent on Earth, from south to north, a distance of up to 3700 kilometres (2300 miles), and from east to west (an even greater distance of 4000 kilometres/ 2500 miles).

The expedition of nineteen men led by Robert O'Hara Burke and William Wills, and funded by the newly independent colony of Victoria, accomplished the first of those challenges, though it claimed the lives of both leaders. Their 1860 plan was to travel overland from Melbourne to the foot of the Gulf of Carpentaria, reducing the overall distance to be covered to 2800 kilometres (1740 miles), and using the Darling River in New South Wales and Cooper's Creek to help them reach their destination. They reached Cooper's Creek after three months, and the party was split, with eight men moving onward. After waiting ten days for supplies to arrive at an encampment just inside the present Queensland border, the decision was made to split the party again and just four men were chosen to push northward to the Gulf. In reality they were still very far from their objective. Although they had a reasonably easy first leg for the journey, encountering waterholes almost daily, the many ridges of the Selwyn Ranges near Cloncurry proved almost insurmountable, with their camels sweating with fear, in pain and bleeding. Moving further north, they ran into the monsoon season and were forced to wade through interminable floodwaters and deep mud. When they finally reached the coast it was to find an impenetrable forest of mangroves.

Maslen's new Amazon

The trip from Cooper's Creek had taken two months and they had used up two-thirds of their rations.

The return journey might be better not described—they were forced to live on snakes, their camels, and John King's favourite horse, Billy. It was also recorded that Charles Gray, the oldest of the party, was found eating some flour in an attempt to ameliorate constant dysentery and was beaten by Burke. Gray died soon afterward. All of the group suffered severe dysentery. In one of the most bitter ironies of nineteenth century exploration, the remaining three men staggered into the Cooper's Creek camp with their last ounce of energy, four months and five days after they had departed, to find the campfire still warm and the site all but emptied of food other than a camel box containing provisions which had been buried beside a tree marked 'Dig'. Convinced that the forward party had perished, William Brahe, in charge of the depot group, and the other members of the party, had finally packed up camp and departed southward to the Darling, having waited a month and five days longer than instructed by Burke, and even then only because one of the men, William Patten the blacksmith, was gravely ill. Burke, Wills and King had missed him by just seven hours. Burke and Wills perished near the deserted camp, being forced to stay near waterholes along the Cooper, and dependent on food from the Yandruwandha people. John King survived, although in pitiable condition, and was rescued in 1861 by Edwin Welch, the relief party's surveyor.

Although he probably did not think so at the time, John McDouall Stuart was to be luckier. Also setting off in 1860, he had mounted a parallel attempt to cross the continent, leaving from Adelaide. He was forced back by the desolate Red Centre of Australia, but at least lived to tell his tale back in South Australia. The dream of a great Amazonian river system draining a fertile inland could not have been more cruel or inaccurate.

RIGHT: If only … Thomas Maslen's fantastical 1827 map of Australia included a huge inland sea fed by numerous tributaries flowing from sweeping mountain ranges.

PART SIX

LANDS OF GOLDEN DREAMS

❧

CARVING UP THE NEW WORLD

DREAMING OF EL DORADO

TREASURE ISLANDS, GIANTS AND
A MOUNTAIN OF SILVER

*LEFT: A seventeenth century edition of Jodocus Hondius's map of South
America which shows Manoa in Guiana.*

*FOLLOWING PAGES: Print depicting native South Americans trading
with explorers in Patagonia by Gallo Gallina c. 1832–34.*

CARVING UP
THE NEW WORLD

The New World and its wealth were rapidly carved up among the European nations. Through the Indies and Central America, the Spaniards were too strong for any other nation to compete, even if they had the stomach for it, and Portugal instead set its sights on South America. So fierce was the competition between the two great seafaring nations that Pope Alexander VI interceded, and in 1493 issued a papal bull that arbitrarily divided the non-Christian lands of the world, including the New World, into two 'zones of influence', one for each of these two rival Catholic countries. In 1494 a formal agreement between Spain and Portugal was signed at Tordesillas in Spain. France was not included in the division of spoils, nor was England.

It seems impossible to imagine now that Rome could calmly have divided much of the non-Christian world between two European nations, without thought or reference to the will of the people whose countries were fought over. The papal bull set the line of demarcation along a circle passing

100 leagues (556 kilometres/345 miles) west of the Cape Verde Islands (an archipelago off the West African coast) and through both the Arctic and Antarctic poles, effectively handing the entire New World to Spain together with the Philippines, while Portugal was awarded Africa, India and the East Indies. The Treaty of Tordesillas, however, drew the circle through a point 370 leagues (2056 kilometres/1280 miles) west of the Cape Verde Islands, putting eastern Brazil under Portuguese influence. In 1533 Pope Clement VII modified the treaty so that France could at last officially partake in this extraordinary carving up of the non-Christian world. Officially, and in reality, given the vast power of the Church at the time, all European monarchs were bound by the papal ruling.

From the time Columbus founded the first permanent Spanish colony, Isabella on Hispaniola, during his second voyage to the New World in 1493, events moved with great rapidity, driven by the rumours of untold wealth to be gained. Puerto Rico was colonised by Juan Ponce de León in 1508; Jamaica was conquered in 1509; and Cuba was taken two years later. The inhabitants of island after island were enslaved and, as Ponce de León had done in Puerto Rico, set to work in the mines and to construction work.

Few voices seem to have been raised against slavery in those early days, other than that of the compassionate Bartolomé de las Casas, who fought hard and long for the rights of indigenous peoples. But in the end not even his role as a priest could protect him from the threats of settlers, and he was forced to leave the New World in 1547 at the age of seventy-two in fear of his life as a result of his uncompromising stance. Even fewer voices were raised against the wholesale destruction of the great cultures of the New World. The native populations were devastated by ill treatment and by diseases introduced from the West against which they had no immunity. Spanish settlement extended from the islands through to Central and South America. Greed was everywhere, from royalty downward.

One of the most lyrical images of the exploration of new worlds comes from the John Keats poem 'On First Looking Into Chapman's Homer' in the nineteenth century:

Then felt I like some watcher of the skies
When a new planet swims into his ken;
Or like stout Cortez when with eagle eyes
He star'd at the Pacific—and all his men
Look'd at each other with a wild surmise
Silent, upon a peak in Darien.

Few poets are loath to twist a fact or two in creating the desired effect, and the great Keats was certainly no exception, but how ugly was the reality of this historic event? It was of course the Spanish conquistador and Governor of Veragua, Vasco Núñez de Balboa, who discovered the Pacific by devious and vengeful means and at the cost of many lives, not 'stout Cortez'. Balboa was probably no worse than many others in the new colonies driven by greed and by a fair degree of superiority and self-righteousness, but he is sufficient to demonstrate the times.

BALBOA

Vasco Núñez de Balboa was the son of a nobleman and a descendant of the lords of Balboa. He accompanied Juan de la Cosa to the Americas in 1500, exploring the coast of eastern Panama and Columbia. He then became a failed plantationer on Hispaniola, and deep in debt, escaped with his dog as a stowaway bound for San Sebastián de Uraba (later Cartagena de Indias in Colombia). Although Balboa was discovered, he won over both the captain and crew, and when San Sebastián was found to have been destroyed by the natives, proposed the city be rebuilt at a more favourable and fertile place, Darién. Hostile natives were awaiting them also at Darién, but the Spanish prevailed. Balboa proceeded to remove Fernández de Enciso from office, and was involved in the removal of Governor de Nicuesa from office (he and a small crew were forcibly put to sea with few supplies in an

'Núñez de Balboa, appalled to find homosexual practices among the natives, has them thrown to fierce dogs who devour them': Theodor de Bry in Grand Voyages: Discovering the New World, 1599.

unseaworthy boat and were never seen again). Balboa became governor.

Once Balboa had been officially recognised as the governor of Veragua, the five Spanish territories of Central America at the time, he took up plundering and slave taking throughout the islands of the West Indies, while informing the authorities back in Spain of his kindness to the native peoples and his diligence in stamping out sinful behaviour.

The utter brutality that he displayed towards homosexuals and transsexuals was not atypical. Homosexuality was considered a normal human variation, completely accepted and by no means a vice in the pre-Columbian world of the Aztecs, Incas, Mayans, Zapotecs, Moches and other tribes. But Balboa, encountering a number of courtiers, including the king's brother, dressed as women and making love to their own sex, was beside himself and spitting venom. The Spaniards quite commonly used their dogs to dominate the native peoples, and Balboa in an act of extreme cruelty ordered that his dogs be turned loose on forty of the men who had been dressed as women. It is said that they were all torn to shreds.

That Balboa's behaviour was far too typical of conquistador behaviour in the New World can be illustrated by the poignant indictment of them made by an Indian who had been sentenced to be burned at the stake. Asked if he wished to be converted to Christianity before dying so that his soul might be saved, the Indian asked whether he would encounter white men in Heaven. When told that of course they would be there, he refused to be converted for, he said, he would not go to a place where men could be so cruel.

Balboa was a man of his time in the New World, a man from a Spain that still had the Inquisition, and a time of emerging imperialism in both Spain and Portugal, the super powers of their day. Courageous as an explorer, a political intriguer with the best of them, plundering and enslaving, often ruthless and brutal, theatrical (one can scarcely imagine a more dramatic moment than when he waded into the Pacific in full armour, holding aloft in one hand a sword and in the other a standard bearing an image of the Virgin Mary to claim the Pacific Ocean and all its adjoining lands in the name of the Spanish king), he was also a born leader of men.

In the end, betrayed by the intrigue of rival factions in Panama and swearing his allegiance to the Spanish king to the end, Balboa was put on trial with four of his followers and, despite the somewhat belated honours showered on him by Spain, was beheaded with his companions. Even at his end, the cruelty that had become so much a part of his world would accompany him: it was recorded that it took three cuts of the axe before he was finally beheaded.

DREAMING OF
EL DORADO

I f the deeply held religious beliefs or the search for an earthly Paradise motivated many quests in the medieval period, by the fifteenth century dreams of riches beyond the most extravagant imaginings, together with the conquest of other lands, became the prime motivation. El Dorado became the symbol of all these searches for elusive treasure and the name entered the language permanently.

The legend of El Dorado began with the Spanish explorer Gonzalo Jiménez de Quesada's discovery of the Muisca nation in what are now the Colombian highlands in 1537. Stories were soon circulated in Quito, the newly conquered Ecuadorian town, of a Golden King, El Rey Dorado. Stories became entangled with other legends, so that finally not only a golden king but also a golden city, called El Dorado, were said to exist.

The Golden King, if not the Golden City, did exist. A century after the discovery of the Muisca nation, the most important novel to be written in the colony of Colombia appeared in 1638, the chronicle of El Carnero, written by the American-born Juan Rodriguez Freile (Freyle). Largely historical, it covered the Spanish conquest, the first century of the New Kingdom of Granada and the founding of Bogotá in 1538. Freile described accurately a religious ceremony that took place on the appointment of a new ruler of the Muisca. The priest-king underwent an initiation, similar in some ways to that undertaken by shamans, withdrawing from the world into a cave, abstaining from women and salt, living only in darkness.

After a period of contemplation away from the noise of the world, the new priest-king's first journey into the light was to Lake Guatavita (near present-day Bogotá) to make offerings to their god. A large raft was made of rushes and decorated. Four braziers were placed on board and lit to burn incense, the smoke mingling with that from the braziers of incense on the shore. Many men and women dressed in the greatest finery boarded the raft and placed at the king's feet great mounds of gold and emeralds as offerings to the god. The king was stripped and his body covered in sticky clay, which was then covered in gold dust. Four priests, also naked, stood beside him, holding their own offerings to the god. When they reached the centre of the lagoon, a banner was raised to signal complete silence. The infinitely valuable cargo of jewels and gold was thrown overboard as an offering designed to restore the harmony of the universe. The banner once again signalled, this time to end the silence, and cheering and the sound of pipes and flutes, dancers and singers came from the shore, welcoming the new ruler of the kingdom.

The Colombian Gold Museum of Bogotá holds the world's largest collection of golden ornaments, some 35,000 items, just a fraction compared with what was taken away by the Spanish invaders. Central to the display in the Salon de la Ofrenda is its most famous object: the brilliantly glowing, perfectly detailed, pure gold model of the Muisca raft.

In 1542 the conquistador Francisco de Orellana led an expedition with Gonzalo Pizarro to find the supposed city of gold, El Dorado. Even the city's pavements were said to be made of the precious metal. The expedition travelled down the Rio Negro and Orellana claimed he found a remarkable civilisation, of well-managed farms and great walled cities. Orellano's tale provoked fascination in Spain and a number of new expeditions were sent, but no evidence was ever found of a hidden city of gold.

THE GOLDEN CITY OF MANOA

Truth rarely gets in the way of a good tale, and the location of El Dorado moved to what Sir Walter Raleigh described as 'the great and golden City of Manoa, which the Spanish call El Dorado', which he believed was located in the highlands of the 'large, and beautiful Empire of Guiana', and founded 'upon a lake of salt water 200 leagues long'. Several expeditions were sent to Guiana (now Guyana) in the hope of discovering gold. One, led by Don Pedro Malaver da Silva in 1530, ended in the death of all the crew at the hands of the Caribs with the exception of Juan Martinez. He appears to have changed his story over time, but at least in one version Martinez lived with the Caribs in a city where the houses were made of gold and precious stones on the banks of Lake Parima, located in Rapunini. The city was called Manoa.

After what was variously described as several months or ten years, he was allowed to leave, laden with precious gifts, and provided with guides to take him to the Orinoco River. There he claimed to have been set upon and robbed. Despite his wounds he reached the island of Margarita off the Venezuelan coast. The monks to whom he told his story clearly believed him. Manoa and the fabled El Dorado were quickly linked and the story spread like wildfire.

Sir Walter Raleigh, who was the most favoured courtier of Queen Elizabeth I of England for some six years (never the wisest of social manoeuvres) found himself challenged for the Queen's favour by the Earl of Essex. Raleigh betrayed his sovereign's affections by having an affair with one of the Queen's ladies-in-waiting, Elizabeth Throckmorton, although he redeemed himself somewhat in the eyes of society by marrying the lady. Like many who offended Elizabeth, he was thrown into the Tower of London by the enraged and jealous queen, where he was forced to cool his heels and his ardour for some time.

Ultimately he was released, and after various naval exploits planned an expedition into Guiana in South America in 1595, rather cheekily sailing up the Orinoco River through Spain's new empire, convinced that the elusive gold of El Dorado was hidden there. As Raleigh also described such rarities as a tribe of headless people, one would think that his honesty might have been challenged. But no. Instead, a cartographer of importance, Jodocus Hondius, included El Dorado on his Dutch-published 1598 map of South America, where it remained until the beginning of the nineteenth century.

In a tale of black humour, another Spanish conquistador, Don Antonio de Berreo, became entangled in Raleigh's search for El Dorado. Don Antonio married in his late fifties a lady much younger than himself called Margarita, the daughter and heir of the rich conquistador Gonzalo Jiménez de Quesada, and through her inheritance became a very wealthy man. In giving his daughter to Berreo, Gonzalo made him take an oath to continue the quest for El Dorado, on which Gonzalo had been engaged for many years. He demanded that Berreo continue the quest 'to the last of his substance and life'. (Berreo was later to tell Sir Walter Raleigh that he had expended 300,000 ducats in carrying out his father-in-law's wishes.) There is no reason to suppose Berreo was eager to conform with his father-in-law's request, although he wrote, 'I judged it no time to rest'. Berreo established a settlement on Trinidad, which was intended to be a launching pad to Guiana and El Dorado, which he planned to reach via the Orinoco River. He made three journeys up the Orinoco in search of the elusive gold of El Dorado. His expeditionary forces numbered hundreds of soldiers, along with porters and horses, each trip resulting in most of his men dying, while his inherited wealth continually shrank. He then settled down, becoming the first governor of Trinidad in 1584, living in the new town of St Joseph, which had been founded by his lieutenant, Domingo de Vera. Together they planned yet another search for El Dorado.

Before landing in Guiana Raleigh stopped in Trinidad and his men set fire to St Joseph, abducting both Berreo and his now elderly deputy, the Portuguese captain Alvaro Jorge, his rivals in the search for El Dorado. Raleigh claimed his actions were justified by Berreo's cruel treatment of the Indians and betrayal of some of Raleigh's

'How the Emperor of Guiana instructed the grooming of noble people when they visited him as guests': Theodor de Bry in Grand Voyages: The Search for El Dorado, *1599.*

crewmen. Raleigh left most of his ships in Trinidad in the port of Curiapan (Punta de Gallo), wandering 640 kilometres (400 miles) by land and river into Guiana, at last releasing his two unfortunate and less than physically fit prisoners in Cumana, Venezuela, when all useful information regarding El Dorado had been extracted from them. The unfortunate men made their way back down the Orinoco and sailed from its mouth back to Trinidad.

In the meantime Domingo de Vera had recruited yet another expeditionary force for Berreo to pursue the search for El Dorado, numbering twenty-eight ships and around 1500 people. By the time de Vera's ships arrived in Trinidad, Berreo had no stomach for further adventure and so Alvaro Jorge, now in his late seventies, took on the captaincy. This final attempt was tragedy on a grand scale: starvation, barbarism and attacks by the natives accounted for most of the expedition. As for Berreo, his wealth exhausted, his daughter's dowry wasted in the pursuit of El Dorado, he made a philosophical comment that might have saved much anguish and many lives had he followed his own advice much earlier: 'In trying to do too much you will end by achieving nothing at all'. He died in 1597 leaving his son Ferdinand equally obsessed with El Dorado and the dream of mending the family fortunes, having learned nothing from his father's latter-day wisdom.

After Raleigh's disastrous Orinoco adventure, his fortunes sunk even further when Elizabeth died and she was succeeded by James I. Raleigh was charged with treason against the king, amid absurd rumours that he was working with the Spanish, condemned to death, then reprieved, but imprisoned for twelve years. During that time he wrote his *History of the World*. When he was finally freed in 1616, like a moth drawn to a flame, he mounted another expedition to find El Dorado, faithfully promising James that he would open a gold mine there without causing an international incident with Spain.

The expedition proved a disaster—Raleigh contracted an incapacitating fever in Guiana, and his lieutenant, Lawrence Keymis, burned a Spanish settlement on the lower Orinoco to the ground. Most importantly in the eyes of James I, however, Raleigh returned to England without the gold of El Dorado. Not surprisingly, the outraged James revived the old charge of treason, and this time there was to be no reprieve. Raleigh was executed in 1618.

RIGHT: Illustration from Sir Walter Raleigh's book The Discovery of the Large, Rich and Beautiful Empire of Guiana with a Relation of the Great and Golden City of Manoa (which the Spaniards call El Dorado).

TREASURE ISLANDS, GIANTS AND A MOUNTAIN OF SILVER

Gold may have been a primary motivation, but silver was also a powerful lure to the expeditionary forces of Portugal and Spain. A legend of boundless silver riches arose as the result of the gifts of silver given by native people to the European survivors of a shipwrecked expedition mounted in 1516 by the Portuguese navigator Juan Diaz de Solis, somewhere around the estuary of the Uruguay and Paraná rivers. It took very little time for the silver objects to become parlayed into a mountain range of solid silver, the Sierra del Plata, lying within a kingdom ruled by a white man.

By the late sixteenth century the Portuguese had named the estuary of the Uruguay and Paraná rivers the Rio de la Plata, under the assumption that it flowed from the Sierra del Plata. As for the silver mountain, it was never found. The nearest region with plentiful silver mines is over 1600 kilometres (1000 miles) away—Argentina, named in 1612, which translates as 'land of silver'.

Even more fanciful and alluring was Ciudad de los Césares, the City of the Caesars. Known by many other names such as the Wandering City, the City of Patagonia, Elelin and Trapananda, the city was said to have been founded by the survivors of a shipwrecked Spanish galleon loaded with vast treasure. The mysterious city appears to be somewhat itinerant, as is the wont of enchanted places, but it is most often located somewhere in an Andean valley in Patagonia. Some say it lies between two mountains, one made of pure gold, the other of diamonds. Still others claim that it appears only fleetingly to humans, or is inhabited by ghosts, or by Patagonian giants.

PATAGONIAN GIANTS

A giant South American race was reported by Ferdinand Magellan during his circumnavigation of the world in the 1520s. The peaceful giants were said to live along the coast of Patagonia and to grow to an improbable 4.5 metres (15 feet). The chronicler of the expedition, Antonio Pigafetta, described an encounter with one of them, recording that the ship's crew came only to the gentle giant's waist, and that he was well proportioned. Oddly, such reports continued through the sixteenth century, one coming from Francis Fletcher, the ship's chaplain on board Sir Francis Drake's ship the *Golden Hind* in 1577, during a three-year circumnavigation of the world. At the time of the sighting, Drake was in the middle of carrying out an extraordinary and exceedingly irregular trial which would end in the execution without authority of one of his captains and supposed co-leader, the aristocratic Thomas Doughty, who together with his brother were accused of actively practising witchcraft and sedition. In such circumstances, an overactive imagination might well conjure giants. Later, Anthony Knivet, who sailed with the English explorer Thomas Cavendish in his second attempt to circumnavigate the world in 1591, claimed to have seen giants 4 metres (12 feet) tall. South American legends record several tribes, such as the Chanak of Peru, whose members were red-headed giants averaging over 2 metres (7 feet) in height.

More than two and a half centuries after the initial report of Patagonian giants, another report appeared in 1766. After successfully completing the fastest circumnavigation of the globe (in less than two years) and returning to London, a 1766 account given by the crew of HMS *Dolphin* under the command of Commodore John Byron spoke of encountering a Patagonian tribe who averaged 2.7 metres (9 feet) in height. The official account of the journey was toned down to record a tall, but not suspiciously so, tribe with an average height of 1.95 metres (6 feet 6 inches). Was the commodore afraid of disbelief, or of suspicions of drunken revelry among the crew under his command that might account for distorted vision, or of gullibility inappropriate to the sobre and rapidly rising commander of one of His Majesty's fleet, particularly one who was looking forward with lively anticipation to further promotion? (Byron finally achieved the status of vice admiral, although it is said that his crews knew him better as Foul-weather Jack, owing to his almost invariable ability to attract hellish seas.) There at least seems to be slightly more probability that the giants existed than the City of the Caesars.

ganes
R.
R.
R. Carr

ONA
LIS
R.

Tonayaca
Paca
Alacama
Caxpiapa

Quintere
raiso

li
nas
ino
radura
ception

Patagonum
regio

ubi incole funt
Gigantes.

A

R. de S. Iuliani

R. de S. Madiere

Apachad

Costa de
las Arenas
Tierra de
Marco

Imperial
en
atio
dina
uanbaro

Carnero

R. del Camaru

CA

G. Pequeno
C. de l. S.

P. de las
Baxas

R. de los Rabudos
Lago de los Coronados

R. de los Palominos

R. de la Cayana

CHI

G. Grande
Costa de
la Cruz

R. de las
Arenas
R. la Celan

Segena

se perdeo

I. de Asencion

THE COUNTRY OF CINNAMON

The search for commercial spices for the tables of rich Europeans, together with gold and silver, were among the driving forces behind the exploration into new lands. One suspects that the drive for Christian converts came a very poor last in the New World. Marco Polo had been one of many who tempted European gourmets with tales of rare and exotic spices. With remarkable precision he had described 7448 islands lying in the China Sea, declaring, 'I assure you that in all these islands there is no tree that does not give off a powerful and agreeable fragrance … there are in addition many spices'. The islands he described were in the general area of the Philippines.

Spices had been one of the objectives of Columbus's expedition, and although he discovered little himself, many merchants had faith in the potential of the Americas to yield great riches in new spices. Where there is hope, there is very soon an obliging legend for adventurous spirits to follow. So the legend of La Canela (the Valley of Cinnamon) arose. Its basis lay in the explorations of Gonzalo Díaz de Pineda in the high Andes. The true story emerged only in 1871, when the manuscript of Pedro Cieza de León was finally published. Gonzalo had discovered some trees in the mountains that had a cinnamon-like scent. He understood from the local people that better trees were under cultivation not far away. The trees morphed into plantations in the way that legends do, and the cinnamon-scented trees that were not cinnamon (it is not indigenous

LEFT: Detail from Willem Jansz Blaeu's globe, 1621, showing the giants of Patagonia.

to South America) beckoned. The story became an irresistible lure for Gonzalo Pizarro (half-brother of the more famous Francisco Pizarro) and his second in command, Francisco de Orellana.

In 1521 they led an expedition from Quito in Equador in search of Pais de la Canela, the Country of Cinnamon. Despite, but perhaps because of, a remarkably large retinue of more than 200 Spaniards and 4000 natives, the expedition failed. Running out of provisions (including 2000 hogs), the party built a boat in the hope that Orellana, accompanied by a small group, could travel down the Rio Napo and reprovision the expedition. Instead Orellana was to find his place in the history of exploration. He failed to find adequate supplies of food, and found the return journey upstream impossible to negotiate.

His party was forced to continue downstream, finally reaching the Amazon and becoming, by accident rather than intent, the first Europeans to negotiate the great river all the way to its delta. Orellana's chaplain, the Dominican Friar Gaspar de Carvajal, who must have prayed with good effect, was a companion on the journey and recorded the entire terrifying adventure in his chronicle, including an encounter he claimed to have had with Amazons, having seen a tribe apparently containing only women and children.

Pizarro was forced to turn back when Orellana did not return. He finally reached Quito two years after starting out, accompanied by just eighty survivors. The sad history of Pizarro's ill-fated adventure in search of the Land of Cinnamon was told later by the brilliant Peruvian historian Garcilaso de las Vega in his *Commentarios Reales de los*

Incas, published in 1617, but later suppressed in the Americas from 1780 to 1918.

TREASURE ISLANDS — OAK ISLAND

Treasure islands are the stuff of adventure and childhood dreams, and exciting novels like Robert Louis Stevenson's *Treasure Island* and Daniel Defoe's *Robinson Crusoe*. The stories are based mainly on the buried treasure of pirates, who seem to have had terrible memories for where they hid their golden hoards, extreme bad luck, or were very careless with maps they had marked with a large black cross and instructions to 'dig here'. Just the same, some islands do seem to have genuine lost treasure or at least a long-lasting treasure story.

Oak Island, a tiny sand-rimmed forested island of about 55 hectares (135 acres) just off the coast of Nova Scotia, certainly offers one such mystery. It is the site of what is possibly the longest island treasure hunt on Earth, and certainly one of the most frustrating. Oak Island is just one of about 300 islands in Mahone Bay. In 1795 a teenager named Daniel McGinnis decided to explore the woods at the eastern end of the island and stumbled on a mystery that remains to this day, and has cost several fortunes and several lives. Daniel found a clearing in the woods with an old block and tackle suspended over a saucer-shaped pit nearly 4 metres (13 feet) wide. His mind immediately sprang to buried treasure — Oak Island had been within the territory of the pirate Captain William Kidd, and rumours had circulated in the seventeenth century that Kidd had buried a treasure trove on an island 'east of Boston'.

Daniel McGinnis returned to the island with two friends, John Smith, aged nineteen, and Anthony Vaughn, who was sixteen. They cleared an area around the site and started digging. Just 60 centimetres (2 feet) down they hit a layer of well-laid slate flagstones. As they dug further, it became obvious that they were re-excavating a shaft that had been filled in at some time in the past. At 3 metres (10 feet), they hit wood, but their excitement at finding an anticipated wooden treasure chest abated. They had hit oak logs. At 8 metres (26 feet) they gave up, convinced that whatever lay below would need a much better organised search team, and they refilled the shaft.

In the summer of 1803 the Onslow Company sailed to the island from Nova Scotia and resumed the work. At 9 metres (30 feet) they again struck oak logs. The dig continued to penetrate something anomalous approximately every 3 metres (10 feet) — charcoal, putty, coconut fibre, more oak logs, stones — until at 38 metres (125 feet) they hit a large flat stone, which was said to have later been carried to the mainland, where it was lost somewhere around 1900. The stone was said to be 60 centimetres (24 inches) long and 40 centimetres (16 inches) wide, and to weigh 80 kilograms (175 pounds). It was carved with symbols that were later 'interpreted' by a university professor during another treasure-hunting venture on the island initiated in the 1860s by the Oak Island Association. Quite a few had their doubts about the professor's translation, particularly as he held shares in the venture. According to him, 'Forty feet below two million pounds are buried'. The 1860s venture went bust in 1864 following a fatality. At the

30 metre (100 foot) level, the excavation had struck a layer of stone which was left overnight by the workers. They returned to find the pit flooded with sea water up to the 9 metre (30 feet) level. An attempt to bore through the base of the pit with an auger brought up evidence of odd layers of metal pieces, oak, spruce and clay.

Since then, numerous attempts have been made to find the 'treasure' including that of the Old Gold Salvage Group in 1909, an attempt in which Franklin Roosevelt participated. Four men died of asphyxiation in a 1960s attempt. That the tunnel is simply a sinkhole seems very unlikely. There was evidence of pick marks down the sides of the re-dug shaft and the soil was said to be noticeably looser than that surrounding the shaft. Box drains fashioned from stones have been verified. But as time goes by and the mystery deepens, ideas of finding the Holy Chalice buried by the Knights Templar or Captain Kidd's lost treasure are receding. Perhaps it was simply a well dug by a would-be settler searching for a permanent water supply who finally hit the briny salt-laden watertable at around 30 metres (100 feet) and backfilled the well to prevent an accident. That would certainly explain the odd mixture of materials recovered from deep underground. (Anyone who has ever backfilled a deep excavation by hand knows that everything available is likely to be thrown in.) Or perhaps it was dug and then abandoned by someone who discovered one of those mysterious maps marked with a big black X.

OTHER TREASURE ISLANDS

In September 2005, the *Guardian* newspaper in England and *New Scientist* magazine both reported the exciting prospect of the discovery of a fabulous treasure, said to be worth around £5.6 billion (US$10 billion). It was found on the real island where Scotsman Alexander Selkirk spent four years from 1704 before being rescued, and inspiring the book *Robinson Crusoe*, published in 1719. Juan Fernández Island lies approximately 660 kilometres (410 miles) off the Chilean coast. The hoard was reported to be buried 19.5 metres (64 feet) down in sand and was said to have been located by a mini robot named Arturio, which had previously been useful in detecting weapons caches. Unfortunately, even a real expert has trouble interpreting Arturio's feedback at such depths. Chilean newspapers speculated on the contents, which were said to consist of up to eight hundred barrels filled with Inca jewels and gold coins, a treasure long sought since the Spanish colonial era. Legend reported that the treasure was buried on the island in 1715 by Juan Esteban Ubilla Eheverria. The bounty was discovered by a British sailor, Cornelius Webb, a few years later, who relocated it to another site on the island.

Another huge Spanish treasure hoard is believed to be located on the Cocos Islands. Then there is the legendary Lost Dutchman's Mine in America. They all have one thing in common: they have cost huge amounts of money and many human lives in the search for what are probably golden mirages.

Lasseter's lost reef

The mystery of Lasseter's lost reef is a treasure story that still attracts hopeful prospectors. The reef is said to be an exposed ridge of gold-bearing quartz up to 20 kilometres (12 miles) long and 6.5 kilometres (4 miles) wide, located somewhere in Central Australia near the Northern Territory–Western Australia border. Lasseter himself described the gold as 'thick as plums in a pudding', but over time, his discovery became a reef of solid gold.

Australia's gold discoveries in the nineteenth century were legendary. They began with the 1851 discovery of gold at Ophir, near Bathurst in New South Wales, by Edward Hargreaves, who had recently returned from the Californian gold rush of 1849. Huge reef nuggets were found in many places in the area, including the enormous rock-and-gold Holterman, which weighed 286.4 kilograms (630 pounds).

Soon afterward, gold was discovered in Victoria, and the state became famous for the many massive pure alluvial gold nuggets which have been found there, including the legendary Welcome Stranger, weighing a massive 71.6 kilograms (158 pounds), valued currently at approximately £1.64 million or US $2.7 million. It was discovered in 1869 under a mere 5 centimetres (2 inches) of soil north-west of Melbourne at Moliagul. The hand-shaped 28 kilogram (62 pound) Hand of Faith nugget, estimated at being worth in excess of £640,000 or US $1,050,000, was found in 1980, lying just 15 centimetres (6 inches) below the ground, at Kingower. Both were found in the area known as the Golden Triangle bounded by Avoca, Castlemaine and Wedderburn. Victoria opened rich goldfields at Ballarat, Bendigo, Inglewood, Wedderburn and other centres, and flourishing towns and cities grew up around the wealth that poured from the ground.

Western Australia was and is a state overwhelmed by mineral riches, including major gold-mining sites such as Kalgoorlie and Coolgardie, Halls Creek, Leonora, Wilga and Kambalda. Gold discoveries began there in the 1850s, but reached a climax with the opening of the Kalgoorlie and Coolgardie fields in the 1890s. Gold fever gripped the country throughout the second half of the nineteenth century, with not entirely impossible dreams of tripping over the next Welcome Stranger.

Harold Bell Lasseter was aged just seventeen in 1897, when he attempted to walk from Alice Springs to the booming Western Australian goldfield of Kalgoorlie. He became lost in the blinding heat of the Gibson Desert, somewhere near the Western Australian border. Delirious, mad with thirst and near death, he was rescued just in time by an Afghan camel driver who took him to the camp of a surveyor named Harding. Forever afterward he was haunted by the memory of having discovered a huge reef of gold-filled quartz while he was stumbling about the desert.

In 1900, he returned to the area to search for the reef, accompanied by Harding. Using landmarks that he still remembered, he claimed to have relocated his lost reef. But neither man could establish the precise geographical location due to equipment failure. During the Great Depression of the 1930s, Lasseter led another expedition to find his glittering reef. The expedition was well funded and equipped by a group of Sydney financiers, who between them founded the Central Australian Gold Exploration Company Limited (CAGE).

A series of disasters overcame the expedition, including the crash of their light plane. When no sign of the reef was found using Lasseter's landmarks, the party finally gave up the quest, convinced that Lasseter was delusional, and returned home. But Lasseter stayed, determined to prove them wrong and believing in his dream to the end. He was never seen alive again. A Northern Territory cattle station owner, Bob Buck, discovered Lasseter's body in a cave. In the diary found alongside his body, Lasseter had written that he had found the lost reef and pegged out his claim, but that nine days after the rest of the party left, his camels had bolted, leaving him without water and food. He begged his wife to remember him as he had been when they met, saying that the flies and ants had almost eaten away his face and that only willpower was holding him together.

Lasseter was buried at Shaw Creek in the Petermann Range, and his diary was returned to his family. A death certificate was issued at Alice Springs giving Lasseter's date of death as 1931, and the *Daily Mirror* in 1931 carried a story headed 'Grim Lure

Lasseter's lost reef

of Gold Tragic Discovery In Ranges'. The newspapers had something of a field day after Lasseter's death. Two women stepped forward claiming to be his wife, and some commented that Lasseter was known to be sparing with the truth. Many thought him a charlatan, but if he was, why did he remain obsessed from the age of seventeen to his lonely and terrible death at fifty-one? Why did he work so long to persuade hard-headed financiers to fund his last expedition? Why did he stay in country that had previously almost claimed his life when the CAGE party left? Whether Lasseter remembered a delusional dream he had when near death in the desert at seventeen or had found a reef bared by shifting desert sands, there is little doubt that he truly believed in its existence. The CAGE Company mounted a second expedition later in 1931 in an attempt to find where Lasseter had pegged his claim. Mining experts on the expedition claimed the country was not gold-bearing.

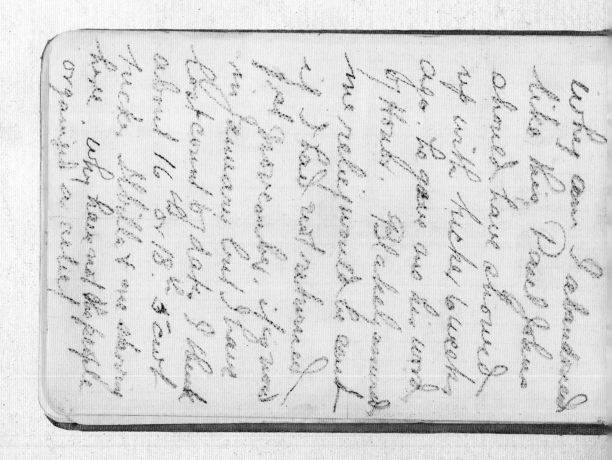

Many expeditions have been mounted since then to find Lasseter's Reef, but none have succeeded. Many were turned back by the extreme harshness of the environment. However, the area is one of constantly shifting desert sand, and a reef outcrop might be exposed only from time to time. A 1979 expedition led by Gerry Nolan, one-time mayor of North Sydney, pilot with the Royal Australian Air Force, flight coordinator on numerous flights to Antarctica, and leader of mineral and water exploration expeditions in Central Australia and South-east Asia, used the landmarks provided by Lasseter and did find a huge unmapped quartz reef that is known to be mineralised, although by no means necessarily with gold.

The details of Lasseter's doomed search for a golden reef were revealed in the diary found with his body. Lasseter claimed to have found the mythical reef, but with his party having deserted him and his camels bolted, he languished with little food and water, recording his progress towards death.

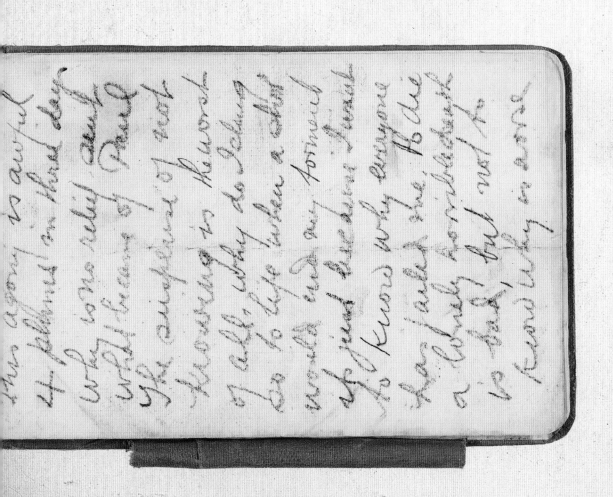

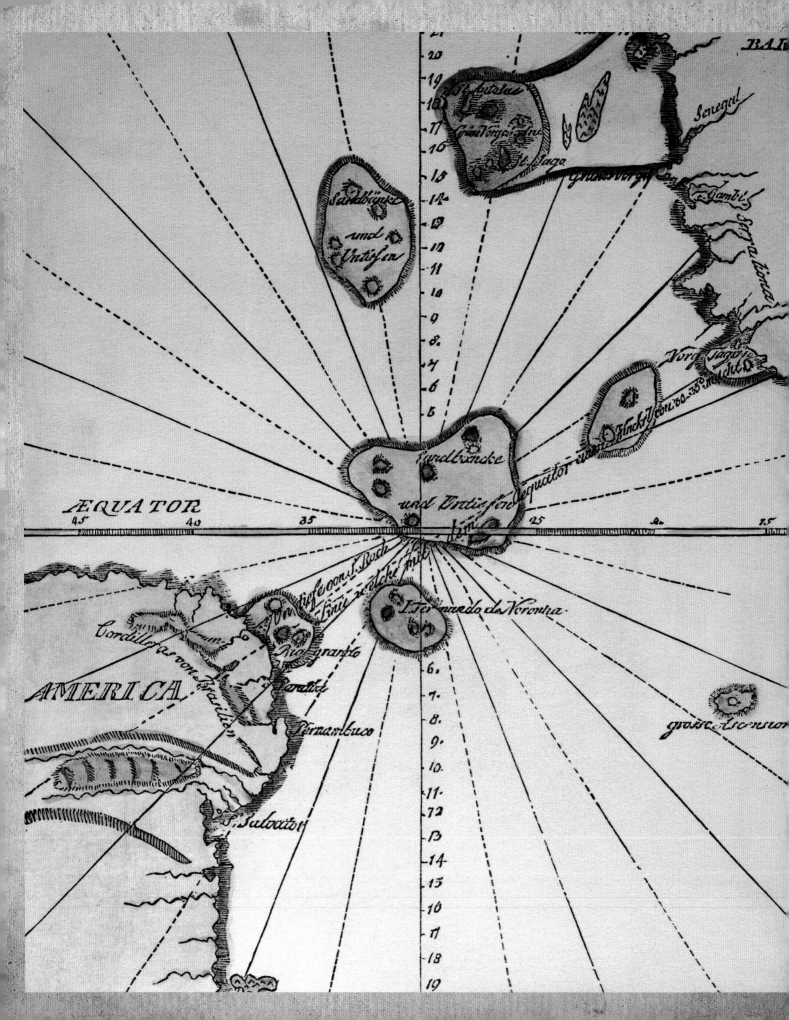

LOST CONTINENTS

∾ ∾

LEFT: A 1785 German map locating the mythical continent of
Atlantis midway between America and Africa.

FOLLOWING PAGES: An artist's impression of Atlantis.

THE GAIA
PRIORITIES

Our planet is not the stable place we might wish it to be. Worlds have come and gone over aeons of time. Gaia may be relatively permanent, until perhaps we have one collision too many with the great chunks of rock hurtling through our solar system courtesy of the asteroid belt. But Gaia truly behaves like a living thing that morphs constantly—a gloriously complex interactive system that acts as if it were a single organism, constantly adjusting to accommodate life so that it may take whatever form it may, whether dinosaurs or humanity. Gaia is completely impartial—a nurturer of life, not of a particular species—as we will discover if we permit runaway global warming to happen.

The ground beneath our feet is a vulnerable crust, no more than 5 to 12 kilometres (3 to 7½ miles) thick under the oceans, and an average of 40 kilometres (25 miles) thick on land. Gaia itself is estimated to be 4.54 billion years old. The Earth's crust, which floats over the much deeper mantle, is not an eggshell-like cover—it is made up of huge fragments, or tectonic plates, broken from the vast parent continent of Pangaea. These plates are constantly on the move, and when they ram into each other, unbelievable forces are set up between two solid objects. On the thin, vulnerable crust we inhabit, those forces translate into earthquakes that can devastate whole regions. In geologically active areas that have thermal springs, volcanoes and volcanic vents, we become uncomfortably aware of the perpetual danger we face from the molten world beneath our feet. In areas like Rotorua in New Zealand, a garden spade dug into the soil can bring forth not the smell of sweet earth, but steam and a whiff of sulphur.

Cyclical glaciation over millions of years has also produced massive land changes, as the water across Earth is locked up in huge glacial sheets, causing sea levels to fall and exposing vast areas of land that were once beneath the ocean. The end of the last glacial period occurred about 10,000 years ago, well within the range of oral history.

Stories of lost lands, of continents sunk beneath the ocean waves, of lands disappearing overnight as the result of great earthquakes and volcanic activity, and of catastrophes on a cosmic scale, such as asteroid impacts on the planet, are known from around the world. Many of those lost places are but dimly remembered, their stories often entering the world of mythology in attempts to explain the inexplicable. Lost lands take on the glow of a Golden Age by virtue of their remoteness in time, inhabited by utopian and sometimes advanced civilisations that represent our universal aspirations.

Yet these persistent memories seem also to resonate with the theory that humanity has lived through many cycles in which civilisations have sometimes reached pinnacles higher than our own, civilisations that enjoyed less mechanistic and material paths, always to be destroyed by unanticipated catastrophes in which all knowledge of history and the sciences was lost and whole populations were reduced to levels only just capable of preserving the species. Catastrophism, at least on a local scale, is an obvious constant in our world, and the theory of lost civilisations that flowered and were wiped out, sometimes in a day, is scarcely a theory but rather a reality. For every Atlantis, there is a provable Santorini and Troy. Darwinian gradualism certainly operates but catastrophism walks beside it.

THE UTOPIAN DREAM

The dream of a perfect world is universal. Fiction has produced many worlds where social justice prevails and everyone leads a peaceful, happy, fulfilling life. But these worlds always exist in the memory of a Golden Age that never really existed, or in intentionally created societies that have failed.

The Greek philosopher Plato receives the credit for creating the vision of Utopia, writing some 2,500 years ago in his *Republic* of a perfect society where equality is achieved, where pacifism is the rule and war used only in defence, where religious tolerance is practised, and poverty and misery do not exist. Sir Thomas More, the remarkable Tudor writer, lawyer, Chancellor of England, adviser to King Henry VIII, and author of, among many books, *Utopia*, was responsible for coining the term and enlarging on Plato's theory of a society created for the common good. As a reward for his brave dreams, a grateful monarch had him beheaded. In fairness, his head was mainly forfeited as a result of his religiously based opposition to the king in the matters of convenient divorces, the maintenance of papal supremacy, and the firm upholding of the laws against heretics. But neither would his novel, contrasting the strife-riven kingdoms of Europe with an idealistic society, as described by what appears to be a lightly disguised archangel Raphael, have endeared More to his king.

The utopian ideal is recognisably the dream of the founding fathers of the United States, although as in all earthly utopias the dream has not been fulfilled.

The nineteenth century, a time of great hardship for many, spawned many attempts to create economic utopias in which wealth would be redistributed to bring hope to the poor in the newly industrialised world. Early proponents advocated the abolition of money and the egalitarian distribution of goods, proposing that all work for the common good for part of each day, spending the rest in creative work. As the century drew to a close, these dreams were seen to be impractical, and more forceful ideas were advanced to create a fairer world. Karl Marx was one who was driven to this view by the poverty that surrounded him.

That wonderfully clichéd and well-rehearsed answer given by nearly every beauty pageant entrant to the critical question, 'What would you wish for?'—'World peace'—probably reflects a utopian vision shared by much of the world. Cliché it might be, but it seems overdue to be tried. We seem to have been more inclined to follow the examples of George Orwell's *1984* and Aldous Huxley's *Brave New World* of late, with a touch of Anthony Burgess's *A Clockwork Orange* for good measure, rather than Plato's *Republic*.

One of the last major attempts to create a genuine utopia was led by William Lane, leader of the emerging nineteenth century Australian labour movement, who despaired of social justice being achieved under the British-ruled colony. Two utopian colonies composed of Australians who shared Lane's dream of a society based on brotherhood were set up in Paraguay, the first in 1893 named the Colonia Nueva Australis (New Australia Colony) and the second, Colonia Cosme, in 1894. From newspaper accounts at the time, it seems the Utopians were regarded as malcontents rather than idealists, but they counted among their number some who would later become famous for other reasons, including Dame Mary Gilmore, Rose Summerfield and Gilbert Casey. Cosme survived until 1909. Brotherhood had reportedly become in short supply. The descendants of the few that remained live there still. The creation of these colonies was reported in places like the United States, Canada and Britain, where similar strong feelings about the need for social justice were running strong.

All the best utopias seem to have been in the magical world of dreams and legend. Most are notably moral, but one worth mentioning for its joyous bawdiness is the medieval Cockaigne, a dream world for the hard-worked peasant and monk. In an interesting slant on Utopia, Cockaigne is an upside-down world where the harsh life of the peasant and lowly monk is inflicted on their rich and powerful overlords, hunger is unknown because the sky rains cheese, and sex is for the taking. It provided many an inspiration at the time for naughty versifying religious students, and probably a healthy outlet for lives subject to endless moral strictures.

'The island of Utopia', title page illustration from Thomas More's Utopia, 1516.

HYPERBOREA— A GREEK SHANGRI-LA

Hyperborea was a utopian land said to lie far to the north of Thrace and beyond the land of the Scythians, a place where the sun never set. According to Pliny the Elder, Hyperborea was a land of warmth, ease and plenty. He placed it at the 'hinges on which the world turns' and at the extreme limits of the stars in their circuit, which could have put it vaguely in Sweden. Pliny describes the tall rocky cliffs, shaped like women, that came to life at night, destroying any ships that ventured into the straits leading to the Sea of Hyperborea. Visitors were warned to pass through the straits only when the sun shone, which it did for six continuous months each year. The inhabitants of Hyperborea were said to sow the fields in the morning, reap at midday, and feast on luscious fruits before retiring to sleep in caves. The first-picked fruits of the season were dedicated to the god Apollo, associated with the sun, who was said to spend the winter with them. Sorrow and disharmony were unknown, and the lives of Hyperboreans were biblically long. When Hyperboreans finally tired of life, they chose their moment of death, first setting forth a great banquet, with much feasting and a celebration of their life, before they threw themselves from a high rock into the sea. Some said they emerged again as white swans, singing the praises of Apollo. It was, in any case and as Pliny remarked, a most serene method of burial.

Hyperborea was a gently governed theocracy ruled by the Boreades, three priest-kings of the god Apollo and sons of the god of the north wind, Boreas. In the temple of Apollo, asses were sacrificed to the god, and the music of lyres and flutes, dance and song constantly celebrated and praised him, while white encircling swans added their sweet music.

Hyperborea was very real to writers of the ancient world. It was bordered on one side by the great Earth-encircling fresh-water Okeanus River, while the high, frigid peaks of the Rhipaion Mountains formed an all but impenetrable barrier to the south. Its largest river, the Eridanos, was one of the few greatly blessed rivers anywhere on Earth to draw its waters directly from Okeanus, and its shores were lined with poplars that produced golden-coloured amber, while flocks of milk-white swans floated on its waters. Lush forests that covered much of the land were called the garden of Apollo. The Rhipaion Mountains were the home of Boreas, held responsible in the ancient world for the bitter winds that blew from the far north that today have names like the Mistral in France and the Meltemi in Greece (known to the ancient Greeks as the Etesian). On the high peaks dwelt fearful griffins, half eagle, half lion, that guarded a treasure of gold, and in the valleys below there lived a tribe of one-eyed men, the Arimaspians, who were almost as fierce as the griffins dwelling above them and, according to Herodotus, always at war with their neighbours.

The same dreamland, virtually unchanged, emerges throughout the ages and in many cultures. In virtually every aspect, Hyperborea was the forerunner of the twentieth century Shangri-la invented by James Hilton in his novel *Lost Horizon*, a place remote from the world and surrounded by high, bitterly cold, impassable mountains, with beautiful fruitful valleys, a river to water the crops, and a perfect gentle climate where spring reigns eternally and the inhabitants live peaceful and impossibly long lives in a state of everlasting youth and happiness.

Greek myths were frequently set within the land of Hyperborea. Phaethon, the son of the sun god Helios, was said to have been struck in the breast by a thunderbolt from the hand of Zeus when he attempted to drive the chariot of the sun. Both Phaethon and his father's golden chariot were almost consumed by flames as they fell into the waters of the River Eridanos. Phaethon's sisters, the Heliades, wept endlessly in bitter grief, and were eventually imprisoned by Zeus within tall poplars along the river's banks. Yet their tears never ended, each droplet turning to amber as it fell.

On their epic journey, the Argonauts were said to have encountered the land of Hyperborea as they returned from the Black Sea to Greece. *Argonautica*, written in Alexandria in the third century BC by Apollonius of Rhodes, described their journey on the stream of Eridanos, where dying Phaethon and his golden chariot had plunged. The Argonauts entered an infinitely sad world, where the

RIGHT: This 1595 map by Ortelius is based on ancient maps of the Roman empire using classical sources such as Salustius, Plinius, Herodotus, Strabo and Dionysius, and shows Hyperborea in the north.

waters still belched steam from Phaethon's terrible wound and they were plagued by the stench of his decaying body. The Argonauts were weighed down with sadness, wanting neither food nor drink as they passed through the region, hearing the laments of the daughters of Helios encased in their poplar trees. Perhaps there was a genuine geographical river described in the epic, one located in a thermal region that produced belching steam and the rotten-egg smell of sulphurous gases. As was his way, Herodotus would have none of this mysterious River Eridanos, considering the name a fiction dreamt up by a poet of the past. As the river has been identified as everything from Europe's Danube to Italy's Po, he is probably, if prosaically, right. Or was Hyperborea a confused and mythologised description of Iceland in summer with its eternal summer day and, equally eternal, winter night and its active thermal areas?

The sacred island of Delos in the Cyclades, which lies about 21 kilometres (13 miles) from the

Aegean island of Mykonos had many mythological connections to Hyperborea. The Hyperborean goddess Leto, goddess of motherhood and a consort of Zeus, gave birth to Apollo and his sister Artemis on Delos. Leto had been relentlessly pursued by Zeus's jealous and vengeful wife Hera from the time she had left Hyperborea and travelled southward, constantly prevented from taking her rest, although she was heavily pregnant. Delos became well known throughout the ancient world as the site of a famous Temple of Apollo.

Pliny related another legend of Delos, describing it as a floating island that drifted for many years before finally settling in its current position. Long before Pliny, Aristotle had written that Delos had appeared suddenly in the sea. Both Herodotus and Pliny the Elder recorded that, for a very long time, the Hyperboreans sent offerings every year of the first fruits from their annual harvest to the Temple of Apollo on Delos. The offerings were at first carried by virgins, who for many years were offered protection and hospitality by the local people. A breach of good faith took place and the Hyperboreans no longer entrusted their virgins to Delos. Instead, they handed their offerings of fruit to neighbouring peoples, who in turn passed the offerings to their neighbours until, after much changing of hands, the tribute reached the temple.

As is the way in the hopelessly confusing, mutable, but wonderfully rich stories of the Greek gods, Hera was both Zeus's wife and twin sister, but she also figures as a daughter of Chronos who, having inherited the throne by castrating his father Uranus, displayed the most unnatural habit of swallowing his offspring at birth.

Gaia and Uranus had warned Chronos that he was fated to be supplanted by one of his own offspring, and he chose to deal with the situation in this particularly direct manner. Finally his more than exasperated wife Rhea gave him a large stone to eat, and he spewed forth the gods Hestia, Demeter, Hera, Zeus, Hades and Poseidon. The beautiful island of Samos, in the northern Aegean, and Argos, in the Peloponnese, were Hera's principal places of worship.

Hera had her own connection to Hyperborea. After her marriage to Zeus, she was presented with many gifts by the other gods, which included a tree bearing golden apples. This was watched over by the Hesperides, the nymphs of the evening, in the garden of Hera, which was said in this version of the story to lie at the foot of mighty Atlas where he held up the heavens in Hyperborea.

In the mythical story of the twelve labours of Heracles, Heracles was required to take three golden apples from the Garden of the Hesperides. Prometheus advised him to ask Atlas to pick the apples, while he instead held up the heavens at their northern axis in Hyperborea, a scheme that worked to perfection.

LEMURIA — THE SUNKEN LAND

In some ways Lemuria has become as famous as Atlantis, another land associated with a golden age. Yet it was first spoken of as recently as the nineteenth century. As the Darwinian theory became broadly accepted among scientists, ancestral species and the centres of origin of species became of increasing interest.

How populations of closely related species or their fossils could exist on either side of great oceans such as the Atlantic, the Pacific and the Indian was a great puzzle to scientists.

Various theories were put forward to explain this migration of species, known as diffusion. Had they survived long ocean journeys on fallen tree trunks or matted reeds? That might just be possible for some insects, and animals such as reptiles, but how could mammals survive? Were they caught up in waterspouts or tornadoes and deposited far from their native range? Were these migrations incremental, the result of island-hopping over perhaps countless millennia until they reached another continent?

It was not until the 1960s that the theory of continental drift, with huge tectonic plates carrying whole groups of flora and fauna away from the mega-continents Laurasia and Gondwanaland, was developed.

One favoured nineteenth century theory postulated continents that had lain in the middle of each major ocean and acted like giant stepping stones for plant and animal migrations. These landmasses were supposed to have conveniently sunk to the ocean floors once having served their purpose.

Lemuria was the name given to one of the 'stepping-stone continents', sometimes located in the Indian Ocean, but sometimes in the Pacific. Sunken continents do exist, including the Kerguelen Plateau in the southern Indian Ocean and Zealandia in the Pacific, but no continent corresponding to Lemuria has ever been detected.

The name of this mythical continent arose with arguments over Darwinian theory. Zoologists were at a loss to explain the distribution of lemurs, a form of small primates. There was a puzzling discontinuity between lemur populations in Madagascar and Africa, India and the East Indies. To provide lemurs with a logical route from one area to the other they literally invented a huge sunken continent dubbed Lemuria which might have acted as a stepping stone for lemurs.

Lemuria might deservedly have become a rather embarrassing scientific dead end if it were not for the Theosophists, and Madame Blavatsky in particular. At the end of the nineteenth and the first part of the twentieth centuries, the occult was the subject of serious study by many. There was great curiosity about hypnotism, séances, card reading,

spiritualism, fairies and many other associated esoteric areas. The classic Noel Coward farce *Blithe Spirit*, with its medium Madame Arcati, was a send-up of the period's preoccupation with séances. Houdini's unfulfilled promise to contact the living after his death was another example of the deep interest in this field.

Madame Blavatsky (born Helena von Hahn), leader of the Theosophy movement, claimed in her book *The Secret Doctrine*, published in 1888, to have studied in Tibet for seven years with great masters of esoteric knowledge, and to have been taught about the lost civilisations of Atlantis and Lemuria. She described a series of Root Races that had gradually ascended the human evolutionary ladder, placing the Lemurians, a people who appear to have had reptilian associations, in the Third Root Race. They were very tall, hermaphroditic, egg laying and were said to have had a cold reptilian brain. Madame Blavatsky claimed they had descended into bestiality, and as a result the Land of Lemuria had sunk below the waves, to be replaced by Atlantis. In time, the story was developed further, particularly with the help of a book called *A Dweller on Two Planets*, written by Frederick Spencer Oliver, in which survivors of sunken Lemuria were described as still living in tunnels beneath Mount Shasta in northern California. A group of 'ancient masters' has long been associated with Mount Shasta.

A considerable body of literature built up around the concept of reptilian humanoid beings. Many appear to relate to Madame Blavatsky's 'dragon men' and 'serpent men' or 'lizard beings', which are said to have great occult knowledge derived from the left path or dark source. Many people still believe in Lemuria and its reptilian humanoids, which often feature in science-fiction novels as well as more-serious books.

The most recent major publication about the reptilians is Whitley Strieber's blockbuster 2007 novel *2012: The War for Souls*. Some also believe that UFOs are not from alien planets but were developed by the Lemurians. Reptilian humanoids are also widespread in various ancient mythologies around the world.

SUNKEN CITIES AND THE LOST CONTINENT OF MU

A lost continent known as Mu is sometimes identified with Lemuria, and like Lemuria it is believed to be of pre-Atlantean origin. Augustus le Plongeon, a nineteenth century antiquarian, traveller and writer, became fascinated with the Mayan civilisation of the Yucatán region of Mexico and investigated Mayan ruins there. Le Plongeon translated ancient Mayan writings, which he interpreted as presenting the story of an ancient continent that had slipped below the sea after a terrible catastrophe. Some of the survivors had created the Mayan civilisation, while others travelled to Egypt, where they founded the ancient Egyptian civilisation.

The theory would have remained an interesting side note in the history of archaeology had it not been for the nineteenth century writer Colonel James Churchward. He became a passionate advocate of Mu, believing that traces of an advanced civilisation, whose people were known as the Naacal, had been left scattered across the Pacific. He cited the gigantic statues of Easter Island as an example of the works of the Naacal civilisation.

However, Easter Island is a geologically young island of independent volcanic origin, arising from deep ocean. The ocean plunges up to a depth of 3237 metres (10,620 feet) within 32 kilometres (20 miles) of Easter Island's shores, indicating that it is not part of a sunken continent. Churchward brought out a series of popular books between 1926 and 1933, including *The Lost Continent of Mu: The Motherland of Man*, *The Children of Mu*, *The Lost Continent of Mu* and *The Sacred Symbols of Mu*, which firmly established the idea of this ancient lost civilisation in the public consciousness. The writer Peter Tompkins built on the idea of Mu as one of the origins of civilisation in his influential 1976 book *Mysteries of the Mexican Pyramids*, in which he said that 'one branch of colonisation ran from Mu to Central America, thence to Atlantis'.

The latest addition to the story of Mu relates to an extraordinary find made in 1988 off the coast of Yonaguni, an island to the south-west of Okinawa in the Japanese archipelago. A team of scuba divers discovered an enormous structure which appeared to be manmade. Local people had assumed it was natural rock, as it lies 23 metres (75 feet) below the surface and was somewhat camouflaged with coral. The entire angular platform is 183 metres (600 feet) long, 137 metres (450 feet) wide, and 27.5 metres (90 feet) high, dwarfing anyone who swims beside it, and strongly resembles a ziggurat with well-defined clean edges and corners. The individual steps are 1 metre (90 inchs) high.

Associated with the main pyramid is an arch and monoliths, and smaller ziggurats are arranged around the main ziggurat. It has been calculated that the land on which the temple complex was formed

12,000 YEARS AGO The most fascinating legend of man is the legend of the lost continent of Lemuria. It is the firm belief of many authorities and archaeologists, that approximately 12,000 years ago, a great civilization flourished in the Pacific, mother country of many colonies all over the globe, among them Yucatan, Egypt, Babylon, and many others. All of today's civilizations are supposed to be the results of Lemurian colonization. (For complete details, see page 144.)

The lost continent of Lemuria, speculated to lie beneath today's Pacific Ocean, may have housed a highly developed civilisation with advanced technology and a sophisticated culture.

has not been above water since at least 8000 years ago. Is this the lost continent of Mu?

Since the 1988 discovery, further underwater exploration has discovered the remains of what appears to be an extensive site with many other structures, carvings, streets and staircases built from what appears to be perfectly cut and fitted stone. Japanese geologists and archaeologists who have documented the discovery and filmed and photographed it in the crystal-clear waters are convinced that the structures are built, and not natural. Researchers have even found masonry tools in the area. Many American geologists continue to contend that it is a natural-rock site. If the structure is not natural, it means that there was an advanced, highly organised civilisation in the East that predates the generally accepted dates for civilisation in ancient Egypt.

Underwater archaeology using modern technology may possibly turn the conventional stories of some early civilisations on their heads. The apparent remains of an immense city, measuring

8 kilometres (5 miles) long and more than 3 kilometres (2 miles) wide, and lying 36 metres (120 feet) below the waters of the Gulf of Khambhat on the west coast of India, were discovered in 2002. Radiocarbon dating suggests the site could be as much as 9500 years old. That would make an associated civilisation 4000 years older than the ancient Harappan civilisation that was centred on the Indus Valley. The structures were discovered by oceanographers using sidescan

sonar to analyse pollution in the bay. Materials so far recovered from the site include masonry, pottery, beads and human bones. The site is believed to have been inundated by rising sea levels at the end of the last Ice Age about 10,000 years ago.

CONTINENTS FROM A LOST WORLD

While this section is largely about places on the invisible atlas, in more recent times a number of

genuine sunken lands have been discovered. Some of them may well have become tangled in ancient memories and legends.

One of the best known is Doggerland, which once stretched between Britain and mainland Europe. It was above sea level in the last Ice Age, when the sea level in the area was about 120 metres (390 feet) lower than it is today. The Dogger Bank, now so rich in fish, was once part of the uplands of

Doggerland. Trawlers have dredged up remains of mammoths from the underwater remains of this once dry and fertile land.

The Kerguelen Plateau lies about 3000 kilometres (1865 miles) south-west of Australia in the Indian Ocean. It was a long plateau created by volcanism about 110 million years ago, about the time of the break-up of Gondwanaland. It is thought to have supported tropical flora and fauna around 50 million years ago. The continent sank about 20 million years ago and now lies 1 to 2 kilometres (roughly 1 mile) below sea level. It has been ripped in two by the Indian Ocean ridge. The only remnants above sea level are the Kerguelen Islands, which include Heard Island and the McDonald Islands, which lie two-thirds of the way from Madagascar to Antarctica and are still wracked by vulcanism from time to time.

The Bering land bridge, or Beringia, was once dry land stretching between Siberia and Alaska. It was around 1600 kilometres (1000 miles) wide at its greatest extent, and was not glaciated. The sea floor remains quite shallow where Beringia was exposed during the last Ice Age. The land bridge allowed the migration of humans from Asia to North America about 25,000 years ago, although earlier migrations were possible, as well as the two-way migration of animals and plants.

Old maps of Terra Australis depicted the east coast as a continuous landmass from New Guinea to Tasmania. They were right in a way. If they had mapped the shores of the Great South Land

LEFT: The submersion of Mu — The great Pacific continent is overwhelmed by a combination of flood and volcanic action.

14,000 years ago that is exactly what they would have found, with New Guinea and Tasmania both attached to the mainland.

New Zealand may now largely consist of two major islands, but it was once a continent in its own right, broken away from the landmass of Australia 60 to 80 million years ago, and from Antarctica even earlier, perhaps 85 to 130 million years ago. Present-day New Zealand is the visible part (less than 10 per cent) of an almost wholly sunken continent named Zealandia, which would have been half the size of present-day Australia, stretching northward to New Caledonia.

Vulcanism has always been a part of Zealandia's history and New Zealand continues to be one of the world's hotspots for vulcanism. The North Island's infamous Taupo Volcanic Zone was the scene of the world's largest volcanic explosion in historic times in 186 AD, and the Coromandel Peninsula is also extremely active.

The wonderfully biologically rich and diverse area now occupied by the Malay Archipelago and the islands of Sumatra, Borneo, Java, Bali and the many other islands that make up modern Indonesia, were once a single landmass known as Sundaland. With rising seas after the last Ice Age, many valleys were drowned, leaving the present-day coastlines. The entire area is volcanically active and is perhaps the world's major hotspot. The earthquake and

tsunami in the region in 2004 were results of that ongoing activity.

The four Hawaiian Islands immediately northwest of Hawai'i, the main island, were once similarly joined to create a much larger island, which has been dubbed Maui Nui or Greater Maui, created by seven volcanoes. A combination of subsidence and flooding as a result of rising sea levels after the last Ice Age reduced Maui Nui to a series of islands separated by shallow sea—Maui, Lāna'i, Moloka'i and Kaho'olawe, the smallest of the islands.

Kaho'olawe was involved in an experiment that might lead one to wonder about human sanity. Admittedly the island was unproductive, because it had a dry climate and had been overgrazed in the thousand years since it was first settled, though it did have a fresh-water source. In 1965 the United States Navy conducted a test called Operation Sailor Hat (operations like these always receive jolly names), designed to find out whether the island and a target ship moored beside it, the USS *Atlanta*, could survive the three massive explosions of TNT detonated on the island. A crater known as Sailor Man's Cap was left behind, and the well with its precious fresh water was cracked. Fortunately the interconnected volcanic vents did not trigger eruptions on other islands. Attempts are now being made to conserve Kaho'olawe, but large numbers of archaeologically valuable sites have been lost.

ATLANTIS

Of all the places in the invisible atlas, none has been more controversial or more discussed than the island of Atlantis. Atlantis strikes a chord as if it is an archetype, somehow connected to the mass consciousness of humanity. It was described as a utopian state with a highly advanced civilisation and scientific knowledge that seemed to have followed a less mechanistic path than our own, a paradisical land with a perfect climate, rich soils and bountiful fruits, where civilised values and social justice were upheld. It has been conjectured to be the same place described by ancient peoples as the Elysian Fields, Eden, the Garden of the Hesperides, Asgard and even Olympus.

PLATO'S ATLANTIS

The entire story of Atlantis rests upon a series of dialogues by Plato, to be hosted by Socrates and intended to entertain a theatre audience during a festival celebrating the goddess Athena. The first two dialogues that describe Atlantis, *Critias* and *Timaeus*, named for the people who presented the discourses, were written in 360 BC. To the everlasting dismay of researchers, only part of *Critias* survives; *Timaeus* is complete; and *Hermocrates*, a dialogue presented by a third speaker has been lost.

According to Socrates who was the host, the company assembled for the discussion was well suited by its nature and education to participate. Timaeus of Locris came from a city in Italy of admirable law, had held the most honourable positions of state and had scaled the heights of philosophy. He discoursed on the origins of humanity and the nature of the universe. Critias of Athens was no newcomer to politics and philosophy, and he recounted the story of a long-lost Golden Age of Athens first recounted to him as a young boy by his grandfather. Hermocrates was hailed as a genius well fitted to any learned discussion and presumably, although we will never know, took as his theme the development of the state and its laws.

Critias and *Timaeus* are often quoted in support of the existence of the lost world of Atlantis, but a careful reading of the dialogues does far more than report on Atlantis. The description is so oddly detailed in parts as to at least give pause to sceptics. Plato must have pieced together much of the material for the discourses from various old sources, and no doubt wove them together into a narrative. The question remains as to whether the story related through the discourses had some basis in remote history. There is always a tendency to debase entire narratives from the remote past on the basis that some segments are dubious. However, the grains of truth left in ancient stories have led to some remarkable archaeological discoveries, such as Troy.

Critias passed on a story he was told at the age of ten by his ninety-year-old grandfather. His grandfather in turn had been told the story by his father, Dropides, who had been a dear friend of Solon, 'the wisest of all sages'—the Athenian statesman and writer of songs and poetry. This, in brief, is the story related by Solon to Dropides, somewhere around 600 BC, and subsequently passed down through the family:

Solon travelled to the town of Sais in Egypt where he stayed for some time, mixing with the learned priests. He came to the early conclusion that neither he nor any Hellene knew about events in the distant past when compared with the Egyptians.

A priest explained that the Egyptians had maintained detailed records of historic happenings wherever and whenever they occurred, and compared this with the records of the Greeks, saying that the knowledge and civilisation of the Greeks had periodically been completely destroyed by 'pestilent streams from heaven', so that the survivors were left like children, destitute of education and recorded history, forced once again to accumulate knowledge and wisdom before they could rebuild their civilisation. The priest stated that many generations that followed immediately after the last deluge had failed to leave a written history, so that mythology had replaced knowledge.

The priest gave as an example of lost Greek knowledge the fact that they had a record of only one deluge, even though there had been many. The Greeks, he said, had no knowledge of an ancient race of Athenians who had created the best-governed and finest city-state of all times. This state had been successfully defended against a powerful empire, the Atlanteans, who had conquered the rest of the Mediterranean world.

Solon was told that this Athenian city-state had been founded 9000 years before and that he and other Athenians were descended from a tiny group of survivors, a seeding community. The old priest told Solon that many honourable deeds and accomplishments of this ancient Athens had been recorded in their own books, but one stood out against all the rest, the conquest of the Atlanteans.

The priest described the Mediterranean and Aegean Seas that lay within the Straits of Heracles (the Pillars of Hercules, modern-day Gibraltar) as being no more than a harbour with a narrow entrance compared with the great sea that lay beyond, which he named the Atlantic Ocean. He described how a mighty power came from Atlantis, a large island lying beyond the Pillars of Hercules. Atlantis was described as being the size of North Africa (called Libya) and Turkey (usually the place intended by the term 'Asia' at the time) combined, and was encountered on the way to other islands and 'from these you might pass to the whole of the opposite continent which surrounds the true ocean'. The strong suggestion is made that North America was either a concept or actually known.

On the island of Atlantis was 'a great and wonderful empire which ruled over the whole island and several others besides together with parts of the continent [Europe]'. The land of Atlantis was apportioned into ten territories. Five pairs of male twins had been sired by the god Poseidon. To the

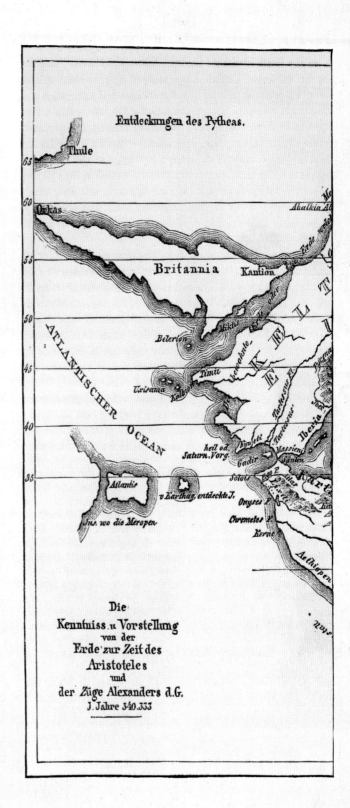

Detail from a map of the ancient world at the time of Aristotle and Alexander the Great showing Atlantis south-west of Britannia.

The mythological city of Atlantis before it was destroyed.

elder of the first pair of twins was given 'his mother's dwelling and the surrounding allotment, which was the largest and best, and made him king over the rest'. This eldest son was named Atlas, and 'after him the whole island and the ocean was called Atlantic'. The remainder of the country was divided between the remaining nine twins.

Atlantis had a very large flat plain in its centre, estimated to be 555 kilometres (345 miles) long, and 370 kilometres (230 miles) across and was very rich and fertile, protected by beautiful mountains on the north side of the island, very precipitous on their seaward side. Atlantis appears to have had a thermal region, as warm and cool springs are mentioned. According to *Critias*, the mountains were filled with 'many wealthy villages of country folk, and rivers, and lakes, and meadows supplying food enough for every animal, wild or tame, and much wood of various sorts, abundant for each and every kind of work'.

According to the priest's story, the Greeks emerged victorious from their battle with the Atlanteans, 'and generously liberated all the rest of us who dwell within the pillars … But afterwards there occurred violent earthquakes and floods; and in a single day and night of misfortune all your warlike men in a body sank into the Earth, and the island of Atlantis in like manner disappeared in the depths of the sea'.

HOW WAS ATLANTIS LOST?

Was there a real island of Atlantis and how did it disappear so suddenly? Did it indeed lie somewhere off the coast of the continent of Europe beyond the Pillars of Hercules? For that matter, did Plato himself

tell the story in good faith, or are we the victims of a wonderful tale that we simply want to believe in? In *Timaeus*, Socrates says that the story of Atlantis 'has the very great advantage of being a fact and not a fiction'. *Critias* likewise calls it 'a tale which, though strange, is certainly true', and told 'on the authority of Solon'.

Many interpretations of the Atlantis story focus on the violent earthquakes shaking and sinking the island, but from the description supplied by Solon this was a mega-earthquake that shook the entire region from outside the Pillars of Hercules to Greece, where its warriors were swallowed 'in a single day'. What appears to have happened was an event on a massive scale associated with the northward-moving African Plate ramming up against the Eurasian Plate, which is responsible for the line of volcanoes and the earthquake zone stretching from the Iberian Peninsula to the Caucasus. The Eurasian Plate extends west of the Iberian Peninsula into the oceanic crust as far as the Mid-Atlantic Ridge.

The region near the Pillars of Hercules is certainly associated with very large earthquakes. The Great Lisbon Earthquake of 1755 is considered to have been one of the most devastating in history. Its epicentre was in the Atlantic Ocean, approximately 200 kilometres (125 miles) west-south-west of Cape St Vincent. The quake has been estimated to have measured approximately 9 on the Richter scale.

In this earthquake the city of Lisbon faced a terrifying sight as the sea withdrew further and further from the shore along the mouth of the River Tagus, revealing muddy flats littered with the debris of centuries, old shipwrecks, broken boats and lost cargo. Forty minutes later a huge wall of water that had been sucked from the seabed reared up as it approached the land, and a massive tsunami swept across the shore and surged far inland, engulfing the main part of the city. The shore had become a killing field.

In some ways the Lisbon earthquake sounds like a virtual replay of the earthquake described by Solon that destroyed Atlantis. Could Greece have suffered a major earthquake that would fit with Solon's description? It's possible the Mediterranean area, particularly from Sicily through to the Aegean, including Greece and Turkey, has seen some of the most significant earthquakes in recorded history.

Even if the story of Atlantis is just that, a story, it may still hold some truth. The priest in Plato's story talks about various deluges that have been lost in the annals of human history, and whole civilisations being destroyed. Perhaps a place such as Atlantis did once exist and the story of its destruction was passed down through an oral history until it became a part of mythology for those who lived in Greece a millennium later.

LOOKING FOR ATLANTIS

Books continue to be written on Atlantis and it seems as if almost everywhere on the planet has been mentioned as a possible location. The Bahamas islands of Bimini, the Azores, the West Indies, Cuba, Bolivia, Antarctica, Australia, Cornwall, the Isles of Scilly, Ireland, the Celtic Shelf, Hyperborea, Thera (Santorini), Crete, Troy, St Brendan's Island, western North Africa, the Baltic, the Black Sea and the Red Sea have all been nominated.

In addition to these current real-world locations, the theosophists in the nineteenth century identified Atlantis with a number of other lost islands and continents, including Lemuria, Poseidon, Hyperborea, Daitya and Ruta, the island of fire of the Dravidas.

According to Solon's account, Atlantis would have been destroyed some 10,000 to 12,000 years ago. As well as placing Atlantis in the Atlantic he noted that at 'the extremity of the island towards the Pillars of Hercules, facing the country which is now called the region of Gades … is Eumelus'. Gades was the ancient name for Cadiz and the area around it in southern Spain.

This has created a geological conundrum. During ice ages, major changes occur in the volume of water left in ocean basins as water is locked up in huge ice sheets covering landmasses. The last ice age ended about 10,000 to 12,000 years ago, when seas are estimated to have been at least 100 metres (330 feet) lower than now, when the ice age was at its peak. At the end of the last ice age, the time to which the story is ascribed, the Atlantic Ocean would have been around 30 metres (almost 100 feet) lower than today. Did the sea level difference expose for a while land that would become known as Atlantis?

We have a few more clues. The city of Atlantis is described as surrounded by a moat-like canal of water. A channel had been cut through relatively high land from the sea to the moat to allow access by boat. According to *Critias*:

Beginning from the sea they bored a canal of three hundred feet in width and one hundred feet in depth and fifty stadia [250 metres or 820 feet] in length, which they carried through to the outermost zone, making a passage from the sea up to this, which became a harbour, and leaving an opening sufficient to enable the largest vessels to find ingress.

The geographic description of Atlantis in *Critias* is of a land raised well above sea level, with a broad internal plain which surrounded a city built on a hill. The plain is in turn surrounded on three sides by mountains, leaving it open to the sun facing south on the fourth side.

The most likely site for Atlantis is based on two reliable translations and cross-referenced with current knowledge in geology, palaeoclimatology and archaeology and places it on the Celtic Shelf, lying south of the British Isles.

Palaeogeographic investigation of Western Europe has located an ancient river originating in the area now occupied by the Irish Sea. The underwater hill, Little Sole Bank, lies on the edge of the Celtic Shelf approximately 57 metres (190 feet) below current sea levels. The average depth of the shelf below sea level is now between 160 and 170 metres (525 and 560 feet).

The dimensions of the plain of Atlantis described in *Critias* fits the sunken plain of the Celtic Shelf. The long-drowned river exited to the sea near the underwater hill. It would certainly have been a perfect location for a city belonging to a seafaring nation. But without detailed investigation by marine archaeologists we will never know if the Celtic Shelf is long-lost Atlantis.

SANTORINI

Many believe the Greek island of Santorini, or to give it its old and re-adopted name, Thera, was the site of Atlantis. Tourism on Santorini certainly promotes it as the lost Atlantis and it is the site for international Atlantis conferences. Santorini is located in the Cyclades group in the Aegean Sea about 117 kilometres (73 miles) from Crete. It is one of the most dramatically beautiful islands in the world, a beauty made more poignant by its vulnerability. The crescent-shaped island partly encloses a pair of small islands with two other larger islands, Aspronisi and Thirasia, close to the coast of Thera. But Thera is not a simple island. It is a surviving segment of a gigantic caldera once known as Strongyli Island, and the small islands it partly surrounds, Nea Kameni (Young Burnt Island) and Palea Kameni (Old Burnt Island), are evidence of a regenerating volcano, the youngest in the Mediterranean.

Santorini is currently listed as one of the Decade Volcanoes under a United Nations program designed to identify potential major natural disaster sites around the world. Santorini is part of a broad belt of vulcanism stretching from west of the Iberian Peninsula through Italy (the Calabrian Arc, which includes Mount Etna, also currently rated as a Decade Volcano; the Phlegraean Fields Caldera, which is a collapsed caldera almost 14 kilometres (9 miles) wide containing cinder cones and many explosion craters just 25 kilometres (15 miles) west of Mount Vesuvius; Mount Vesuvius, also listed as a Decade Volcano; and Mount Stromboli) and Greece (the Hellenic Arc, including Santorini) to the Caucasus. This line of fire results from the convergence of two huge tectonic plates, the

FOLLOWING PAGES: The great earthquake of Lisbon was one of the most destructive natural disasters in recent history.

Edgar Cayce's Atlantis

Psychics, theosophists and others have added to the original description of Atlantis, including Edgar Cayce, the Sleeping Prophet of America. Cayce was a deeply religious man who had great psychic gifts from childhood onward. He was responsible for some remarkable prophecies (and misses), and also for hundreds of authenticated medical diagnoses and recommendations for cures for patients who were completely unknown to him and often living far away. Although he was a committed Christian and a man of relatively little learning, in a trance state while doing past-life readings he frequently spoke of Atlantis, describing it in detail and remembering not only a life he had lived there but also attributed past Atlantean lives to many for whom he made readings.

Yet the details of Cayce's Atlantis do not fit Plato's descriptions. Cayce described a huge continental mass in the Atlantic, stretching almost from Europe to the Gulf of Mexico, and far older than the world described in Plato's dialogues. He predicted that temple ruins from Atlantis would be found near Bimini in the Bahamas. Cayce described a highly developed race, whose knowledge of science was advanced and certainly in advance of the science of Cayce's day: he described fire crystals that sound very like lasers, advanced flying ships and electronic transmissions. This is not Plato's paradise of swords, spears and shields, sailing boats, delightful mountain villages and lush gardens. Cayce described the Atlanteans as misusing their great technology and causing the destruction of their primary power source around 50,000 years BC. A second major catastrophe hit in 28,500 BC, breaking the back of the giant continent and leaving three large islands, Aryan, Og and Poseidon. The final destruction took place in 10,500 BC. The surviving Atlanteans escaped and migrated to other parts of the Earth. Is it possible that Plato's Atlantis was one of the three remnants of the original continent? That would be just feasible if it were not so difficult to harmonise such a huge mid-Atlantic continent with modern geological knowledge.

RIGHT: 'Aronnax views the lost city of Atlantis and the eruption of an underwater volcano', woodcut after drawing by A. de Neuville from the 1870 edition of Jules Verne's Twenty Thousand Leagues Under the Sea.

northward-moving African Plate and the Eurasian Plate. Around Santorini the geology is highly complex, with a mass of micro-plates.

Santorini has suffered up to twelve massive eruptions around 20,000 years apart, with minor eruptions in between. The last 'minor' eruption occurred in 1956, taking many lives. Houses broken in half still overhang black cliffs as testimony to its violence. But an eruption on a cosmic level happened on the island known as Strongyle ('the round') or

The eruption of the Santorini volcano, illustration from Etudes sur les Volcans *by Julius Schmidt, 1881.*

Kallista ('the beautiful') c. 1500 BC. The exact date is controversial and ranges between 1500 BC and 1650 BC, depending on how the explosion is dated.

Somewhere before 2000 BC, the town of Akrotiri was built on the sea coast of Strongyle and became a thriving outpost of the Minoan civilisation, which was centred on Crete. It grew into an important port city in its own right. Excavations at Akrotiri which, similar to Pompeii, was buried under deep ash in the c. 1500 BC explosion, have revealed the remains of a sophisticated and prosperous Bronze Age complex of impressive tall buildings, squares, and many large and beautiful houses. The houses, often multi-level constructions, are ornamented with exceptionally fine frescoes that seem unusually gentle, depicting saffron gatherers, a fisherman with his catch, leaping dolphins, antelope, a flotilla of ships and ladies at leisure. The culture appears to have diverged from that of Crete, and at its height Akrotiri was not ruled by Crete but became an independent plutocracy. Water was piped through the city in a twin-pipe system suggesting that geothermal water was delivered to houses along with fresh water, and houses had water closets linked to a sewerage system.

Only a fraction of the site has been excavated, though Akrotiri may have been a very large and affluent city for its time. As in Pompeii, many of the houses appear to belong to members of a wealthy and well-educated class.

Unlike Pompeii, no bodies were found in the ruins of Akrotiri, although enough artefacts were recovered to indicate widespread trade with countries as far away as Egypt, Libya, Syria and Anatolia. The evidence shows that a minor eruption took place before the catastrophic event, and that a number of tremors probably acted as a warning sign. The entire population appears to have escaped in a well-ordered evacuation, taking most of their belongings before the second catastrophic eruption about two months later. At the time of this eruption, the caldera, which has been reformed many times over the last several hundred thousand years, was an almost complete ring around an enclosed harbour, with a single entrance lying between Thera and Aspronisi.

The eruption was centred on a small island in the centre of the caldera close to the present-day island of Nea Kameni and it literally blew apart the caldera. The eruption is now rated as one of the three largest volcanic explosions in the last 5000 years, third only to the eruption of the Taupo Caldera in the North Island of New Zealand in 186 AD, generally considered the most violent volcanic explosion within historic times and on a scale that utterly dwarfs that of Vesuvius in 79 AD, and Mount Tambora in Indonesia in 1815. The Tambora eruption is estimated to have had more than four times the energy of the Mount Krakatoa eruption of 1883 and created pitch darkness as far as 600 kilometres (370 miles) away for two days. The reputed duration of darkness caused by the destruction of Atlantis was seven days.

Strongyle would have produced a column of ejecta 40 kilometres (25 miles) high, compared with Taupo at 51 kilometres (32 miles), and Tambora at 43 kilometres (27 miles), and the debris was carried over the entire Aegean and eastern Mediterranean. Sea water rushed into the crater, turning instantly to steam. It has been calculated that the volume of ejecta from the explosion was in the region of 65 cubic kilometres (40 cubic miles).

The Bermuda Triangle

The infamous Bermuda Triangle first came to public attention on 5 December 1945, with the mysterious and famous disappearance of Flight 19 from Fort Lauderdale in Florida. Five US Navy Avengers were sent on a routine training mission under the leadership of Lieutenant Charles Taylor. Soon after take-off, Taylor found that his compass was malfunctioning. Familiar with the topography of the Florida Keys, Taylor chose to continue the flight by following visual references, but he became totally disoriented as a storm began to build. He was still in contact with Fort Lauderdale, but reception became increasingly bad, and for some reason he did not switch to emergency frequency. Taylor believed they were flying along the Florida coast. Thus, when they turned east, they were flying directly out to sea—and were never seen or heard from again. A search party in a Martin Mariner was dispatched—also to never be seen again.

There are logical explanations for failed Flight 19. Taylor was said to be feeling less than well, and had tried to swap flight duties with other officers. The other pilots in the flight were qualified, but inexperienced. Were they so inexperienced that none could read a compass? Or did all five have malfunctioning compasses or, worse still, no compasses? Were they all so timid that nobody spoke up when they headed into the wild blue yonder of the Atlantic, with inadequate fuel? Even in a gale, it is possible to drop closer to the land and get visual bearings, particularly something as simple as distinguishing sea from land. Perhaps a couple were too overawed to speak out, but surely not all. Pilots are rarely the most reverential of people. The Mariner that was sent out to search for them reportedly blew up almost immediately after take-off, a not-unheard-of event, because of faulty gas tanks. Whatever really happened, none of the planes was ever seen again—but as with most things, the logical explanation is probably the right one.

'The non-gravitational vortex, in which ships are mysteriously lost in the Atlantic Ocean', by Hyatt Verrills, from the magazine Amazing Stories, *June 1930.*

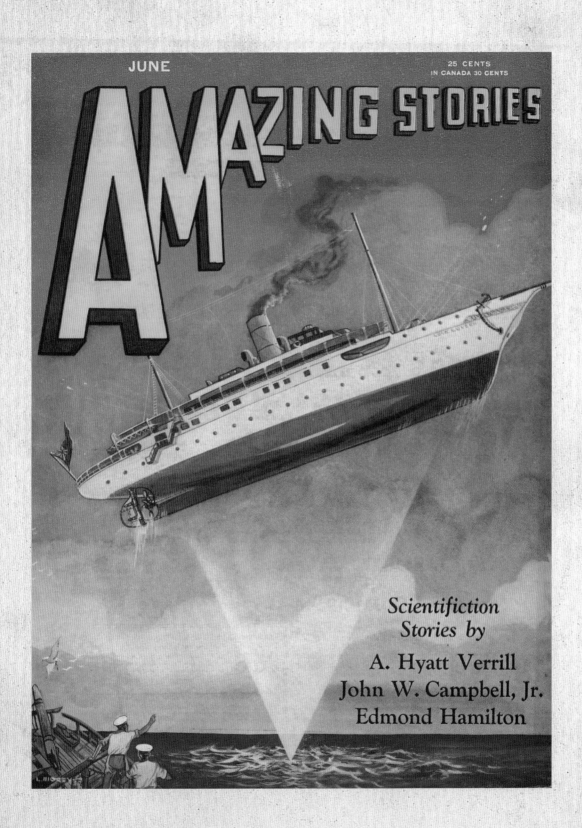

An immense tsunami followed the eruption, so huge that it affected the entire region. Islands in the vicinity were hit by waves past imagining, estimated on the basis of studies carried out on islands such as Crete to have reached heights between 160 and 250 metres (525 and 820 feet). As far away as Tel Aviv the tsunami, calculated on the basis of sea-level changes, was still a monstrous 7 metres (23 feet) high. The waves are calculated to have sped to the surrounding islands at the rate of 160 kilometres (100 miles) per hour.

Like the tsunami that followed the Lisbon earthquake, this tsunami would have sucked the ocean beds dry far out from land before returning repeatedly with murderous force. Some have suggested that the Santorini explosion may have been recorded in the Bible as the story of the Israelites fleeing from the Pharaoh in Egypt. Certainly a similar event would account for the description of the parting of the sea.

The Santorini event happened in four phases, and tsunamis continued to wrack nearby islands and surrounding coastlines, generated not just by the explosive force of the eruption but also by the collapse of the caldera, and perhaps also in response to successive massive earthquakes. The largest of the waves that slammed into Crete wiped out the towns of Mallia, Zakro and Phaestos, and laid waste to much of the great Minoan civilisation. Ash smothered the east and centre of the island, preventing cultivation of food for decades, and Crete also suffered severe earthquakes. Santorini remained uninhabited for 500 years.

There are many parallels between events on Santorini and the story of Atlantis. The island had a wealthy city, Akrotiri, which was clearly at the forefront of modernity, with what appears to have been an independent secular government. The island had traded very widely and would have simultaneously acquired much knowledge. The architecture of the city was very advanced and even included the use of buttressing to resist seismic events, and the water was managed with sophisticated engineering. Atlantis was described as being built with black, red and white stone. Such stone does exist on Santorini and, more importantly, these are the colours associated with the beautiful Minoan palace of Knossos in Crete.

Akrotiri's population, and their property and pets, were rescued over a short period, indicating both order and compassion. The exquisite frescoes in the houses, with their almost Elysian subjects, indicate a highly civilised people. Akrotiri certainly qualifies as a utopia of its era. The geography of the island also fits well with some aspects of Plato's Atlantis. Before the explosion, there was an outer ring of island with a single narrow channel between the islands of Thera and Aspronisi, leading into the large inner harbour; Atlantis was described as being laid out in concentric circles, with a canal leading into its great harbour. Plato described an island of plentiful water, which Strongyle once had (and Santorini now singularly lacks). Like the Atlanteans, the Minoans' civilisation was destroyed while they were at the height of their power and influence.

The story of such a massive eruption, which must have killed many, and not just in the Greek islands, would have remained vivid in the imagination of those who lived in the region a millennium later. The large, beautiful, modern city, with its emphasis on science, architecture, engineering and the arts, lost in the horrific explosion that blew Strongyle apart, may well have become woven into the fabric of the Atlantis story recorded by Plato.

However, some things stand in the way of Akrotiri actually being Atlantis, first and foremost being that it did not stand outside the Pillars of Hercules. Its people were rich seafaring traders, but there is no indication that they ever fought progressive wars along the Mediterranean coasts of North Africa and Europe, or occupied those countries. The description of the island does in some ways conform to Plato's Atlantis, but Akrotiri was located on the seaward side of the outer island and was not approached by a canal. The very large central plain ascribed to Atlantis is missing. Lastly, the time frame is completely wrong, separated by at least 8000 years. Plato is unlikely to have been unaware of at least the approximate timing of the Santorini eruption.

ATLANTIS IN THE NEW WORLD

Many other places have been thought to be Atlantis, and two in the New World are worthy of particular mention. One, which has been briefly touched on with reference to the Fountain of Youth (see page 77) is the area around the Bahamas in the West Indies, a site Edgar Cayce nominated as part of Atlantis (see page 284). The second refers to a triangular area bordered by Fort Lauderdale in Florida, Bermuda and Puerto Rico, which encompasses the Bahamas, that has acquired a number of names, including Hoodoo Sea, the Devil's Triangle and the Bermuda Triangle (see page 288). It is associated with many mysterious disappearances of ships and

planes over a long period. Christopher Columbus was reputedly the first to experience the mysterious influence of this area, claiming that the compasses of his three ships *Nina*, *Pinta* and *Santa Maria* went crazy in this area in 1492, a phenomenon that he attributed to his proximity to Paradise. At the same time, the crews sighted lights in the sky. The lights, seen on the first night they were in the area, may have been a meteorite crashing into the sea, and those of the second sighting were possibly caused by summer lightning. A number of ships have been mysteriously abandoned in the zone, and some ships have simply disappeared. Phenomena associated with malfunctioning compasses and altimeters have also been reported. Of course, there is a logical explanation for almost all these events. There almost always is. But the frequency of such events is unusually high.

The idea that Atlantis was in the Bahamas brought together the phenomena associated with the Bermuda Triangle and Edgar Cayce's prophecy that ruins from the lost continent of Atlantis and its advanced civilisation would be found near Bimini. The well-known Arawak Indian story of the Fountain of Youth was also associated with Bimini. It was said that the anomalies affecting instrumentation in the area of the Bermuda Triangle were caused by force fields or high energy rays emitted by the fire crystals that had once powered Atlantis and were still operating on the drowned continent.

It is certainly difficult, given our current knowledge of plate tectonics, to imagine that a huge continent once lay in the middle of the Atlantic Ocean, but there are a number of similarities between the cultures of the two continents lying

Coral Castle and Atlantis

Florida provides another mystery that some believe has connections to Atlantean knowledge. Coral Castle remains a mystery to this day. It is located near Homestead, south of Miami, and is famous for taking a direct hit from Hurricane Andrew in 1992, a Category 5 hurricane that roared in across the Bahamas, making landfall at the southern tip of Florida and virtually levelling Homestead. Modern buildings were splintered to matchwood, but Coral Castle remained unharmed although it was directly in Andrew's deadly path. The castle was built by just one man, Edward Leedskalnin, in the hope that he would one day share it with the girl he loved, whom he always called his Sweet Sixteen. It would never be. She married in Latvia and he never saw her again. Edward was a tiny man, just 150 centimetres (5 foot) tall and weighing 45 kilograms (100 pounds). He was born in 1887 and emigrated to North America from Latvia before the First World War. After working in a lumber camp in Canada he contracted tuberculosis and moved to Florida, where he bought a piece of land near Homestead with his small savings.

Edward had the poorest of equipment, a very old bicycle and a few basic items like chisels, hammers, wedges, chains and a hoist. For over twenty years, until 1923 he worked only at night and in secret, cutting out enormous blocks of coral to build his castle. What is inexplicable is how this small, quite frail man moved the blocks of coral, most of them weighing more than 5 tonnes. The average weight of the stones used in the Great Pyramid of Giza in Egypt is 2.5 tonnes. The monolithic revolving gate at Coral Castle is fashioned from a single block that weighs 9 tonnes. It is fitted with such precision that there is a 6 millimetre (¼ inch) gap on either side, and it is so perfectly balanced that it opens with the touch of a finger. No engineer has been able to explain how it was built to such a level of precision with such primitive equipment. The square-based tower has been estimated to contain 243 tonnes of huge coral blocks, perfectly fitted together.

There is evidence that Edward was deeply interested in metaphysical studies, and read widely on such subjects as cosmic forces, though his education never formally progressed past fourth grade. Various astronomical symbols are scattered through the grounds. No one ever saw him working. He would always stop if anyone arrived, behaving very sociably until they left, but always laying down his tools. Some boys once watched him secretly and described how they saw him 'floating' great blocks through the air. But testimony of this sort is far from reliable. When the site of his castle was threatened by development in 1936, he bought 4 hectares (10 acres) at Homestead with his life savings and dismantled and moved the massive, almost finished, castle 16 kilometres (10 miles) to its present site. For the only time in the entire saga he hired help to transport the vast blocks overland. But he insisted that he would load the blocks on to the truck and trailer while the driver was absent. On one occasion the truck driver had to turn back to retrieve something he had left at Coral Castle. Arriving back just thirty minutes after leaving the site, the driver was shocked to find the trailer already fully loaded with the gigantic coral blocks. Edward was nowhere to be seen. The driver swore it was impossible to have completed the loading in the given time, even if a steam-driven derrick had been used. He left feeling most uneasy.

When pressed, Leedskalnin was quoted as saying: 'I have discovered the secrets of the pyramids. I have found out how the Egyptians and the ancient builders in Peru, Yucatán, and Asia, with only primitive tools, raised and set in place blocks of stone weighing many tons'. Some, including perhaps Solon, would have said that the secret was passed down from Atlantis to the Egyptians.

each side of the ocean, not least that of pyramid culture which could be linked by a lost continent between them. The construction of pyramids is far more widespread than commonly imagined. Pyramids have been reported in the far north of Queensland in Australia, in China and Japan, and in recent times numbers of possible ancient pyramids appear to be emerging in Europe.

THE BOLIVIAN ATLANTIS

Unlikely though Bolivia might be as a site of the utopian world of Atlantis, it does warrant a mention because, whether by coincidence or not, a submerged island that was destroyed by massive earthquakes lies in Lake Poopo, which is virtually an inland sea. The island meets many of the specifications of Atlantis in Plato's description. The site comes with a legend that closely parallels the Poseidon legend of Atlantis, complete with male twins and an equivalent god. South America is certainly the approximate size of the lost continent of Atlantis, and it does lie opposite the Pillars of Hercules, if very remotely. The plain described by Plato could match the Altiplano of Bolivia, which is

roughly rectangular. There are hot and cold springs, as described in Plato's dialogues, and plentiful red, black and white stones. The area is also quite rich in minerals, including gold and silver. The mysterious orichalcum which, according to Plato, covered the interior pillars, walls, floor and outermost wall of the Temple to Poseidon and Cleito in Atlantis so that it 'flashed with the red light of orichalcum', was also used to line the ceiling of the Poseidon temple, together with gold and silver.

There are also records of it being used in the Temple of Solomon in Jerusalem. Orichalcum was by no means common, and knowledge of it seemed to be all but lost in Plato's time, yet it was also made in Bolivia under the name tumbaga. It was a very malleable alloy of copper, silver and gold, which was easily cast, hammered and polished. The proportions of the metals used appear to have varied, although up to 95 per cent of gold could be used. Tumbaga, the name adopted for the alloy by the Spaniards in the New World, was widely used by the Aztecs, particularly for religious objects. A sunken galleon off the Great Bahamas yielded 200 bars of tumbaga when discovered in 1992.

THE HOLLOW
EARTH THEORY

In the late seventeenth century, the astronomer Edmund Halley put forward the notion, fantastic even for the time, that the Earth was constructed from four concentric spheres, rather like a Russian doll. The Earth inside this hollow Earth was populated, and it was illuminated by an inner sun. He postulated that the Aurora Borealis was evidence of gas escaping from a hole located at the North Pole in the Arctic. (In fairness to Halley, who was a brilliant astronomer and mathematician capable of predicting the precise time of return of the comet that bears his name, his theory was based on an attempt to explain the variability in the Earth's magnetic field.)

This odd but explicable theory was augmented by the Swiss mathematician Leonnard Euler, who proposed replacing the three inner earths with a sun supposedly 960 kilometres (600 miles) wide. It would be interesting to see the original mathematical proof of that calculation. He postulated also, without the assistance of mathematics, that an advanced civilisation inhabited this inner world. The Scottish

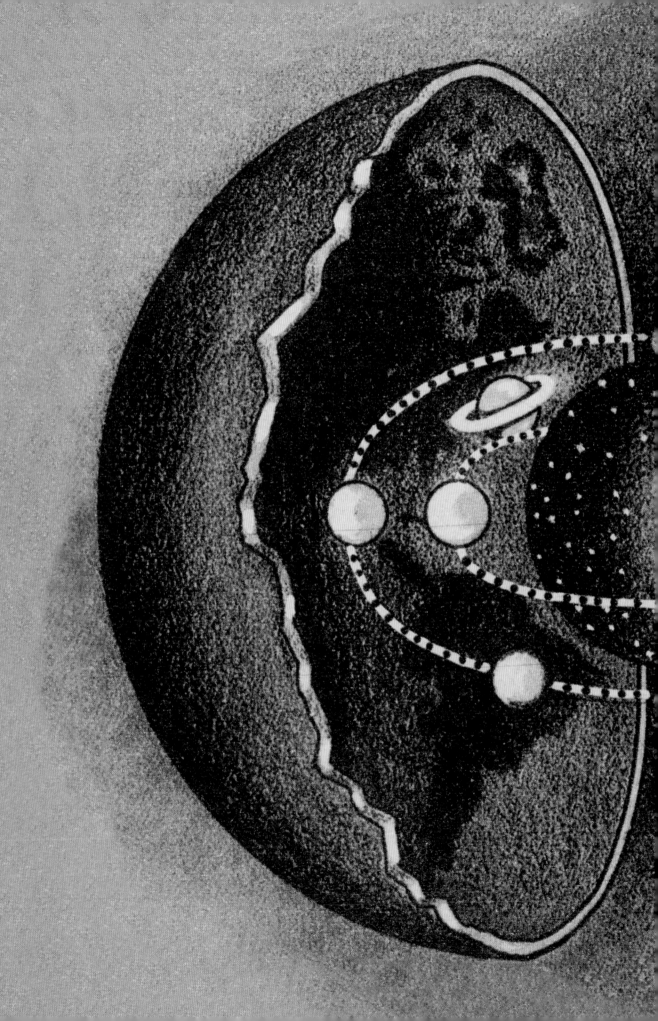

PREVIOUS PAGES: German scientist Karl Neupert's diagram of the hollow Earth, 1935, presents an inner solar sysetem at work.

mathematician Sir John Leslie could not leave well enough alone and proposed that there were two suns within the Earth, which he named Proserpine and Pluto.

In 1818 John Cleves Symmes, Jr, a rather eccentric American ex-army officer and businessman, brought the theory back to everyone's attention, even though it seemed to ignore all current knowledge of the Earth's geology. He proposed, like Halley, that the Earth was a hollow shell, which he claimed was 1280 kilometres (800 miles) thick, enclosing three inner shells that had openings extending from the innermost shells through to the two poles. The openings even became known as Symmes Holes in his honour. Like the Rupes Nigra theory (see page 152), which proposed an imaginary geography at the North Pole with a giant hole through which the waters of the world fell, the Hollow Earth theory took on a life of its own. Symmes demanded that an expedition be undertaken to prove the theory and raised money for the purpose. A newly incumbent president of the United States, Andrew Jackson,

ruled against the expedition in 1829. Symmes died that year, but one of his followers, a newspaper editor named Jeremiah Reynolds, continued to call for an expedition to discover the Symmes Holes. Reynolds so successfully offended those in power that he was not included in the exploration of Antarctica, the great US Exploring Expedition of 1838–42, despite being largely responsible for its instigation. Far from bringing back news of an enormous hole at the South Pole, the expedition brought back useful information about the last continent discovered on Earth, Antarctica.

There is no end to human ingenuity in marshalling ideas in favour of a pet theory, but Marshall Gardner was in a league of his own. In the nineteenth century the world was fascinated to hear news of the discoveries of several perfectly preserved woolly mammoths in ice in Siberia. In his 1913 book *A Journey to the Centre of the Earth*, Gardner proposed that they had lived within the Earth, warmed by the inner sun, and had wandered out of the northern Symmes Hole and frozen to death in Siberia, which explained their perfect state of preservation. And to think we attribute great imagination to those who lived in the medieval period!

HAWAIKI
— HOMELAND OF THE
POLYNESIAN PEOPLE

Lost homelands take on the glow of Utopia, and the Polynesian people seem in many ways to have taken their Utopia, and the name of their legendary homeland, with them. It changes little in different parts of the Pacific—Hawaiki in New Zealand, Hawai'i, Avaiki or as on Easter Island, Hiva.

The story of their migration from their legendary homeland has proved far more interesting and complex than the original theory of passive migration. The Polynesians have ancient oral traditions of migrating from a sinking mountainous island called Hawaiki, travelling in long canoes of the type still used today. It now seems that their beloved Hawaiki lay within the islands of eastern Asia. Taiwan has been proposed as this homeland, although clearly it did not sink and does not correspond with the homeland described in oral history. Far from being passively carried on currents and by the wind, at least parts of their journeys could only have been made by sailing against prevailing winds. The Polynesians used classic early methods of reckoning by the heavens, just as were used in Europe, and a trick well known to Columbus of following birds to locate land. They carried with them all they needed to survive and thrive in new places, including tools and valued food plants, such as the sweet potato (kumara). To prove the feasibility of this theory, which is well backed by science, ocean-going canoes have been constructed according to original techniques and successfully sailed over the likely routes using ancient navigational methods. To maintain genetically healthy populations a fleet of such canoes would have been involved in migrations. The Maori people recorded in their oral history that the journey to New Zealand (Aotearoa) involved around forty large boats.

There is just one small problem with the theory of movement from east Asian islands to the Pacific, which suggests that Polynesian migration patterns were more complex than this. The sweet potato is native to tropical America. How did they carry the sweet potato with them if they came on a one-way trip from eastern Asia? The bright orange-fleshed kumara, *Ipomoea batatas*, was certainly a staple food from the beginning for the Maori, who arrived in New Zealand c. 1000 AD. Sweet potatoes have been domesticated in South America for 5,000 years.

A nineteenth century illustration of Tongariro and Ruapahu, which are part of the Taupo volcanic zone, the site of the largest volcanic explosion in historic times.

IN A GALAXY
FAR FAR AWAY

What will we do without Terra Incognita, without a playground for our fertile imaginations? Without lands beyond the Pillars of Hercules and in the mysterious Orient of medieval times, or at the uppermost reaches of the Nile and the Mountains of the Moon? As the world shrank as a result of our exploration and we finally managed to sort out its geography, we seemed to have left ourselves with no dark and unknown place for the imagination to roam. At the end of the nineteenth century, the gap began to be filled with exploration of the mystical arts, from a revival of sorcery to hypnotism, tarot and contacting the dead. Scientists also put forth new ideas, explaining the dispersal of species by creating imaginary continents that obligingly disappeared on cue beneath the oceans.

But as we recovered from two nightmare world wars that had shown us monsters far more horrific than any we might conjure from the realm of Terra Incognita, we found fresh challenges. The inner world of psychology came of age and became both a serious study and a fashionable preoccupation. Alexander Pope, the deliciously caustic-tongued satirical eighteenth century poet, was frequently quoted: 'The proper study of Mankind is Man', although a second cautionary quote from Pope might well have been remembered: 'A little learning is a dangerous thing; Drink deep, or taste not the Pierian spring'. Hollywood certainly drank deeply of such things, embracing the more chilling aspects of studying humankind with films that at their best included those of Alfred Hitchcock, which tapped into the fascination audiences have with terror, and as he is quoted as saying: 'They like to put their toe in the cold water of fear'.

Technology finally provided us with the gift of fishes, the ability to roam underwater, even to unimaginably crushing depths in bathyscapes, providing a new frontier. Sciences like marine biology and oceanography became both fashionable and fascinating, as the underwater world yielded up its secrets and its mysterious dramatic geography.

In 1957 the stars seemed to come within our grasp when the Russians stunned the world by placing a satellite called *Sputnik I* into orbit around the Earth. Our world would never be the same again, and the phrase 'Space, the last frontier' would be used interminably in newspapers, magazines and books. With the Cold War between Russia and the United States well advanced, the event spun off into what became known as the Sputnik Crisis, and led to the space race. *Sputnik I* burned up on re-entry in January 1958, after three months in orbit.

But the door had been opened not only to the world of rocket science and astrophysics, but also to the world of imagination. Science fiction and fantasy novels became mainstream as the real possibility of encountering other worlds and intelligent life became a possibility, no matter how remote. We looked backwards too. Had the human race been visited by civilisations far more scientifically advanced than ours? Was there any evidence in ancient records that might point in that direction?

Although some of the books that emerged were more fantasy than science, others were serious attempts to come to grips with unexplained mysteries on the planet, such as the Nazca Lines on the high desert plateau of Peru that appear when viewed from high above like a giant map left for ancient astronauts. Whether a theory is right is not so important as the fact that we are trying to make sense of the human time line, no longer accepting the conventional interpretation of our own story but questioning everything and delving for new concrete evidence.

We may well prove to be the children that the Egytian priest in Plato's dialogues called the ancient Greeks, thinking we know our history but with no true idea of our remote past. We are beginning to piece together a new story. It will be a fascinating trip. Our world has proved to be neither stable nor truly known. If all else fails us in our search for challenging new worlds to explore, modern physics has provided us with an infinity of worlds in parallel universes and dimensional planes. We seem to have discovered so many new territories, so many places for our imaginations to roam and create new dark monsters, that if we have any sense of adventure we will find more excitement in our future than we ever did when Terra Incognita bordered the maps of the world.

RIGHT: Space, *the next realm to imagine and explore.*

Further Reading

Ashe, Geoffrey. *Atlantis: Lost Lands, Ancient Wisdaom*. Thames and Hudson, London, 1992.

Ashe, Geoffrey. *Quest for America*. Pall Mall, London, 1971.

Baker, Sir Samuel White. *The Albert N'yanza; Great Basin of the Nile, and Explorations of the Nile Sources*. Vol 1. Adamant Media Corporation, Chestnut Hill, Massachusetts, 2001.

Bartlett, Robert. *The Making of Europe: Conquest, Colonisation and Cultural Change, 950–1350*. Penguin, London, 1994.

Bawlf, Samuel. *The Secret Voyage of Sir Francis Drake: 1577–1580*. Penguin, London, 2004.

Bergreen, Laurence. *Over the Edge of the World: Magellan's Terrifying Circumnavigation of the Globe*. Harper, New York, 2004.

Bergreen, Laurence. *Marco Polo: From Venice to Xanadu*. Reprint edition. Vintage Books, New York, 2008.

Bricker, Charles and R.V. A. Tooley. *A History of Cartography: 2500 years of Maps and Mapmakers*. Thames and Hudson, London, 1969.

Brown, Lloyd A. *The Story of Maps*. Dover Publications, New York, 1980.

Cook, James. *Journals of Captain Cook on His Voyages of Discovery*. Beaglehole, J.C. (ed.). Cambridge University Press, Cambridge, 1967–1974.

Dampier, William. *Memoirs of a Buccaneer: Dampier's New Voyage Round the World, 1697*. Dover Publications, New York, 2007.

Defoe, Daniel. *A General History of the Pyrates*. New edition. Dover Publications, New York, 1999.

Ehrenberg, Ralph E. *Mapping the World: An Illustrated History of Cartography*. National Geographic, Washington D.C. 2005.

Elliott, J. H. *The Old World and the New 1492–1650*. Cambridge University Press, Cambridge, 1970.

Ellis, Richard. *Imagining Atlantis*. Alfred A. Knopf, New York, 1998.

Exquaemelin, Alexander O. *The Buccaneers of America.* Alexis Brown, translator. Dover Publications, New York, 2000.

Flint, Valerie. *The Imaginative Landscape of Christopher Columbus.* Princeton University Press, Princeton, New Jersey, 1992.

Fitzhugh, William. W. and Ward, Elizabeth I. *Vikings: The North Atlantic Saga.* Smithsonian Institute Press, Washington D.C. 2000.

Fernandez-Armesto, Felipe. *Before Columbus: Exploration and Colonization from the Mediterranean to the Atlantic, 1229–1492.* Macmillan, London, 1987.

Fowles, John. *Islands.* Little Brown, Boston, 1878.

Friede, Juan and Keen, Benjamin (eds.) *Bartolomé de Las Casas in History.* Northern Illinois University Press, Dekalb, Illinois, 1971.

Fuson, Robert H. *Legendary Islands of the Ocean Sea.* Pineapple, Sarasota, 1995.

Graves, Robert. *The Greek Myths: The Complete Edition.* Penguin, London, 1993.

Green, Peter. *Alexander of Macedon, 356–323 BC: A Historical Biography.* Reprint edition. University of California Press, Berkeley, California, 1992.

Hapgood, Charles H. *Maps of the Ancient Sea Kings: Evidence of Advanced Civilization in the Ice Age.* Adventures Unlimited Press, Kempton, Illinois, 1996.

Harley, J.B. and Woodward, David (eds.). *The History of Cartography: Cartography in Prehistoric, Ancient, and Medieval Europe and the Mediterranean.* Vol 1. The University of Chicago Press, Chicago, Illinois, 1987.

Harwood, Jeremy. *To the Ends of the Earth: 100 Maps That Changed the World.* David and Charles, London, 2006.

Holm, Bill. *Eccentric Islands: Islands Real and Imaginary.* Milkwood, Minneapolis, 2000.

Ireland, J. de Courcy and Sheehy, David C. (eds.) *Atlantic Visions.* Books Press, Dublin, 1989.

Johnson, Donald S. *Phantom Islands of the Atlantic: The Legends of Seven Lands That Never Were.* Walker and Company, New York, 1994

Joseph, Frank. *The Destruction of Atlantis: Compelling Evidence of the Sudden Fall of the Legendary Civilisation.* Bear and Company, Rochester, Vermont, 2004.

Mandeville, John. *The Travels of Sir John Mandeville.* New edition. Penguin, London, 1983.

Mann, Charles C. *1491: New Revelations of the Americas Before Columbus.* Vintage, New York, 2006.

More, Sir Thomas. *Utopia.* David Wootton, translator. Hackett Publishing Company, Indianapolis, Indiana, 1977.

Moreland, Carl. *Antique Maps.* Phaidon Press, London, 1994.

Morison, Samuel Eliot. *The European Discovery of America: The Northern Voyages: A.D. 500–1600.* Vol 2. Oxford University Press, New York, 1992.

Morison, Samuel Eliot. *The European Discovery of America: The Southern Voyages A.D. 500–1616.* Oxford University Press, New York, 1974.

Mumford, Lewis. *The Story of Utopias.* Peter Smith, Gloucester, 1954.

O'Meara, John J. Introduction to *The Voyage of Saint Brendan.* John J. O'Meara, translator. Colin Smythe, Gerrard Cross, England, 1991.

Phillips, J.S.R. *The Medieval Expansion of Europe.* Oxford University Press, Oxford, 1988.

Polk, Dora Beale. *The Island of California: A History of the Myth.* Arthur H. Clark, Spokane, WA, 1991.

Polo, Marco. *The Travels*. Ronald E. Latham, translator. New edition. Penguin, London, 2004.

Preston, Diana. *A Pirate of Exquisite Mind: Explorer, Naturalist, and Buccaneer: The Life of William Dampier*. Walker and Company, New York, 2004.

Ritchie, Robert. *Captain Kidd and the War Against the Pirates*. Harvard University Press, Cambridge, Massachusetts, 2005.

Romm, James S. *The Edges of the Earth in Ancient Thought, Geography, Exploration, and Fiction*. Princeton University Press, Princeton, New Jersey, 1992.

Scafi, Alessandro. 'Mapping Eden: Cartographies of Earthly Paradise' in *Mappings*, Denis Cosgrove (ed.). Reaktion, London, 1999.

Severin, Tim. *In Search of Robinson Crusoe*. Basic Books, New York, 2002.

Shipman, Pat. *To the Heart of the Nile: Lady Florence Baker and the Exploration of Central Africa*. HarperCollins, New York, 2004.

Sobel, Dava. *Longitude: The True Story of a Lone Genius Who Solved The Greatest Problem of the Time*. Walker, New York, 1995.

Sondergaard, Lief. 'At the Edge of the World: Early Medieval Ideas of the Nordic Countries' in *Medieval Spirituality in Scandinavia and Europe*. Bisgaard, Lars (ed.). Odense Press, Odense, 2001.

Strommel, Henry. *Lost Islands: The Story of Islands That Have Vanished from Nautical Charts*. University of British Columbia Press, Vancouver, 1984.

Sigurosson, Gisli (ed.). *The Vinland Sagas*. Penguin, London, 2008.

Snyder, John P. *Flattening the Earth: Two Thousand Years of Map Projections*. University of Chicago Press, Chicago, 1993.

Thomas, Nicholas. Cook: *The Extraordinary Voyages of Captain James Cook*. Walker and Company, New York, 2004.

Weatherford, Jack. *Genghis Kahn and the making of the Modern World*. New edition. Three Rivers Press, New York, 2005.

Whitfield, Peter. *New Found Lands: Maps in the History of Exploration*. Routledge, London, 1998.

Wilford, John Noble. *The Mapmakers*. Revised edition. Vintage Books, New York, 2000.

Yeoman, Guy. *The Quest For The Secret Nile: Victorian Exploration in Equatorial Africa 1857–1888*. Chaucer Press, London, 2004.

Acknowledgements

Special thanks to Diana Hill who inspired and supported this book and Emma Hutchinson who so enjoyed creating its wonderful visual appeal, both of them treasures at Murdoch Books Australia. Thanks also to Hugh Ford and Susanne Geppert for the gorgeous look of the book, and Linda Brainwood for finding the maps and artwork.

Image Credits

AKG Images: pages 61, 110–111, 115, 215, 227, 248, 263, 282–283

Beinecke Rare Book and Manuscript Library, Yale University: pages 230–231

Corbis: pages 2, 16, 148, 177, 196, 234–235, 278

Granger Collection: pages 130–131, 244–245, 256, 285

Library of Congress: cover, pages 38–39, 190

München Bayerische Staatsbibliothek: page 37

National Library of Australia: pages 151, 206, 212–213, 218–219, 230–231

Picture Desk/Art Archive: pages 2, 12–13, 56–57, 72–73, 78, 88, 90–91, 94, 99, 118—119, 124–125, 134–135, 145, 157, 162–163, 174, 238, 243, 300

Photolibrary: pages 4–5, 9, 10, 19, 22–23, 26–27, 32–33, 42–43, 47, 49, 52–53, 54, 64, 70–71, 82–83, 87, 102, 106–107, 122, 140–141, 154–155, 160, 166, 180–181, 186–187, 200–201, 208–209, 222, 232, 258–259, 266, 271, 272–273, 277, 286, 289, 296–297, 303

State Library of New South Wales: pages 254–255

Index

First published in 2009 by Pier 9, an imprint of Murdoch Books Pty Limited

Murdoch Books Australia	Murdoch Books UK Limited
Pier 8/9	Erico House, 6th Floor
23 Hickson Road	93–99 Upper Richmond Road
Millers Point NSW 2000	Putney, London SW15 2TG
Phone: +61 (0)2 8220 2000	Phone: +44 (0) 20 8785 5995
Fax: +61 (0)2 8220 2558	Fax: +44 (0) 20 8785 5985
www.murdochbooks.com.au	www.murdochbooks.co.uk

Publisher: Diana Hill
Editor: Emma Hutchinson
Cover design: Hugh Ford
Internal design: Susanne Geppert
Picture Researcher: Linda Brainwood
Production: Alexandra Gonzalez
Text copyright © Judyth A. Mcleod
Design copyright © Murdoch Books Pty Limited 2009

National Library of Australia Cataloguing-in-Publication Data:
Author: McLeod, Judyth A.
Title: The atlas of legendary lands : fabled kingdoms, phantom
            islands, lost continents and other mythical worlds / Judyth McLeod.
ISBN: 9781741961416 (hbk.)
Notes: Includes index.
Subjects: Cartography–History.
            Early maps.
            Geographical myths.
            Discoveries in geography.
Dewey Number: 912.09

A catalogue record for this book is available from the British Library.

Printed in CHINA.